OUTSIDE IS AMERICA

OUTSIDE IS AMERICA

U2 *in the* U.S.

CARTER
ALAN

FABER AND FABER

Boston · London

Library of Congress Cataloging-in-Publication Data

Alan, Carter.
    Outside Is America : U2 in the U.S. / Carter Alan.
        p.   cm.
    ISBN 0-571-12926-9
    1. U2 (Musical group) 2. Rock musicians—Ireland—Biography.
3. Rock musicians—Travel—United States. I. Title.
ML421.U2A8   1992
782.42166'092'2--dc20
    [B]   92-3302
                                                                           CIP
                                                                            MN

Cover design by Lorna Stovall
Cover photographs by Deborah Padova

For Shirley and Hilda

CONTENTS

PREFACE

A DAY DOES NOT PASS lately without someone asking me, "How's the book doing?" It has become a relentless pursuer, this question, fueled originally by my resolve to produce the volume you are holding right now. You see, when first thinking about attempting the mammoth task of writing a book, I figured that if I told everyone about my plans, I'd be too embarrassed *not* to write it. That plan certainly succeeded in motivating my efforts at the beginning of the writing process, after which the project was a joy to work on, but it also informed dozens (hundreds?) of friends and acquaintances about my plans. It has become an essential bit of conversation in most of my encounters (but how did my dentist find out?). Don't misunderstand me, I welcome people's interest and concern about the project, but be assured I won't be telling anyone about my next book until it's done!

Seriously, I've been astonished at how rapidly and completely word about this book has spread. It's a testament not only to how popular U2 is, but how very important the band is to people. Belief in this group has meaning, fills a niche in our lives, enriches the regimen, opens eyes and ears, points fingers, and doesn't just go quietly away when the CD is over. Some think that artists like this are born with the talent to affect us deeply, but in U2's case it was a series of learning experiences —especially the mistakes—that brought them to the top. It's also easy to forget that this journey took the band members a decade to accomplish—not exactly the kind of overnight success with which they've often been tagged. U2, a sum greater than the talents of the four principle individuals involved, owes its success mostly to curiosity and courage.

Never satisfied with staying in one place too long, the band members have always leaped from a comfortable artistic berth toward something more indistinct or even completely unfamiliar to them. Taken along on the journey, we can only count on the fact that things will sound different once we get there.

Though U2's aim has always been a sort of continuing quest to satisfy its artistic urges, the drive has been to accomplish this on the world's rock and roll stage. Even as four baby-faced freshmen in America on their first tour in December 1980, the members of U2 were moving toward the goal of becoming known — maybe not as headliners at Madison Square Garden, but the Paradise Theater would certainly do. That ambition seems common — every band wants to be successful — but U2 accompanied it with a resolve to preserve the highly prized personal relationship it enjoyed with its supporters. Although the band would sometimes take necessary steps to block an ever-curious media, the fans have never been shut out.

Outside Is America is as much the fans' story as it is U2's. Because of this, a current fanzine list is included and most of the photos in this book were taken by U2 fans from across the country. I've met a lot of compatriots on the road over the years and encourage anyone to write who has comments about the book or wants to share an experience. Send an SASE to U2/Outside Is America, Box 5965, Marlborough, MA 01752. This isn't an official pipeline to the band or a part of U2's excellent fan magazine *Propaganda*, but it is a direct line of communication to me.

As the title implies, this book concentrates on U2's American story, the viewpoint stemming from my personal encounters and interviews with the group as well as music industry sources. Although I occasionally talked about writing a book on U2 prior to 1987, nothing was formally put down on paper until after the *Joshua Tree* tour. Originally intended to appear before U2's latest album, *Achtung Baby*, this book was delayed by the extra time taken to finish the manuscript and conduct the necessary publishing business. In the end, the delay offered me the opportunity to examine U2's most radical musical change yet, so the book includes a look at *Achtung Baby* and the 1992 Zoo TV tour.

The interview material was assembled from a 1983 WBCN radio visit with Adam, Edge, and Larry, a 1983 phone call from Edge at the US Festival, a 1984 radio interview with Bono, a chat with Edge and Adam for Island Records in 1984, Boston conversations with the bassist and guitarist for WBCN the following year, another Island Records interview with Bono and Edge in spring 1987, and a syndicated radio conversation with the entire band that September. Although these interviews were not expressly intended for a book at the time they were conducted, they do reveal firsthand information about the band members and their developing artistic motivation when put in chronological sequence.

I've been a fan since August 1980 when I first heard "A Day Without Me," and as a disc jockey became professionally involved when I played the import single on WBCN–FM in Boston that same month. Twelve years later I'm still a fan because U2 has never ceased to move forward and inspire me — if the group was releasing its third retreading of *War* at present, I wouldn't be writing these words. It's a never-ending story, really; U2's is the sort of open-ended creativity that allows me to boldly predict another decade of enriching music from this band that I'm sure I will continue to follow.

April 1992

ACKNOWLEDGMENTS

My heartfelt thanks to the following who in some way helped in the completion of this book:

Lisa Abere, Mike Abramson, Andy Allen, Frank Barsalona, Tony Berardini, Steve Berkowitz, Bob Catania, Ellen Darst, Debbie Ditulio, Randy Ezratty, Dave Fanning, Jay Fialkov, George Gerrity, Terri Hemmert, Jimmy Iovine, Kurt Itil, Keryn Kaplan, Frank Kearns, Anne-Louise Kelly, Kevin Killen, Jill Kneerim, Harvey Kojan, Sam Kopper, Larry "Cha-Chi" Loprete, Tristram Lozaw, Mitch Maketansky, S. Kathleen Maki, Dave Marsh, Lynn McDonnell, Paul McGuinness, Sheila McGuinness, Larry Moulter, Deke O'Brien, Oedipus, Deborah Padova, Lisa Petraitis, Marianne Philbin, Rachel Phillips, Steve Rainford, Peter Ratajcak, Lisa Robinson, Dan Russell, Donna Russo, Linda Ryan, Nina Ryan, Ken Shelton, Barbara Skydel, Jim Tausch, Betsy Uhrig, Steven Van Zandt, Norm Winer, Peter Wolf, Robbie Wooten, Zoe Zanakis, and the members of U2.

OUTSIDE IS AMERICA

1

BE CAREFUL
OF WHAT YOU
WISH FOR

BRIGHT LIGHT flooded Cleveland's cavernous Richfield Coliseum, illuminating busy specks on the floor as they stacked thousands of folding chairs on long metal carts and pushed brooms through piles of crushed soft drink cups and other more grimy refuse. Above them, figures moved through the arena's surrounding rows, cleaning off the brown, yellow, and tan plastic seats. On the huge stage dominating one side of the floor, workers rushed about in perfect order, packing musical instruments and electronic gadgets into black cases and dismantling the huge steel truss of lights and speakers that had hung overhead all evening. With an ease and efficiency born from repeating these tasks nearly every night, the crew quickly disassembled the elaborate stage and packed it into tractor-trailer trucks waiting silently for their trip to the next concert.

U2, the rock and roll band that had started from scratch in Dublin only seven years earlier, was in the middle of a 1985 coast-to-coast American trek that would only touch down in the gargantuan sports arenas of the land. Generous radio airplay and television exposure of the band's latest single, "Pride (In the Name of Love)," was selling *The Unforgettable Fire*, U2's most recent album, as fast as copies could be pressed. Tonight's sold-out Cleveland performance had been a joyous, sweaty delight, so there was ample reason for U2 and its staff to celebrate afterward during everyone's first breather of the day.

Invited to partake freely in the happy mayhem backstage, I waded into the crowd of musicians, U2 management staff and crew, media representatives, and the concert promoter's guests. Since 1980, when I'd first played U2's music on the American airwaves as a deejay at Boston's WBCN–FM, my friendship with the band and their committed staff had deepened. That relationship had allowed a detailed look at U2's rapid and stunning rise from a band struggling to fill tiny rock and roll clubs to this latest level where they were selling out massive sports arenas.

Fresh from his dressing room shower, U2's bassist Adam Clayton smiled as he walked by me on his way to greet some lucky fans who had been anxiously waiting forty-five minutes to meet a band member. With a Heineken in one hand and a Marlboro in the other, the curly-haired blond strode into the bare, concrete-walled room. Many of the fans, who had been relaxed and chatting easily with one another, stiffened perceptibly as Adam entered. It wouldn't take long for him to offer a handshake and an autograph to each person, putting everyone quickly at ease in his typically friendly manner. U2's guitarist, the Edge (or simply Edge in conversation) was close behind. His receding black hairline belied an age of only twenty-four, and the thoughtful, studious manner in which he spoke also made him seem much further along in years. Tonight, the man credited with popularizing a whole new guitar technique radiated his usual warmth and spoke humbly about what everyone present considered a brilliant U2 performance.

For years, Bono, the band's lead singer, had enjoyed his reputation as a commanding and wildy energetic front man in the spotlights, but if he ever perceived his performance as second-rate, he would sink into an inconsolable gloom. On this occasion, however, Bono happily roamed the backstage corridors, black derby perched atop dark, shoulder-length hair, his peaceful and reflective side shelved for the moment as he searched for the one musician in U2 usually referred to as "the quiet member." At twenty-three, the group's drummer, Larry Mullen, Jr., was younger than his bandmates, but he too seemed more mature than his years. Larry's dashing resemblance to the late James Dean, complete with crew cut and a passion for motorcycles, was a look that many of U2's female fans found irresistible. The drummer's distaste for attention, however, frequently made him quite difficult to locate. Tonight, though, Bono easily found him behind the stage laughing it up with a few members of the band's road crew.

The mingling went on for another forty-five minutes before shouts drifted into the corridor. "The limos are ready to go! If you want to be stuck out here in the middle of Ohio, you can miss them!" The voice belonged to Dennis Sheehan, the man entrusted with running U2's entire traveling troupe, and his words were not to be taken lightly. From Cleveland, the band had driven for a half-hour past miles of lonely fields and farms to reach Richfield Coliseum earlier that day. Now, after the exhausting setup and performance of U2's massive show, it was time to return to the hotel. Dennis appeared from around the corner to emphasize his threat in person. The short, medium-built man approaching middle age generally possessed a gentle and pleasant disposition. An expert organizer who had once helped road-manage Led Zeppelin, the epitome of rock-star excess during the seventies, Dennis was one of the best and everyone knew it. He'd proven it time after time in nearly three years with U2. Everyone, including the band members, was quite used to obeying his orders instantly.

Three long black Cadillacs stood ready in the Coliseum's indoor parking lot. Most of the entourage crammed into the first two; only Adam, U2's management assistant Keryn Kaplan, and I stepped into the third. Keryn, a black-haired woman in her late twenties, worked in U2's New York City management office. With a razor-sharp business sense honed on Wall Street and an unquenchable love of the band's music, she was an integral part of U2's team who had been pulled away from her desk job to help out on the tour. There was no more work to be done tonight, though, so she lounged back in the plush rear seat and closed her eyes as our car glided through a concrete tunnel and outside to the brightly lit parking lot. Adam glanced through the window. "We have company," he remarked with amusement. Clustered by the backstage tunnel entrance was a group of a dozen cars, conspicuous in the immense and empty Coliseum parking lot, and doubly so when all their headlights suddenly flashed on.

"Well, they're determined," Keryn remarked. Now wide awake, she glanced at her watch and noted it was just short of one in the morning. "It's been almost two hours since the show ended." The cars jumped out in ragged disarray behind the trio of limousines as they neatly exited the lot and gained speed on the open highway. The intent of the trailing posse was clear: follow U2's convoy all the way back to Cleveland to find out where the band was staying or where it was going to party. The pursuers showed no scruples about the speed limit as they quickly made up for lost ground, their bright lights gaining rapidly in the limo's rearview mirrors. A pair of headlights accelerated out of the pack and a red Chrysler appeared on our left while a white shape tucked snugly in behind. Keryn knew that our pursuers couldn't peer in through the limo's tinted glass, but she could plainly see a pair of excited girls bouncing and waving from the speeding Chrysler. "Don't you think they're getting a bit too close?" she asked Adam with genuine concern. The bass player continued to smile, but yelled to the driver, "Are you okay up there?"

"We'll be all right, sir," the chauffeur replied confidently, but then added, "as long as one of those drivers doesn't screw up." A gold Pontiac with a half-dozen girls and one guy pasted in the driver's window rapidly pulled alongside in the breakdown lane. Now, with the Cadillac boxed in on three sides at sixty miles per hour, even Adam was beginning to look worried. Unruffled, our chauffeur closed the distance with the limousine ahead, tightening up the tandem formation so no cars could wedge in between. The fanatic escort easily maintained its position, however, even gaining enough ground to surround the Cadillac in front of ours.

"They . . . they really are starting to get close," Keryn noted as she stared at the Pontiac and the excited faces within; they seemed unaware of the danger of hurtling along the bumpy and potholed shoulder. With everyone waving their arms crazily at the limousine, there didn't appear to be any one person actually taking responsibility for holding on to the wheel. "Well, since they are quite willing to kill themselves to see us, perhaps I should let them have a look," offered Adam, who promptly lowered the window and stuck out his head. Hands stretched out across the gulf toward the bass player's beaming face as the careening Pontiac swerved to less than four feet away. One of the girls held out a wildly flapping piece of paper for an autograph. "This is crazy!" Keryn screamed. "They're gonna go for it and we'll be wearing that car in a second!"

A bridge appeared out of the darkness, its concrete and steel supports eliminating the breakdown lane just a short distance ahead. The shoulder narrowed to the left, forcing the Pontiac along with it until a collision with the limo seemed certain. Adam's friendly wave changed into a sudden frantic warning. At the last second, with options dwindling fast, the Pontiac's driver finally slammed on the brakes, dropping the shouts, waving arms, and piece of paper abruptly behind us. The Pontiac fell in with the rest of the escort, which was now content to merely shadow U2's caravan.

"Well, that was exciting wasn't it?" offered a slightly pale Adam, prompting a round of nervous laughs.

Our convoy reached the city limits and turned onto a beat-up boulevard heading downtown with the line of pursuers still strung out behind. In moments, the limousines had arrived at the Stouffer Hotel, the drivers parking in tight formation, bumper to bumper, to effectively barricade the entrance from the street and most of the sidewalk. It was a good move because Bono, Edge, Larry, and Adam were unprepared and simply too tired for the huge crowd that had massed around the block waiting for them. The chauffeur prepared to step out, walk around the car, and open Adam's door, but the bassist was well ahead of him, offering his hasty thanks while jumping out onto the street. Looking back into the limo, he shrugged, "You just can't keep a secret in Cleveland, can you?" Then, after a quick wave to the fans, he sprinted to a line of security guards and through the hotel doors just as the crowd surged forward to engulf the limousines.

Avoiding its fans had never been U2's style in the past. Over the years, the band had fostered a reputation for accessibility, and there were very few occasions when the band members had deliberately avoided a gathering of supporters. The group was famous for surprising clusters of fans waiting patiently after shows for any glimpse of the foursome. A frequent scenario featured the band members appearing through a backstage door, walking quickly toward their tour bus, then breaking rank to gladly converse and sign autographs. Usually, one of U2's management staff, checking his watch frequently and mumbling apologies, would be forced to break up the friendly session and drag his charges onto the idling transport. In a 1983 radio interview with me at WBCN in Boston, Edge admitted: "It's the moment I actually meet the people that enjoy our music that's very special. We cannot control what people think of us, [but] when we meet people, we just underline the fact that we are the same as they are. We may be in a privileged position in a creative field of music, but other than that, there's essentially no difference."

That viewpoint was demonstrated during the same interview when one of my studio assistants appeared with a scrap of paper passed to him by a small group of fans gathered in front of the station. The U2 supporters had shown up during the live radio interview with Edge, Adam, and Larry, hoping to meet the musicians. Larry read the short greeting and noted the seven signatures scrawled underneath, then asked, "Can you let them in?"

"I really can't," I apologized. "It's strictly against station rules."

"Are you sure?" Larry persisted. He finally made such a nuisance of himself that an agreement was struck to admit the fans into WBCN's front office, where they could at least listen in on the rest of the interview. Larry happily supervised the operation, assuring the delighted group that they would meet the other band members as soon as the interview ended.

U2 had also built its loyal following with an unusual candor onstage. Even when the band was just a young and determined unit touring exhaustively across America for the first time, the members recognized that the audience was as essential to the chemistry of each show as the performers. U2 treated fans with a tremendous amount of respect, working hard to inspire them during live performances. Still teenagers when they first toured America in 1980, the band members possessed an idealism and unflagging belief in their music, matching it with the courage to express their ideas openly onstage. U2 balanced its inexperience with an uncommon honesty, admitting from the very beginning that what the audience saw was what it got. The band hid behind no mask, intending its presence onstage to be naked and real, for better or worse.

In a *Boston Rock* magazine interview after the group's debut Boston appearance in December 1980, Bono stated: "A lot of bands will go to the far right or the far left just to make 'new' sounds, but they leave emotion behind. People can see through pretend—if a band can't do it for real, then people shouldn't go to see them. Emotion is everything." His intent, he said, was to inflame the audience with U2's own zeal so that, "instead of directing your energies negatively, into busting somebody's head open, you can direct them positively, into letting yourself go and appreciating what's going down onstage."

That honesty had a powerful and kinetic effect on the small number of converts who picked up import copies of U2's debut album *Boy* in 1980 and attended the earliest Stateside club appearances. The band's direct emotional challenge quickly transformed the few curious onlookers into a unified vanguard of U2 enthusiasts. Most witnesses left U2 concerts convinced they'd heard the truth, and that the subjects Bono had been singing about were of real concern to him, not just a collection of rhymed words. The new followers were drawn to the group with a double bond unusual in popular music—not only were they moved by the band's passionate performance, but they also left with a respect for U2's message. There were few bands who could deliver such a jolt of adrenalin and inspire such loyalty, so word about the four young Irishmen spread rapidly through the musical underground.

America's well developed network of rock and roll clubs and bars doesn't offer much in the way of profit for bands on the road, but it is the cheapest avenue to follow for new groups struggling to promote their name and music. Major record labels that regularly subsidize their bands' touring costs keep the bottom line in view as well, preferring to test a group's efforts at this relatively inexpensive level. A memorable performance might prompt those in the audience to tell their friends, adding to the size of the crowd when the band returns. If the group is touting a new album or single, fresh converts might buy the discs or re-quest that the songs be played by their favorite local radio stations. The tremendous added exposure of airplay and (since the debut of MTV during the summer of 1981) video-play can significantly increase the size of a group's audience. When the response is great enough, bands can look forward to moving out of the 200- to 2,000-person capacity clubs and into larger theaters that hold between 2,000 and 8,000 people. In an attendance bonus, minors normally excluded from bars by state drinking laws can attend theater concerts. As exposure of its music and resulting album sales increase, a band might find itself comfortably sell-ing out sports arenas with a capacity of over 10,000 persons. The final stage, reached by only a few superstar performers at the peak of their popularity, involves enormous concert productions in football stadiums seating over 50,000 fans.

Although the colorful success stories of groups that lug massive stages with complex sound and light systems through America's largest stadiums and arenas are easily recalled, most bands fail to step up from the rock and roll club circuit and remain little known. These hopefuls' attempts are sometimes thwarted from within by clashing personalities, but even a solid unit needs the right combination of professional ele-ments and luck to become a hit. Expanding a group's toehold takes pro-motion and advertising, commercial exposure through hit records, and the largest question mark of all: acceptance by an always unpredictable audience. Out of the thousands of new bands that release music in a giv-en year, only a handful build their careers to the point of successfully selling out theaters. This statistic alone establishes U2's rise from an anonymous club support act to stardom as a definite phenomenon, but the short period in which it occurred — barely seven years — truly makes this one of popular music's most impressive success stories.

In 1983, U2 scored its first major American breakthrough with the album *War*. After that, the ranks of its followers swelled considerably until U2 was easily selling out 20,000-seat arenas like the Richfield Coliseum all across the country. By 1988, with a pair of number one sin-gles and the cover of *Time* magazine, U2's popularity had increased tenfold. While the combined sales for the group's first two albums had barely totaled 100,000 copies in America, U2's *The Joshua Tree*, released in 1987, sold in the millions and garnered Grammy awards for album of the year and best rock performance by a group. The initial eight-day dash across the eastern United States in December 1980 had earned a few hundred dollars a night; U2's worldwide tour in support of *The Joshua Tree* grossed over $40 million.

Can a group that thrives on a close relationship with its audience maintain that key ingredient while riding an incredible wave of popularity? Has U2's emotional potency waned in the gigantic stadiums where, to most of their audience, the band members appear as mere dots onstage? Was sufficient warmth transmitted by the group's concert movie *Rattle and Hum*, sent out to film screens across America in place of an actual concert tour in 1988? U2 has accepted these compromises in order to satisfy its audience's demands for contact. Has the group, by virtue of its need to interact closely with its new massive audience, fought into a no-win situation?

In November 1984, during a live phone interview with me on WBCN, Bono revealed his fears concerning success. "I like to be able to talk to people, I like to be able to spend time with people. I don't like when they see me as anything other than a person. [When] people start relating to me as some sort of pop star, I get real freaked out." Three years after that, during an interview for Island Records, I asked Bono if U2 could survive the incredible storm of popularity that had come with *The Joshua Tree*. He replied: "I think the chances of succeeding . . . success are pretty slim. I mean, surviving success with a sense of humor, for instance. But we're only halfway down the road here—in fact, not even halfway! I don't know where all this is gonna lead us, [but] it's a lot of fun finding your way when it's uncharted territory."

2

U-WHO?

EVERY SEPTEMBER the city of Boston sits on the invisible border between an endless summer and the annual fall invasion of a quarter million students. Almost overnight, hundreds of rental vans and station wagons converge and clog the maze of streets around Harvard, M.I.T., Emerson, Boston University, Tufts, Northeastern, Boston College, and many others. Demolished U-Haul trucks, peeled open on Storrow Drive after their drivers fail to notice the famous low bridge warnings, are a common sight. But for every one of those crippled, a hundred break through every fall to deposit their cargoes on dormitory steps across the city.

In 1980, the students were eager reinforcements for Boston's burgeoning rock and roll scene. Attendance at the local decibel dives was at an all-time high and many who labored in classrooms at the Berklee College of Music and other fine arts institutions constantly replenished New England's pool of musical talent. Most of these young players had to rethink their classical training to adapt to the rock and roll spirit of the times. The inner city clubs — Cantones in the financial district, the Rat(hskeller) in Kenmore Square, and the Club just across the river in Cambridge — had been attracting steady crowds by hosting local rock groups playing original songs. Bands bearing the latest hip sounds from New York City or England found Boston an essential stop that often boasted the largest, most enthusiastic audience of their entire tour.

The catalyst for all of this activity was punk — the gritty, unglamorous musical bastard that had crawled from the basements of New York City over four years before. Reacting to what they believed was a clogged mid-seventies rock and roll scene rife with rock-star conceit and lofty instrumental excesses (endless solos and burdensome arrangements), supporters of the new attitude refocused on rock and roll's roots — where energy and emotion mattered more than technique. A New York City quartet of scrawny mop-tops in leather known as the Ramones were the earliest American perpetrators of punk rock. Spitting in the face of convention with a steady guitar-bass-drum buzzsaw and lead singer Joey Ramone's pervasive monotone, the band's debut album, *The Ramones* (1976), presented fourteen songs, each clocking in at around two minutes. This concise collection had much more in common with the Beatles' first few albums, which were jammed full of short singles, and with 1950s efforts from Jerry Lee Lewis, Carl Perkins, and Eddie Cochran, than with the seventies mini-opera of Queen or grandiose art rock from Electric Light Orchestra.

To most of those who had heard the first Ramones album in 1976, the music seemed like a joke, but its ground-breaking revolt would inspire a host of others including important English bands like the Sex Pistols and the Clash. Brand new names began appearing on the record shelves: the Dead Boys, the Stranglers, Wayne County and the Electric Chairs, the Buzzcocks, Eater, Sham 69, the Vibrators, Richard Hell, Eddie and the Hot Rods, the Adverts, Johnny Thunders' Heartbreakers, and Generation X. Mainstream consumers recoiled in horror, dismissing the music as caustic and incompetent, but the punks established a beachhead anyway. Raw, perhaps naive optimism fueled their early days, creating a unified movement out of a thousand individual efforts across the globe. It was a guerrilla attack with a noble purpose: to take control of rock and roll from the current hierarchy and place it back in the hands of the commoners.

As time passed, though, the noble spirit waned. Some of punk's most vital bands attracted a host of fans who were not motivated by the desire to help create a new world, but inspired instead by the nihilistic charisma of the personalities onstage. Some punk heroes were elevated to and accepted star status, a process many early supporters equated with joining the enemy. In 1979, the massive pop and disco hit "Heart of Glass" from Blondie plus the Clash's *London Calling* album and its single "Train in Vain" gave the music a mass acceptance dreaded by punk diehards. The new attitude had flowed into the mainstream and noticeably affected popular taste, but its original vitriolic sting was steadily diluted and soon absorbed.

Eventually, the original buzzsaw sounds from the Ramones

evolved into a scene characterized by a variety of styles. Talking Heads led the fascinated into a land of off-beat melodies and black-inspired rhythms, Elvis Costello and Nick Lowe developed as songwriting crafts-men inspired by the folk tradition, while Jamaican reggae flavored the pop tunes of the Police. The Specials, Madness, the Selector, and the English Beat took England by storm with their revival of ska, an up-tempo form of reggae. Electronic melodies and rhythm powered Devo's jerk and quirk, the primal street-pulse of Suicide, and fledgling efforts from a seminal "dirty" lineup of Human League. Joy Division studied the gloomy artistic intentions of sixties predecessor Velvet Under-ground. Unabashedly embracing outrageous pop fashion, Adam Ant conjured up swashbuckling pirate imagery with eye shadow, mascara, and dramatic buccaneer costumes.

In the pages of music magazines, American critics were quick to extol the importance of the punk movement, but other media outlets were far less enthusiastic. A network of radio stations coast to coast made up the most powerful medium available to expose music, but in-dividual programming managers were unwilling to gamble on the radi-cal new style. Without airplay, American punk bands were severely hampered from breaking out of their local areas. Especially hard hit were British and European groups that enjoyed popularity at home, but found business in the U.S. anything but lucrative. In spite of enormous fame in England, the Jam failed to ever rise above playing a loose net-work of small punk clubs across America. Paul Weller, the band's out-spoken guitarist, constantly leveled attacks at the indifference of U.S. radio, trying unsuccessfully to goad the stations into playing his music. The Boomtown Rats, a massively successful group in its native Ireland as well as England, was similarly frustrated. In a 1981 interview with me for *Boston Rock* magazine, lead singer Bob Geldof charged that Amer-ican radio was "the worst in the world"; he resented that his band was "expected to make safe records for radio."

Commercial radio stations that played rock music were split into two camps. Top 40 stations, also known as contemporary hit radio (CHR), played singles — individual songs released by record companies in hopes that the songs would become hits with the listening audience. The most popular singles — an arbitrary playlist of forty varying slightly from station to station — were featured on the air as frequently as possi-ble, the idea being that listeners would hear their favorite music more often and stay tuned in. The abrasive sound of punk was likened to jack-hammering by Top 40 programmers. Even the more liberal-minded album-oriented radio (AOR) stations, which featured less familiar album tracks not released as singles, turned a deaf ear to the new style. AOR stations, previously on top of every fresh turn in rock and roll, were more concerned in the late seventies with the airplay benefits of Fleetwood Mac's hits than the angry art of the Sex Pistols' album. Even the later, more palatable musical forms that rushed into view behind punk were mostly avoided by AOR, as those stations continued to play the same standard fare of mainstream groups that had been successful for years.

The punk scene did find a friendly radio medium, however, at noncommercial stations based on college campuses all across the United States. Most were subsidized organizations that didn't need to streamline their programming and maintain a viable commercial sound that would sell advertising. Nearly every major city had at least one noncommercial outlet on the low end of the FM dial playing anything from Kentucky bluegrass to Mozart, John Coltrane, or John Cage. When punk sounds were introduced onto some of these stations, the individual local scenes around them benefited immediately. Word of mouth about new bands was complemented by actual airplay of their music, and information concerning the latest groups' tour schedules was easily accessible.

New England's first college station to feature the sounds of punk, WTBS–FM (renamed WMBR after its call letters were purchased by TV mogul Ted Turner) pumped out a mere ten watts of broadcast power from the campus of M.I.T., as opposed to the 50,000 watts generated by many commercial FM outlets. Its antenna's position high atop a Cambridge building, however, permitted the tiny signal to broadcast over the whole of metropolitan Boston. Hosting a variety of public affairs and alternative music shows that included reggae, soul, blues, and jazz, the managers at WTBS were proud of their fresh-sounding programming. The station welcomed nonstudent volunteers, and in 1975 a bespectacled visitor with the unusual habit of dyeing his hair various colors began a weekly radio show designed to expose the new sounds of "underground" rock and roll. Oedipus, as the quietly intense deejay was known, soon proved a wily visionary on his "Demi-Monde" program, becoming the punk scene's first radio disciple and its most active exponent in the Northeast.

A recent college graduate with some deejay experience, I was marking time in 1976 as a highly overqualified house painter while applying for work at every Boston radio station I could locate. Since a paying radio job continued to elude me, I had volunteered at WTBS and nailed down a weekday morning shift styled after traditional AOR. Centered around typical favorites like Steve Miller, Supertramp, Blue Oyster Cult, and Jethro Tull, the show soon began featuring an ever-increasing mix of the punk sounds that Oedipus was then doling out. His belief, that seventies rock had lost an essential energy and that the new spirit rising out of New York City and London could be brought into Boston, was prophetic. Soon the attendance at area clubs began to increase, a wave of new bands crawled out of their rehearsal spaces, and record store sales of local music and punk rock became noticeable — then respectable.

The boiling activity on "the street" came to the attention of Boston radio powerhouse WBCN–FM, which hired Oedipus in 1977 to ply his knowledge on weekend nights over its massive New England–wide broadcasting range. One of America's first album rock stations, WBCN had survived from its psychedelic days of 1968 to become a very successful radio outlet. Although the station's success depended on regularly featuring the most popular rock artists of the day, a commitment to expose new music added to its appeal, making the decision to hire Oedipus a wise one. His "Nocturnal Emissions" program earned increasing notoriety, and by the following year he was elevated into a regular radio slot every weeknight. In a development that surprised me, I was invited by WBCN to follow in his footsteps, occupying the weekend shifts Oedipus had just transferred from.

On a boiling August afternoon in 1980 I headed toward WBCN in an ancient Green Line trolley, sweat dripping freely while I gazed through the rust-locked windows. If I could catch BCN's music director Jimmy Mack in a good mood, there might be some free albums thrown my way. Exiting from the train, I detoured through seedy Kenmore Square for a regular visit to New England Music City. Carefully stepping over the tossed bottles and melted chewing gum hazards, I made my way into the record store and found Greg Reibman, a salesman and also fellow deejay at WTBS, hunched over a box with pricing gun in hand. It was a prized shipment of fresh releases from across the Atlantic. Consistently demanded discs from the Buzzcocks, the Sex Pistols, and the Clash formed the bulk of the shipment, but there were also a few new items, including singles from England's most talked-about new group, a Liverpool outfit known as Echo and the Bunnymen — which expounded the latest musical trend dubbed "the psychedelic revival." I noticed records from another psychedelic entry, the Teardrop Explodes, ska discs by the Selector and the English Beat, a forty-five released by sixties mod revival group Secret Affair, and two singles from a band called simply U2.

The first single's shiny white paper sleeve was dominated by a black and gray front cover photograph of a train station with one lonely, waiting figure. There were no clues offered concerning the identity of U2's members, but printing on the back cover revealed that the song "A Day Without Me" had been recorded in Ireland. Greg and I listened to the single while he priced his import shipment. A brief guitar stiletto echoed out of the speakers, answered by a repeating double-note sequence. The crystalline introduction repeated three times before a massive drum crash announced the guitar's soaring melody. Compared to the primitive homemade quality found on many new bands' singles, this recording delivered a solid high-fidelity knockout punch. The singer's words slammed out earnestly, but without the snarling emotional affectations that many punk vocalists added in place of genuine angst. The single's B-side, "Things to Make and Do," was an engaging instrumental driven by more of the band's distinctive guitar work. Greg handed me the second forty-five, entitled "11 O'Clock Tick Tock," which provided more information about the group: a photo on the back of a blue picture sleeve identified the four band members as Larry, Adam, Bono, and the Edge.

Purchasing "A Day Without Me," I left the store for the short walk to WBCN's studios. After slipping into Jimmy Mack's office, I played the usual waiting game until he managed to get off the telephone. Young and hyperactive, Jimmy devoured new records, spending much of each working day discussing their merits with record company promotion reps. He was also responsible for recommending to his immediate boss, program director Tony Berardini, which albums and singles should be placed in the main studio to be featured on the air. Unlike most stations, whose program directors select every song on the air and when to play it, WBCN's deejays at that time were permitted to choose the music for their own shows, and we could arrange the favored cuts in an hourly framework merely suggested by Tony. The major restriction to this "loose" format was that songs not placed in the studio were off limits unless Jimmy gave special permission for them to be featured on the air. Sensing that "A Day Without Me" possessed the sound, production, and style of a WBCN hit, I hoped to receive that special permission.

Any commercial radio station, whatever the musical format,

can only exist for a short time without playing music that an audience wants to hear, or listeners will simply tune elsewhere. Selecting new songs to play that will become desirable to listeners involves a programmer's intuition and use of available information. Compiling an artist's previous sales history, current retail indicators, telephone request activity, and concert attendance can provide strong evidence for gauging a new single's hit potential. None of these factors, however, can completely guarantee that a song will be successful. At some point, a programmer has to rely on an intuition steadily honed by listening to music and seeing what works on the air and what fails. A successful programmer is often referred to as one who has "good ears," and Jimmy's ears were highly regarded. His immediate excitement over the U2 single confirmed my belief that this song could be a hit. Having read about the group in England's *New Musical Express*, Jimmy confirmed that the band was indeed from Ireland. He gave his blessing to feature the song on my weekend radio program.

Nighttime airplay on WBCN soon spread U2's name throughout the local area. I took "A Day Without Me" over to WTBS where it quickly became the second most requested rock song on the station, right behind "Rescue" by Echo and the Bunnymen. The few available copies of U2 discs were snapped up instantly from record store racks, and with frequent reorders sold quickly throughout the fall. If I hadn't reserved an import copy of U2's debut album before it arrived in October, New England Music City surely would have sold its two copies before I could intercept one. Entitled *Boy*, the album featured "A Day Without Me" plus ten new songs, including the latest English single, "I Will Follow." Jimmy, Tony, Oedipus, and I were united in our agreement that *Boy* deserved WBCN's special attention, but Tony decided to hold back heavy airplay until Island Records officially released the American version of the album in February. He knew that WBCN's exposure would prompt listeners to scour record stores for the few copies of the British import that were available. Why not wait a couple of months until Island had prepared its American promotional campaign and there were plenty of domestic albums available in the stores? Tony believed that coordinating the radio attack with a strong retail campaign would make *Boy* a huge seller in Boston.

A unique set of circumstances, however, forced U2's name into the local spotlight just a few weeks later, accelerating WBCN's involvement with the band. The station had agreed to cosponsor the Boston appearance of a Detroit group named Barooga at the Paradise Theater on

December 13. The band's latest album on Capitol Records was receiving heavy airplay at the station, and local Capitol promotion man Tony Chalmers was counting on a packed club to build more attention and excitement for his act. To promote the event, he had arranged for the admission price to be lowered and provided WBCN with a large number of tickets to give out on the air. If all went well, Barooga's "beer-drinking and hell-raising" style of rock, not far from Bob Seger's Silver Bullet ranch, would turn the night into a massive sweat-fest. Then, unexpectedly, U2's name began to appear in concert ads as Barooga's warm-up act. It was an awkward billing, as the two bands approached rock and roll from opposite directions. Barooga represented the old school fueled by blues and boogie with lots of the soloing that had dominated seventies AOR rock, while U2 was the young aggressor racing out of the basement with an atmospheric punch, concise songs, and a marked lack of instrumental excess.

Jimmy confirmed that U2 was definitely scheduled to open the show, and he informed me that Tony had instructed him to get more U2 music on the air as soon as possible to support the event. He placed *Boy* in WBCN's record library and encouraged the deejays to feature it. Since another import copy of the album wasn't readily available, Jimmy cheerfully impounded mine. Free to play *Boy* on the air, the disc jockeys responded in earnest, but my original favorite, "A Day Without Me," was soon surpassed in airplay and requests by "I Will Follow" and "Out of Control."

December arrived, and along with the winter chill came disillusionment for rock and roll supporters. Purists had to accept that punk rock was in the throes of change as the style fragmented into the many less threatening facets of what was now known as "new wave." Mainstream listeners and punks alike experienced a massive trauma when John Lennon was murdered in New York City on December 8. As one of the few established artists who had successfully bridged the gap between sixties idealism and the punks' restless energy—two seemingly distant camps which actually shared many goals—Lennon had influenced the lives of many U2 supporters. Now the Irish band, which had begun its first tour of America in New York City two days before the assassination, plowed doggedly on through its concert dates, fighting through their own sense of shock and the grim numbness that hung over each audience like a black cloud.

Five nights after Lennon's death, Barooga and U2 rendezvoused at the Paradise Theater in Boston. Unlike many of the dives that featured rock and roll bands, the Paradise was clean and well maintained, with ample lighting and an excellent sound system. The club had always been a hotbed of activity, hosting an interesting variety of performers since opening its doors in 1977. It was a neutral ground — where punk rockers hung out to watch the Dead Boys one night and rhythm and blues freaks hit boogie heaven with NRBQ or Bonnie Raitt the next. With a capacity of over five hundred, the Paradise was a popular choice for many national groups on introductory tours and also marked a plateau that local bands struggled to reach. Filling the Paradise was proof that a group had captured Boston's attention.

Arriving early, I was surprised to see a large gathering of leather jackets already waiting in line. Usually an audience trickled into the club while the warm-up band was playing, and often the bartenders were the only ones present when the group walked onstage. However, with showtime still minutes away, a crowd of nearly 150 already jammed the area in front of the stage, many of the faces familiar to me from the local punk scene. They applauded loudly when the four members of U2 appeared in the spotlights and the lead singer looked up with some surprise to mumble a greeting. Without wasting time, the guitarist eased into low, ominous guitar chords to introduce "11 O'Clock Tick Tock." Solid and loud, the drummer crashed into action with an aggression unexpected from someone who looked like he'd been kidnapped from a boy's choir. To the right, the bassist paced back and forth under a profusion of blond curls, steadily measuring out a fat rhythm swath. As the melody burst into brilliance, the singer whirled around and charged recklessly into the lyrics.

Bono was a tireless figure in motion for the entire show, yet it was the Edge who attracted most of my attention as he held court on the left side of stage, coolly laying out the same chiming guitar sounds that made U2's debut album so distinctive. He stood stoically amid the raging energy pouring off the platform, seeming lost in thought and rarely looking up at the audience. Far from the stereotype of the lead guitarist who struts haughtily onstage like a Greek god deigning to perform for mere mortals, the Edge was self-assured yet reserved in his manner. Displaying a rare economy in his playing, he stuck to chords and echoed tones rather than showy lead solos.

U2's undeniably strong charisma in those first few moments eroded somewhat as the band encountered some technical problems. An overblown echo effect on Bono's microphone threatened to sabotage his effort during the opening number as well as the next two songs: a suite of "An Cat Dubh" and "Into the Heart," both featured on *Boy*. Just as the electronic annoyances were being worked out, another difficulty arose as Bono began struggling to hit some of the higher notes. The audience didn't seem to notice the squeaking feedback and missed notes, though, responding instead to the band's energetic and emotional performance. The singer's rambling monologues exposed a breathy, nervous excitement, but Bono soon settled down to reveal a sampling of the wit for which he would become well known in years to come. "We intend to spend a lot of time next year in this country — probably because it's so large." Bono also exhibited his improvisational skills, striking a collective nerve when he borrowed a few lines from John Lennon's "Give Peace a Chance" and inserted them into the middle of a U2 original, "The Electric Co."

U2's eager attack fueled an emotional reaction from the crowd that amazed the group. After the Edge took charge for "Things to Make and Do," Bono emerged from the shadows and stared onto the dance floor with eyes wide. Grabbing the mike, he admitted, "There's a lot of people here tonight who weren't supposed to be here." Then the band tore into more music from *Boy*, ending its set with "Twilight" and a sweaty, out-of-breath version of "I Will Follow." Even though the time allowed for the opening slot was short, U2 was permitted to acknowledge the wild applause by jumping back onstage to churn out a second rendition of "11 O'Clock Tick Tock." (The practice of performing a popular single twice in one show was quite unusual in America, but common with European groups.) That should have been the end of the warm-up, since U2 had used up more than its allotted amount of stage time, but the audience insisted on more. The tumult prompted the Paradise stage manager to usher the surprised members back into the lights once more, where an amazed Bono reached out for the mike and said, "This is our first ever . . . I don't know what!" I believe he meant "second encore in the States." The group complied with a suitably frenzied version of "Out of Control."

U2 had succeeded in taking the clean studio sonics of *Boy* into a powerful new dimension onstage. The exciting show made me resolve to see this band again as I trudged off the dance floor and up to the bar. Sweating people filed past, many rushing off to see the Martha and the Muffins concert across town. Such an excellent early attendance usually indicated a busy night ahead for the Paradise staff. Now was the time that Barooga's fans would reach the club to overwhelm the audience that had cheered U2 on. At the moment, though, fleeing patrons were passing in droves through the club's front door and out into the street. I moved in the opposite direction, since the backstage pass Tony Chalmers had given me to meet Barooga after their show would also work now to admit me into U2's dressing room upstairs.

The band members didn't see me enter since they were all jammed around a window that looked out into the main room where they had just played. Fans exiting the club spotted the foursome staring down at them and waved excitedly back. The only person in the room who noticed me was Anne Marie Foley, a friend who worked at a local record store. She had reached the dressing room only moments before and had already introduced herself to the boys. Now, as if she'd been best friends with everyone for years, she loudly announced, "Hey guys! This is Carter Alan from WBCN; they've been playing your record!" Four heads whipped around as Anne Marie jumped right into the introductions. When she got to the guitar player she said, "Carter . . . this is the Edge. The Edge, this is Carter. That's too formal, can we just call you Edge?" The guitarist couldn't have had time to consider disagreeing; he just nodded with an amused smile. Another figure walked into the room. "This is Paul McGuinness," Anne Marie added. The latter, with black rimmed glasses over serious brows and a cigarette gripped tightly in his fingers, stepped forward and firmly shook my hand. "I am the band's manager and we're very happy that you've chosen to play our record. In fact, since you are already playing it, you can consider yourself to be the first American station to do so."

Paul McGuinness was clearly very intelligent, but he wasn't afraid to admit that he lacked much knowledge about the American media. I was in the process of answering his many questions about radio when a seventh person burst through the door, his commanding presence ending all discussion in the room. Anne Marie introduced him as George Skaubitis, a local promotion man for Warner Brothers, the record label that would be distributing U2's American album for Island. George waded in and began pumping hands with the surprised band members. "I just want to tell you guys how much I loved the show and the new album!" He dug into a brown paper bag he was carrying and said, "I know I don't have a record to promote yet, but I just couldn't resist." Skaubitis beamed as he opened his hand to reveal a small white button with a black U2 logo on it. "I went out and had a couple hundred of these made up for the show!"

"Surely you didn't have to do this!" McGuinness remarked. "But I'm very appreciative and impressed that you took the time to do it."

Bono grabbed the bag from George's hand, pulling out some of the little treasures and throwing them around the room while he yelled, "Look boys, the label's made badges for us!"

While we all admired the buttons and reached for our own handful, Adam pointed out the window and announced, "Everyone appears to have left." We crowded around the pane to see an almost deserted room with barely thirty people — including bartenders — scattered about in the semidarkness. U2's drummer, quietly reserved so far, raised his eyebrows toward Edge, whose sober stage demeanor was now replaced by excitement. Bono stared through the window, shaking his head. It was now obvious that the Boston audience, after delighting U2 with its warm reception, had nearly disappeared. This set off a fit of jabbering in the dressing room until Paul McGuinness observed that Barooga was going on. Anne Marie used the sudden lull in conversation to ask, "Does everybody want to go to a party?"

"I think I'd like to watch Barooga first," said the manager as he turned from the window. The four band members agreed, so everyone exited to hear some of the Detroit group's set.

I followed Bono through the backstage door into the club's main room. To Barooga's credit, the band was churning out a full-tilt set for the few who remained. I felt bad for the group, especially because WBCN had been playing Barooga's latest album a great deal, but clearly few listeners had liked it enough to want to come to the show. Tony Chalmers waved us over to his spot at the bar, offering to buy a round for our entire group, courtesy of Capitol Records. The U2 members stayed for most of the show while I kept company with Chalmers. Barooga's disheartened record company promotion man drank more than his share of scotch — and I was right there with him — but I'm sure he wasn't too wrecked to notice the trace of a smile on Paul McGuinness's face as U2 sucked down Capitol Records' beer.

3

LOST IN AMERICA

U2 WAS SIGNED to Island Records, a subsidiary of Warner Brothers. This meant that *Boy* was marketed and distributed to retail, and promoted to the media by Island's parent company, Warner Brothers. As a member of the Warner Brothers artist development staff, Ellen Darst helped shepherd a number of the label's artists through early career difficulties, introducing them to radio and music retailing VIP's in the process. Assigned to the U2 project in November 1980, Darst had another task as well: to inspect the band while on tour and gauge U2's stability as a working unit and its potential in the American market. Her opinion would figure heavily in Warner Brothers' plans for the band. Conservative in appearance, with short black hair and conspicuous eyeglasses, Darst took her official role with dead seriousness. However, it was obvious upon meeting her that she had a friendly and easily approachable nature, as well as an eager enthusiasm for music and her job.

Ellen missed U2's Boston show, but had seen the opening tour date at the Ritz in New York City on December 6. That performance became U2's American debut because the original opener at the Penny Arcade in Rochester on the fifth was canceled. Ellen also witnessed U2's second concert, in Washington, D.C., and was moved by the band's energy and zeal. She told me, "They were all over the place and real rough, but it was so . . . compelling!" Backstage, Ellen was impressed with the band members themselves. "A lot of the English bands had a very cynical attitude about record companies, which I found insulting. You'd work your heart out trying to make things happen and they'd just look at you and say, 'Why are you wasting our time?' But U2, they were clued in, interested and receptive, with none of that negativity I'd seen from other bands. What they lacked in finesse, they made up for in commitment. I could also see that although Paul [McGuinness] was very green, he was extremely smart." The minitour of eight dates, some with Barooga, had been his hastily arranged plan to introduce the group to a few select cities. Ellen pointed out, "They just wanted to do a little Northeast tour. Paul didn't care who they toured with; they could have been opening for Ringling Brothers!"

Premier Talent arranged U2's tour. Headed by a consummate businessman named Frank Barsalona, who had started his company in the mid-sixties by signing on British Invasion bands like Herman's Hermits and the Animals, Premier had become an undisputed leader in booking rock and roll bands, largely through Barsalona's uncanny instinct for discovering new, untested artists. This ability had fostered an agency stable which boasted at one time or another the talents of Led Zeppelin, Jimi Hendrix, the Who, Jethro Tull, and a fledgling performer named Bruce Springsteen. Barsalona first heard about U2 from Island Records president Chris Blackwell. As he related to me, "Chris had great taste, a little off-beat, but great taste! So, whenever he came up with an act, I was always interested." Blackwell's intense enthusiasm about an Irish rock and roll quartet he'd found convinced Barsalona. "Before I'd do anything with an act, I would have to see them. But [with U2] I never did. I told Chris I'd take the act just like that, sight unseen. I booked them without having heard anything, either, because Chris didn't have a tape to play me."

Barsalona had no intention of allowing U2's American debut to take place in New York City, but the Rochester cancellation left him no choice. "You usually book a week or ten days [of concerts] outside of New York and work your way in," he said. That way, when a band reached the Big Apple, it would be seasoned enough to perform for a host of important music critics and record industry big shots. Another stumbling block was that the last-minute scheduling of the minitour forced Barsalona to book U2's New York City performance on a weekend night. "The Ritz usually had dance bands every Friday, Saturday, and Sunday night and they filled the club with people who wanted to dance. I knew the place would be packed, but not with people who wanted to see U2."

Fully prepared for a possible disaster for the unknown Irish band, Barsalona admitted that what transpired that evening was "incredible." Except for a tiny core of supporters up front, nobody paid much attention to the four band members as they walked onstage and plugged in. "But with every song," Barsalona remembered, "a little part of the audience started paying attention. It was almost like a wave. When they were about sixty percent through, they basically had the whole audience. I still get chills when I think about it." Barsalona was so enthusiastic about the show that he rushed into U2's dressing room afterward to shake the hands of the four surprised band members, whom he'd never met, and pledge them his complete support.

U2's dramatic coups in New York and Boston dominated Ellen Darst's glowing report to her superior, Warner Brothers senior vice president of artist relations Bob Regehr. The band's initial success and its obvious commitment confirmed what Regehr already suspected, and he quickly became one of U2's greatest allies within the company. This was critically important because artists on subsidiary labels are often regarded as bastard children, promoted only after the primary label's artists have been properly taken care of. Ellen remembered: "He had so much confidence in their ability to get on. He pushed Warner Brothers [to promote U2] probably beyond the level they would have for an unknown band on a subsidiary label." Regehr's efforts helped garner the vital support funds required to mount U2's planned coast-to-coast visit in the early spring, and he continued to focus positive attention on Warners' Irish find even when three years of effort produced only lean sales for the band's first two albums.

Released in October 1980, the U.K. version of *Boy* featured a front cover photo of a young lad named Peter, a neighbor of Bono's whose face was filled with wonder and curiosity — an appropriate image for U2's first musical exploration. The black, white, gray, and silver artwork included costly extras: an inner sleeve made with heavy paper stock as well as custom record labels that pictured the same youth from the cover. If nothing else, the elaborate packaging demonstrated Island U.K.'s belief in its new signing. The American version of *Boy* released in January 1981 featured the same lineup and order of songs as the overseas version, but the artwork and packaging were quite different. All images of the young boy featured so prominently on the import were replaced with polarized photos of the band, stretched to distort each member's appearance. Ellen Darst recalled that there was a "vague worry at the label that there might be a homosexual impression left from the boy's waist-up nakedness." The concern was obviously strong enough to prompt Island's extensive revamping of *Boy*'s artwork. (Later pressings would return the censored boy from the U.K. cover to the U.S. album, printing the facial shot on a previously blank side of the inner paper sleeve.)

Both the import and domestic versions of *Boy* featured the same 1980 recordings from Windmill Lane Studio in Dublin, produced by Steve Lillywhite. "I Will Follow" opened the album with a simple ringing guitar figure that formed the backbone of the entire song. Edge never strayed too far from a basic melody, which was hitched to Larry's runaway drum crash and Adam's fat, booming bass lines. Around the traditional rock instruments, a glockenspiel could be heard chiming energetically, and near the beginning of the song's brief slow section, one could hear glass breaking. "I Will Follow" became U2's next European single and its first in America (the group's only domestic single until February 1983). The next song, "Twilight," had been previewed in rugged form on an Irish single in spring 1980. Lillywhite polished U2's performance with a crystal-clear recording, but left a raw feel to the song as well, with Edge's brief guitar solo echoing flatly off the back wall of the studio. Predating "I Will Follow," this was one of U2's earliest compositions, but even in 1983, during a radio interview, Adam Clayton informed me that he still regarded "Twilight" as one of U2's "great tracks."

"An Cat Dubh," "Into the Heart," and "Out of Control" completed side one. Known informally at WBCN as "the trilogy," the suite's first two songs flowed smoothly into each other as one piece, with "Out of Control" grafted on from another studio session. Translated from the Gaelic as "The Black Cat," "An Cat Dubh" entered on Edge's banshee guitar wail, drifting through a gloomy melody and Bono's ominous lyrics. A synthesizer in droning ostinato joined with softly rumbling bass to close the nightmarish tale and introduce a lovely guitar figure and answering glockenspiel which began "Into the Heart." This brief and beautiful look at the wonder of adolescence passed quickly into the pounding beat of "Out of Control," an early composition that originally appeared in embryonic form on the band's first release, the Irish EP *U-2-3*, in 1979. A beefy boogie, "Out of Control" was a crowd pleaser usually reserved for encores by the time U2 visited America.

The marriage of U2 with producer Steve Lillywhite was fortuitous for the stellar sound quality his recording process attained. *U-2-3*, as well as the following singles, "11 O'Clock Tick Tock" and "Another Day," sounded bland and timid next to the powerful ambience of "A Day Without Me," the first song that Lillywhite and U2 recorded together. His studio expertise and creative chemistry with the quartet introduced technical possibilities to the band members' raw ideas, pushing their songs into new musical territory. The relationship, which would continue to develop over two more albums, was not unlike George Martin's legendary association as producer and musical mentor with the Beatles. Lillywhite's presence stimulated U2 to write fresh material in the studio, crowding many of the band's older live standards off the album. "An Cat Dubh" and "Into the Heart" were written just prior to recording, as was "I Will Follow," which the band worked out on paper only three weeks before sessions began.

"Stories for Boys," which began side two of the album, had also been introduced two years before on *U-2-3* and was vastly improved this time around. After "The Ocean," a moody, low-key interlude, U2 returned to glorious heights with "A Day Without Me." The soaring guitar break in the song's middle section was reminiscent of a Jimmy Page guitar riff at the center of "How Many More Times?" on Led Zeppelin's first album. When asked about the similarity, Edge professed to be completely ignorant of Led Zeppelin's song and was curious to hear it. Bono's lyrics were sparked by the 1980 suicide of singer Ian Curtis, who had fronted the English band Joy Division. Eventually U2 would continue the tribute by regularly incorporating that band's masterful "Love Will Tear Us Apart" into its set.

"Another Time, Another Place" covered ground already presented in "Twilight," but "The Electric Co." was made of sterner stuff, enduring as a U2 concert staple for years to come. Heavily echoed at times, this tale of electroshock therapy overcame Lillywhite's unusually murky recording to become one of the album's strongest moments, even though its definitive version wouldn't appear until a live recording was released in late 1983. In sharp contrast to the booming, cathedral-sized sonics driving "The Electric Co.," a small-room intimacy permeated the recording of "Shadows and Tall Trees," which closed the album on a pensive note. Once a much faster and rocked-out song in U2's early Irish concerts, "Shadows and Tall Trees" featured the voices of Bono and Edge in delightful harmony on the choruses, accompanied by soft, lilting guitar and nearby drum taps.

Bono admitted to me during an interview conducted for Island Records in 1987 and released on a promotional album, "my lyrics tried to capture the elusive message of the music," rather than being written beforehand with a specific song style in mind. Indeed, the songs that made up *Boy* showed the young writer as a questing artist painting pictures. Observations from his own life seemed to have found fertile ground in U2's music, with youth growing into manhood as the dominant theme. Love was a newly discovered treasure worth cherishing and sacrificing for in "I Will Follow"; "Twilight" painted youth as a mystery regarded by the elderly with envious eyes; infinite possibilities beckoned on a shoreline in "The Ocean"; and the enigma of life's tightrope journey fascinated the narrator of "Shadows and Tall Trees." *Boy* was a reflection of the band members' own growing pains, and the frankness with which U2 shared these secrets was an early indication of the honesty that fans would come to expect from the group.

Press reaction to the album was mixed. *Variety*, a trade journal for the entertainment industry, offered only a terse, lukewarm reaction: "New British ensemble is not shy about playing three chord rock on their occasionally interesting debut." Mark Moses, writing in the *Boston Phoenix*, had a more pointed response: "On the softer songs the group aims for 'ethereal' and ends up with 'overwrought.' " Although the April 1981 *Rolling Stone* review of *Boy* was often approving, writer Debra Rae Cohen reacted negatively to all the praise and hype the English press and Island Records had been heaping on U2. She appreciated the band's potential, but recognized that the album was filled with the flaws and inconsistencies of a young and inexperienced group. Cohen also paid particular attention to "Shadows and Tall Trees," describing the song as "seemingly interminable" and "rambling without resolution."

Some writers, however, responded positively to the debut. In February 1981, *Rolling Stone* writer James Henke wrote a favorable review about the quartet. Having listened to an early import copy of the album, he wrote: "*Boy* does indicate that U2 is a band to be reckoned with. Their highly original sound can best be described as pop music with brains. The lyrical guitar lines slice through every song, while the vocals are rugged, urgent, and heartfelt." Full of praise, *People* magazine began its review of *Boy* with a comparison to another new arrival: "The Pretenders are not rushing their second album; that's good, because they're going to have to face some mean competition from, among other bands, U2."

Boy was only marginally successful in America: it struggled to number ninety-four on *Billboard*'s Top 200 chart of best-selling albums. But even if it didn't sell widely, the album was still considered by many a strong artistic statement. In 1983, *Trouser Press*, a respected monthly music magazine based in New York City, would look back at U2's debut with a glowing summary in its *Guide to New Wave Records*: "A musical package delivered to disc with great skill by producer Steve Lillywhite.

Unquestionably a masterpiece, *Boy* has a strength and beauty that's hard to believe on a debut album made by teenagers." Perhaps the best view, however, was somewhere between the emotional superlatives and critical hostility — a middle ground that Jim Green effectively staked out in the May 1981 issue of *Trouser Press*: "This is a startlingly good but flawed debut LP. U2's grim self-absorption runs the risk of making them look like prats. Maybe taking that risk, and succeeding despite/because of it, is what separates *Boy* from the rest of the boys."

With press reaction to *Boy* divided and American radio play of the album limited, Paul McGuinness and Warner Brothers wanted to put U2 back on the road at the earliest opportunity. They were counting on the band's formidable performance skills to leave a lasting impression on the small audiences that would turn out at this early stage. Ellen Darst joined up with U2 on March 3, 1981, at the opening concert in Washington, D.C., serving as record company liaison between the band and the media. She handled the first two weeks of touring in the eastern United States, then took a two-week break while Larry Butler, her counterpart on the West Coast, hitched up with the band in California. Ellen rejoined U2 in Texas and accompanied the tour as it wound its way back east to finish in Pittsburgh. The arduous seven-week visit, during which U2 performed in thirty-five cities, began a busy year that would see the band return to the United States for two additional tours.

U2's March–April road trip was quite different from others that Ellen had experienced in her career. In an interview for this book she recalled: "When a band came over from England, the record company would give them a certain amount of money to do showcase dates. They'd go to New York and Boston, San Francisco and L.A., maybe Texas or Atlanta, but they wouldn't do other dates [across the country]. This was a different kind of tour. The band traveled with the crew and the gear on the same bus. Nobody I've ever worked with has done that." The novel approach for a young and untested band presented extra problems, as Ellen related. "Every day you have the bus, you're spending money, so you stop in Ames, Iowa between Minneapolis and Chicago [and play]. These are routing dates — [like] Oklahoma City between Dallas and Tulsa." Even though U2 had to perform extra concerts to help absorb some of the tour costs, Ellen found that the band members didn't mind a bit. "They thought of themselves as a live band; they just wanted to go out and play."

Unlike reviews of its album, response to U2's concerts was almost universally positive and followed the group across the country like wildfire. The *Washington Post* reported most favorably about the tour opener at the Bayou: "U2 brought to their performance a sense of refinement that has been lacking in rock for some time. U2, like the Police and the Clash, are taking new wave to the next, higher, musical level." The following night in Philadelphia prompted a strong response from the *Courier Times*: "The last time this fast-rising group played the Bijou Cafe, it was to an audience of about 50 persons. But this time it was to a full house of churning bodies, dancing to the fine musical art of this bunch of rockers." Albany was the next stop, where U2 performed at J. B. Scott's to a crowd of four hundred. The *Schenectady Gazette* heaped praise on the show, stating that it "confirmed the excellence of the group's debut album, *Boy*."

Flush with the success of these shows, U2 pulled into Boston on March 6 for the fourth stop of its tour. Steady airplay and a strong word-of-mouth reaction to the group's memorable appearance in December had quickly sold out U2's return to the Paradise, prompting the addition of an early show which had also sold out. It was obvious to Warner Brothers and Paul McGuinness that, with over a thousand people attending the group's first headlining concerts in Boston, the city had become one of U2's strongest bastions of support. It made sense to use the Paradise as the location for Warner Brothers' planned recording of a U2 live show. The resulting tapes would be pressed into an album as part of the "Warner Brothers Music Show" series, which was sent to radio stations across the country. It was hoped that the program would acquaint radio programmers and their audiences with U2's prowess in concert and heighten interest in the band.

U2's first Paradise show was a superb rush of energy and excitement, ably captured on tape by Sam Kopper, a former WBCN disc jockey who ran his own mobile recording studio called Star Fleet. The performance got off to a shaky start when Larry's bass drum pedal broke after the first song. But Bono didn't let the potential disaster upstage the band, filling the repair time with comments, including a playful poke at having to do two sets in one night. "Only show-bands with guys in red suits who are balding have to do that back home!" Once the problem was fixed, U2 quickly worked up to full steam again, with the instrumental unit holding tight around Bono's spirited singing. Between songs the singer took the opportunity to salute the Boston groups he knew, including the evening's opening act, La Peste, and also Mission of Burma and Someone and the Somebodies. When they were called back onstage for an encore, the band members took their places as yells for "Out of Control" dominated the uproar. U2 complied, with Bono's introduction and Adam's bass pulse setting off a riot of cheers. After leaving the stage, the dazed foursome was called back again by a continuing tumult from the audience. U2 used the unexpected opportunity to perform "11 O'Clock Tick Tock" and "The Ocean" once again.

The second show that evening, also recorded by Star Fleet, featured U2 in a much more abandoned state, with precision sacrificed in favor of sheer energy. Afterward, upon listening to the playback, the band members preferred the first set and edited it into a usable radio program. They were obviously pleased with the material, since several songs eventually showed up as live B-sides of U2 singles. The encore of "Out of Control" appeared as flip side to the American "I Will Follow" single, which was pressed quickly and released in April. During the summer, initial pressings of a new English forty-five entitled "Fire" would feature a second seven-inch disc containing the live Paradise versions of "11 O'Clock Tick Tock," "The Ocean," and "Cry/The Electric Co." When U2's second album, *October,* appeared in late fall 1981, the U.K. single of "Gloria" was backed with the Paradise version of "I Will Follow." Ellen Darst commented to me that there was a purpose behind this. "Very early on they were looking for interesting B-side material. It's partly just the way they do things, but it had a lot to do with the perspective you get as a band from England or Ireland where the economy is depressed — they were into the idea of a good value. So if you put a single out, rather than it just be a track from your album, you made it attractive to your fans and worth the extra money spent on a single."

As the tour progressed, U2 won its most important critical accolades in New York City and Los Angeles. After a concert at the Ritz, *New York Times* critic Stephen Holden called the performance "a strong showing." He added, "For such an accomplished band, U2 is unusually young. Ranging in age from eighteen to twenty, its members met three years ago at a Dublin secondary school. Yet their sound makes them one of the most harmonically sophisticated rock bands to emerge in recent years." In Los Angeles, with only one major radio outlet, KROQ–FM, exposing U2's music, it was a gamble to play the Country Club with its thousand-person capacity — a half-empty club wouldn't look good in any review. But, as showtime approached, the hall did fill up with fans as well as the curious. Ken Tucker from the *Los Angeles Herald Examiner* found U2's set "vivid and enthusiastic." Robert Hilburn, an arts writer for the *Los Angeles Times*, applauded, "Gradually, the economy and intelligence of the music, coupled with the purity and heart of [Paul "Bono"] Hewson's vocals, broke down the audience's reserve."

The band, however, did not consider the important critical successes any excuse to take shortcuts in their road schedule. U2 played a wide variety of theaters and bars, as Ellen remembered: "In Tulsa we played this Texas swing-style ballroom with these huge painted pictures of country-western stars from forty or fifty years ago. I don't know if he was from there, but it was considered home to Bob Wills. The university gig [at Washington University in St. Louis] was in a chapel. That was kind of rousing in a way." In Chicago, U2 packed 750 people into a more traditional rock club called Park West, but also played at the University of Chicago's International House with a dollar admission charge and free beer. The group played its final show on April 21 at Decade in Pittsburgh, then took a ten-day break before another leg of the tour began in Gainesville, Florida. The band members used the time to vacation in the Bahamas, but also met Steve Lillywhite at Nassau's Compass Point Studios to record a new song. When it appeared two months later, "Fire" became the band's first charting U.K. single.

Racing around the United States in their cramped mobile quarters, the band members finally returned to Boston on May 28, 1981, with only four days remaining in their exhausting tour schedule. Ellen arranged a midday interview at WBCN with deejay Ken Shelton. Far from the image of ragged, road-weary veterans that I expected to stagger through the door, Bono, Edge, and Larry walked in smiling and obviously eager for the session (Adam had somehow "gotten lost" and failed to show). Also apparent was that the three displayed none of the swaggering arrogance that characterized many European punk or new wave bands. "You are a group of young gentlemen," began Shelton. "What is the oldest age of the group?"

Bono replied with mock seriousness: "Well at the moment, I'm taking charge of leadership—being twenty-one. I was twenty-one last week."

"Just twenty-one!"

Bono nodded and added, "The Edge and Larry are nineteen."

"Is that right?" Larry piped in while looking at Edge. The guitarist smiled and replied: "I don't know, I think after about nineteen you start going senile. I think Bono's on his way out."

Larry took the brunt of some good-natured abuse when Shelton singled him out for failing to participate more in the interview. "The shy one in the background, that's Larry. Does Larry get a microphone to sing during his performance while he's drumming? Or, Larry, do you just drum?"

"Well listen, I can hardly play the drums . . . "

Edge offered, "Larry makes so much noise when he's hitting things that he just tends to be quiet when he isn't."

Shelton looked at the guitarist. "Larry, the cute quiet one, have they put him in *Sixteen* magazine yet?"

While his bandmates laughed, the drummer looked aghast. "No, they never will!"

The three proved themselves witty conversationalists, but Bono was easily the most loquacious. He brought up the unexpected topic of American television weathermen whose reports were "like a puppet show," introduced his request for the Who's "My Generation" by calling it "the first rock record ever," and then explained the band's selection of David Bowie's "The Jean Genie" by saying, "They've allowed us in here to play some records. I don't know why, [maybe] because we haven't got a record player on the bus. I'd like to play this record, 'Jean Genie.' It was a very important record, certainly, when I was . . . I think I was fifteen when this record came out. It seems that Bowie influenced, more than anybody, this whole new explosion of music over the past few years."

One of the interview's more serious segments revealed some background to U2's songwriting. Shelton asked, "You dealt with a topic [on *Boy*]; it is a theme album of sorts."

Bono responded: "It's different. As a lyric writer, I'm more interested in people than politics, and more interested in why people should want to hit each other over the head with a broken bottle rather than where they do it . . . it being Northern Ireland. Everybody is violent, I feel."

"The album deals more directly with an individual's passing from childhood to manhood."

"Very loosely," Bono replied. "It's not a concept album, the lyrics are autobiographical. I just write about things that affect me, and I had a quite, sort of, violent adolescence."

"Violent . . . ?"

"Violent mentally."

U2 had easily sold all the tickets for that evening's appearance at the Metro, a Boston club with two and a half times the capacity of the Paradise. Preceded onstage by a solitary piper, the band teased the impatient audience just waiting to explode by opening delicately with

"The Ocean." Once the four blew into "11 O'Clock Tick Tock," however, there was no looking back as U2 slammed through a fast-paced, almost frantic set. Bono introduced a raw version of "I Fall Down," which would appear, with piano parts added, on the band's next album. "Over the past few months we traveled by bus over most of your country . . . and in the back of the bus this was found." The inspiring lyrics spoke of failure and a resolve to pick oneself up and try again. The band followed with "Fire," the song it had recorded in Nassau the previous month. "We release a single in England in two weeks!" the singer shouted. "This is the second time we ever played this—'Fire'!" Edge throttled his way into the song with a snappy, rhythmic melody punctuated by sharp, strident blasts at the end of each verse. Adam and Larry moved solidly behind with an airtight, rolling beat. As a preview of U2's next album, "Fire" seemed to indicate that very little would change in the band's trademark instrumental approach.

U2 appeared to be regressing back to its punk roots as the songs kept flying by at a faster pace. "Stories for Boys," "Out of Control," and "Boy/Girl" raced by in quick succession. Bono surprised the crowd by injecting a full verse of the Monkees' "I'm a Believer" into the middle of the latter song. By the time U2 blasted its way to a final monstrous chord, the air conditioning had long since surrendered and the deliriously charged and soaking-wet crowd was applauding with wild abandon. As Paul McGuinness watched the satisfied throng tumble outside into the warm night, he was pleased to observe that his band's live show kept "getting better and better."

But now it was time for U2 to leave the continuing refinement of its live set. Island wanted a new album in the fall, so the group was scheduled to spend most of its summer locked in the recording studio in Dublin. The result, a surprise by any fan's standards, would herald U2's return to America in November.

4

THE FIRE INSIDE

U2 HAD EMERGED from the aftermath of punk rock's explosion, adding certain musical refinements to the aggressive style and replacing the negative angst with its own hopeful and uplifting message. The band's debut album and string of performances in support of it demonstrated that U2's members, particularly Bono with his lyrics and onstage demeanor, were quite willing to make the extra effort to get that message across. As the group's career entered its next phase with the release of a second album, Bono emphasized in an unpublished March 1982 interview with Boston-based *Concert* magazine, "We can't turn our backs to the audience, we've got to reach out." The statement confirmed that U2's commitment to its audience hadn't wavered one bit as the band also seized the opportunity of its new release to reach out creatively and widen its musical horizons.

Prior to the release of *October*, U2 gave a hint of the forthcoming album with the "Fire" single in Europe. The chart hit was backed with "J. Swallo," an interesting collage of odd martial beats, ghostly vocal chants, a somber guitar melody, and creepy keyboard drones. Sounding suspiciously unfinished, "J. Swallo" was an early indication that this group wasn't afraid to express an experimental side. Years later, Brian Eno would help the band further explore this readiness to experiment and risk sounding rough or unfinished. Appropriately, U2's new album, *October*, reached record stores in the U.S. and Europe by the end of October 1981. The color cover photo of the band members standing on a Dublin dock by the River Liffey removed the mysterious cloak of the previous album's artwork, but the music contained within certainly didn't follow the same trend. *October* reflected both sides of the "Fire"/ "J.Swallo" single — some of it focused and powerful, the rest seemingly unfinished and adrift. Ira Robbins, writing in the *Trouser Press Record Guide*, agreed, finding some of the songs to "rank with the group's best work" and "several others that fall just short, mostly the result of incomplete songwriting efforts."

U2 recorded ten of the songs on its new disc at Dublin's Windmill Lane Studios during July and August, adding the earlier Nassau recording of "Fire" to complete the album. Once again, producer Steve Lillywhite's atmospheric touch prompted the band to incorporate new sounds and ideas in the studio. Edge mastered the piano as recording began, adding a fresh alternative to U2's basic rock attack, especially on the refined version of "I Fall Down," which retreated from its aggressive concert beginnings into airy acoustic territory. Another new texture for U2 was heard in the bright trumpet flourishes used to color the middle of "With a Shout." Vincent Kilduff, who later joined the popular Dublin band In Tua Nua, was invited to add uilleann pipes to the album. Somewhat similar in appearance and sound to the more familiar bagpipe, this instrument's eerie tone conjured up images of rural beauty, especially on the song "Tomorrow." The stunning opening track, "Gloria," featured an unusual middle break highlighted by a rare Adam Clayton bass solo shadowed by the sound of thick glass being broken in the background.

This exciting atmosphere of experimentation, however, was often compromised by the need to remain on schedule. U2 had flown back from America at the end of May, performed in Holland and London the first week of June, and was scheduled to begin sessions for *October* in July. "We had three weeks to prepare to record that album and we got only three or four songs out of it," Bono told *Trouser Press* in March 1982. The band members composed most of *October* at Windmill Lane. To add to their difficulties, a leather satchel containing the lyrical ideas Bono jotted down while on the road had been stolen during the previous tour. Bono entered the studio empty-handed, inventing most of the album's lyrics on the spot as he immersed himself in the band's music.

In the 1982 *Concert* magazine interview, Bono confided, "The lyrics are like a puzzle because, on *October*, I didn't know what I was saying a lot of the time. Things came out of me on that record that I wasn't even aware were in there. People accuse me of not being specific enough in the lyrics and that is a fair criticism, but I think there is more power in imagery because it can do more things — people can react on more levels." Edge spoke to me about Bono's improvisational abilities in a 1985 interview for WBCN: "I think he probably produces work he's more comfortable with when he has time to think about what he's doing. But, as an outsider, I think his most interesting work is done when he's really put on the spot."

A close examination of Bono's newest lyrics revealed that something critical to the core of U2 was unfolding. With the release of *October* it was obvious that the band was openly embracing spirituality, that their faith was an integral part of how they wrote, performed, and lived. Although it was Bono, Edge, and Larry who had experienced the exciting spiritual growth, Adam, the only non-Christian, quite willingly contributed to and shared in the band's total vision as displayed in its music.

U2's essentially nondenominational belief in a personal rapport with God was revolutionary in Ireland, where Catholics and Protestants were constantly embroiled in a conflict as inbred and vicious as racism in America. Larry had been brought up as a Catholic, Edge's home was Protestant, and Bono's Protestant and Catholic parents had been united in a rare, frequently scorned, mixed marriage. By stepping out of their sectarian pasts, this band made clear its distaste for the oppression and manipulation of organized religions. Their desired goal was something more intimate.

U2 voiced its questions openly, not professing to have all the answers and not parading its conviction like a right-wing religious group with a political agenda. The band members' faith, as critical as it was to them, was never revealed for the purpose of exploitation. On the other hand, U2's spiritual side was too important to conceal, as it inspired the band members' honest passion for life. In most rock music, spiritual matters are treated as taboo, or at least out of place. Some wondered whether U2 would convert to a religious band and leave behind most of their fans. Bono dispelled this worry early on, emphasizing in the *Concert* magazine interview: "We're not a Christian band. There's too many people standing up and saying this is the way, that is the way, the other is the way. If there's anything to what I say, it should be seen in my life."

Bono offered a brief, piano-accompanied tribute to the enduring love of God on *October*'s title track and also found himself improvising a song of thanks and praise in "Gloria." As he mentioned in the *Concert* interview: "I didn't think, 'Hey, I'm going to write about my belief in God,' it just came out. We improvise, and the things that come out, I let them come out." Bono found himself resorting to ancient Latin phrases to convey his emotion. "Our manager came up with some

Gregorian chant records and I listened to the way people did it in the past. I felt it worked in ['Gloria']."

After "Gloria" and "I Fall Down," Bono sang about breaking down personal barriers in "I Threw a Brick Through a Window." Larry's deeply echoed drum crashes and rumblings inspired the disconcerting image of distant artillery blasts slowly approaching, while Edge added a set of tough, crunching guitar lines that advanced into heavy metal territory. Completed by the full-speed anthem, "Rejoice," followed by "Fire," the first side of the album was a rock and roll tour de force, while side two detoured into less defined musical territories. (On compact disc versions, "side two" begins with track six.)

The haunting sound of uilleann pipes introduced the second side, softly accompanying Bono's hushed voice at the beginning of "Tomorrow." During a WBCN interview in 1985, Adam admitted that the track was still "very poignant" to him. "I like the way the song builds from that lilting Irishness into something very stormy and defiant in the end." The storm came as Edge blasted through with a series of guitar explosions echoed violently by the chilling scream of the pipes driving to a cacophonous climax. Bono revealed to me that the memory of his mother's funeral had haunted the lyric writing of "Tomorrow," images of the ceremony becoming metaphors of violence and fear. In the 1982 *Concert* magazine interview, he stated that the song was "[a] comment about the situation in Northern Ireland. In Northern Ireland the door is an image of fear . . . it's like a knock at the door, black car outside, don't answer that door 'cause you don't know who might be out there." But, he added, "there are other levels [as well]."

Rolling tom-toms announced "With a Shout," a rock-steady locomotive in which Bono crossed Biblical time and distance to defiantly rally for a march to Jerusalem, or a reawakening to God. A similar affirmation of faith followed in "Scarlet," with Bono simply chanting the word "rejoice" regularly through a slow and beautiful landscape of guitar, piano, and martial drumbeats. U2's power was also restrained during "Stranger in a Strange Land" before "Is That All?" rocked the album to a spirited finale. Edge transplanted one of his strongest riffs, from the band's live instrumental "Cry," to the basic melody for "Is That All?" The song, however, sounded awkward and undone. Without any substantial lyrics, only a disjointed ad-lib from Bono, the studio recording did nothing to improve on its more fiery live original. The song title itself seemed to comment on most of *October*'s second side, which presented the band as a courageous musical entity unafraid to wander along pastoral roads of folk and classical experimentation, but which obviously suffered from songwriting and lyrical anemia.

Paul McGuinness met with Bob Regehr when the new album was delivered to Warner Brothers, and admitted that *October* was probably not filled with the hit singles that the label had hoped for. Regehr remained confident, however, of U2's long-term potential, and agreed to issue the album on schedule without any changes. McGuinness persuaded Regehr to approve (once again) the disbursement of life-giving tour support funds. U.S. concert dates were then confirmed beginning November 13 in Albany, New York, at the familiar J. B. Scott's. Designed to reinforce U2's presence in its strongest areas of support, the month-long excursion of twenty-three shows included three packed nights at the Ritz in New York City, a near sell-out of L.A.'s 4,400-seat Palladium (making it the tour's most attended North American concert), and live FM radio broadcasts in Boston, Cleveland, and Long Island. However, the trek also brought U2 across Michigan's heartland, down to Nashville, and through Hartford, Connecticut, for the first time.

U2 blazed into Boston on November 14 to perform at the Orpheum, an old downtown theater. Frank Barsalona believed the band could fill most of the 2,800 seats, more than twice what U2 had sold out in Boston previously. Once again, his intuition proved correct — steady summer airplay of the "Fire" import and the more recent radio success of "Gloria" had attracted many new fans and re-primed the already converted. In short order the concert sold out and arrangements were made to broadcast the show live on WBCN. The taping of U2 at the Paradise in March had been an attempt to expose a fledgling band's breathless live show to a wider audience, but the planned broadcast of the Orpheum concert just eight months later would document the return to Boston of four conquering heroes.

Backstage before showtime the members of U2 huddled together to focus their attention and to pray, then they blasted onto the big theater stage like a Molotov cocktail. Pouring its unrestrained energy into the crowd for seventy minutes, the band exuded a greater self-assurance and precision than ever before. The maturity was most evident in Bono as he clearly exhibited his increased confidence and courage to take greater risks. Always a fair singer who covered up any vocal deficiencies with his generous charisma, Bono had never shrunk away from attempting notes outside of his range. Even though he had missed many of those in the past, more were now landing squarely on the mark. U2's front-man was also mastering the art of using his mistakes in pitch to create a different feel in the melody. Frequently Bono jumped for the "off" notes deliberately, endeavoring to do what experienced soul singers make a regular practice of—losing themselves in a song's emotional feel to play freely with its melody and timing. Ever earnest in his efforts to draw the audience closer to the band onstage, Bono led the crowd through a spirited and soulful sing-along during "11 O'Clock Tick Tock."

Edge's stage role had also matured beyond the already compli-cated task of providing both the rhythm and lead guitar parts from U2's studio tracks. Now a regular part of the band's stage equipment, an elec-tric piano was essential to the refined "I Fall Down," which vastly im-proved on the faster guitar-driven version heard at the Metro in May. While Edge played the keyboard, Bono strapped on a guitar to handle the simple rhythm. The singer constantly joked about his six-string abil-ities, but even as an admitted novice, he was still competent enough to play the song. Edge's piano also made it possible to perform the title piece from *October*. Larry accompanied the beautiful solo piano notes with shimmering chimes and an unadorned woodblock beat while Bono cried out his words and then added a stirring vocal coda.

One week after U2's Boston show, the Ritz was filled for all three of the band's performances, but the typically frosty New York au-dience was far less enthusiastic than its New England counterpart. The immobile crowd eventually gave up its chill during a raging set that nearly duplicated the Orpheum show. Afterward, local scene-makers flocked to the group's small upstairs dressing room, and Ellen Darst tried in vain to stem the tide of "guests" being admitted in alarming numbers by the club's bouncers. Within minutes, as the regular au-dience cleared out of the theater, a perspiring crowd of visitors and party-crashers were squeezing by one another and knocking elbows in the tiny room. A jovial Frank Barsalona mingled in the sea of bodies while Adam Clayton and Paul McGuinness moved about comfortably, drinks in hand as they greeted friends and new faces. The other three band members were much more subdued; Bono and Edge appeared only briefly and Larry was impossible to find at all.

Perhaps the drummer's course was best, since a tough schedule had been mapped out for the band in New York City. After U2's second performance at the Ritz ended in the early morning, the members grabbed a few hours of sleep at the Mayflower Hotel before being roused for a day-long session at Kingdom Sound on Long Island. The attempt at recording a new song with noted producer Sandy Pearlman, who had worked with Blue Oyster Cult and the Clash, resulted in a tough eight-hour workday before U2 returned to Manhattan for its final Ritz concert. Another exhausting performance, a few hours of rest, then the four were driven out to Kingdom for a second day-long session. The following morning the band members returned to the Long Island studio for a final time, to mix the recording into a usable stereo tape. Then they dashed west across the Hudson for a 4:30 P.M. soundcheck and midnight show at the Hitsville North nightclub in Passaic, New Jersey. But U2 fans would never get to hear the results of the Kingdom Sound session, which was viewed by the band as an experiment to test the waters with a new producer. U2 felt that the recording hadn't jelled, so the song was never released.

U2 then hopped down the New Jersey Turnpike for a Thanksgiving performance in Bruce Springsteen's stomping ground. Close by the beach and Asbury Park's main cruising circuit, the tiny Hitsville South nightclub looked like any innocuous roadside bar with a minuscule stage accustomed to hosting local cover bands. Inside, though, enough punk rockers and fans had flocked to the club to nearly fill its seven-hundred-person capacity. U2's load of equipment filled up most of the stage, leaving the band little room to pace back and forth. In camouflage T-shirt, Bono surveyed the crush of black leather in front of him while his bandmates took their places. Larry worked his way, with great difficulty, through the jungle of wires, amplifiers, and speakers to reach his drum stool. Perhaps influenced by the claustrophobic surroundings, U2 blasted into a buzzsaw version of its *October* live set, pausing only sporadically to gulp some air and offer a few slower songs. Bono restlessly prowled the small stage, squeezing with difficulty past Adam and Edge as well as the obstacle course of microphones, speaker cabinets, guitar cords, and foot pedals.

It was at the Hitsville South gig that I first witnessed one of the mischievous stage stunts that would get Bono into so much trouble in the future. I was joined up front in the crowd by some friends from Boston and New York, forming a tight knot against the stage. Bono spied our group halfway through the show and, with a smile, turned around and suddenly dropped backward off the stage on top of us. For a few shaky moments, his passively stretched body, slippery with sweat, was dangerously close to crashing to the floor. Someone groaned, "Ohhhhh, don't let him fall!" Scrambling to prevent this, our group gave a mighty shove and neatly deposited Bono back onstage as the rest of the audience roared an approval. It didn't make much sense to wipe his sweat from my shoulders, since by that point everyone in the room was just as soaked as Bono.

After the show, I began searching for the backstage area; I didn't have to look far. There was no adjoining room or office that U2 could run to after finishing, so the band members just clustered to the side of the stage. Usually the area served as a storage place for the club's beer supply, and I found Larry sitting wearily on a keg with the band's instruments and equipment scattered among the dull silver containers. Once most of the audience had left, Bono tried to change out of his sweat-soaked clothes, but he was constantly thwarted by curious young women who hung back to witness the event. Finally a pair of roadies sheepishly held up a large towel in front of Bono while he changed garments and laughed loudly at all the fuss.

U2 flew home for a Christmas break with plans to return to America in the spring. Behind the scenes, however, there were serious concerns that the financial lifeline for the *October* campaign might be cut. In a massive business move, Island Records was transferred from the mighty distribution wing of Warner Brothers over to smaller Atco Records. A subsidiary of Atlantic Records, which was part of the Warner empire, Atco could hardly be expected to exceed the distribution success and promotional clout of its predecessor. Fortunately for U2, Bob Regehr would still have financial power until the transfer was completed, and that included funding approval for the spring tour. Despite the knowledge that the business move would eliminate his future involvement in a project he had held dear, Regehr remained supportive until the end. "He could have easily justified not investing any more money in U2, but he really believed," Ellen remembered. "When the split happened, Warner got to keep a couple of the next Steve Winwood records [on Island], but Regehr was always saying that he wished they had taken U2."

Warner Brothers' national promotion department also worked diligently until the transfer. George Gerrity led a dedicated staff of regional record company reps who phoned radio stations and urged programmers to give the band a chance. Their efforts resulted in airplay of "Gloria" on at least three dozen significant album rock stations. The label was also successful in placing U2's video clip of the single on America's new MTV network, which had begun continuous broadcasting on August 1, 1981. Filmed on a barge in the middle of the River Liffey barely three months after MTV began broadcasting, the "Gloria" clip became an early mainstay on the channel. It was accompanied occasionally with a video of "I Will Follow" filmed live in concert earlier that year. College radio embraced *October*'s less commercial stance, not only discovering rich airplay resources in "Gloria," "Fire," and "I Fall Down," but dipping into the album's other tracks as well. All of this radio and video activity kept *October* selling throughout U2's two-month absence from America. The album debuted on *Billboard* magazine's Top 200 album sales chart on November 7, 1981. It peaked at number 104, but did manage to remain on the survey for sixteen weeks.

On the *October* project, the combination of album and college radio airplay spread the word to a large number of listeners, but to nowhere near the degree that the American contemporary hit radio stations, playing their top forty songs over and over, could do. By their very mainstream nature in 1981, these hit-oriented stations usually excluded the grittier proponents of rock and roll, favoring more commercial dance music or universally loved ballads. Failing, in Warner Brothers' opinion, to deliver a viable single that could be brought to the CHR stations, U2 was prevented from the big national score— a hit on *Billboard*'s Hot 100 singles chart. Combining CHR airplay with acceptance on album and college radio, the new factor of MTV, and heavy touring was a grand-slam mix that usually brought a band enormous fame. CHR airplay alone was often enough to create overnight superstars; album radio exposure combined with frequent touring could also boost a band's career. Eventually MTV by itself would possess the power to make or break stars. Even so, the audience had the ultimate power to reject a band even though it might achieve massive airplay and/or tour heavily. For now, Warner Brothers retrenched, content to build U2's airplay base on album and college radio, then consolidate its advances with another concert swing across America.

On February 11, 1982, U2 opened its new tour on board a five-deck riverboat straight out of the pages of Mark Twain. S.S. *President*, docked in New Orleans, had had its huge paddlewheels removed to make way for more efficient twentieth-century propellers, but the stately colonial grandeur inside was beautifully preserved. A spacious grand ballroom that once held scores of waltzing couples would now host a churning mass of 1,500 U2 fans. As with most areas of the country, support from New Orleans' major rock stations was nonexistent, but word-of-mouth reaction to U2's previous visit as well as generous airplay at Tulane and Louisiana State University's non-commercial radio stations managed to sell out the show anyway. On board the *President*, U2 and its manager were sequestered, appropriately enough, in the captain's cabin. Prompted by the sudden dull throbbing of engines and a lurch as the ship was cast off and surged into the muddy waters of the Mississippi, Paul McGuinness joked, "This is the first time we've played a venue and the venue left."

Within moments of U2 hitting the stage, the restless crowd went into action as Edge slammed out the opening guitar salvo to "Gloria." The audience bounced almost violently through that song as well as "Another Time, Another Place." At the center of the crush, a body of pushing and shoving slam dancers defended their territory. Slam dancers were common at hardcore concerts, where ultra-fast rock made normal dancing impossible. Jumping and bouncing into each other or climbing onstage to dive back into the seething mass, hardcore dancers made attendance at a rock and roll show a contact sport. No one managed to get up and leap from U2's stage, but at one point a few ice cubes were hurled in Bono's direction. The singer promptly emptied a beer on the front rows in retaliation.

As the floating concert hall returned to home dock and tied up, the band members ended an incendiary hour-long set and retired to their cabin for plates of red beans and rice. McGuinness revealed to me: "We almost had to forget this tour. It was almost canceled before it started."

"Then we found out that we were going to do a couple of weeks with the J. Geils Band," Adam added.

"We're playing Florida and the West Coast with them," said Bono, who was busily jamming his foot into a heavy military-style leather boot. "But first, we're going to get lost in Texas! Yee-haw!"

McGuinness elaborated: "We're going through Texas, the Midwest, and finishing up in Colorado before we join up with J. Geils in Florida at the beginning of March. Then, as their opening act, we'll play arenas for the first time."

The J. Geils Band was enjoying its first-ever chart-topping success with the "Centerfold" single reaching number one in January and its accompanying *Freeze Frame* album selling over a million copies. After fifteen years of live touring and a dozen albums, the Boston band was now embarking on its first guaranteed sellout tour in U.S. arenas. Barbara Skydel, Premier Talent's second in command, knew that U2 needed the extra exposure and came up with the idea of pairing the two bands on tour. The J. Geils Band didn't require a warm-up act that could help sell tickets, but wanted to locate "a good packaging band, somebody that wasn't just filler," according to Geils lead singer Peter Wolf. "If you put on a great show from beginning to end, it's better for everyone. Because if the opening act is strong and doesn't bore people, [then] the audience isn't restless," he told me.

Frank Barsalona had urged Wolf, his client and friend, to check out U2's show at the Paradise the previous spring. The Irish band's performance excited Wolf, who readily agreed when Skydel suggested the tour combination. He observed: "We wanted a band that was coming up, a band that you really dug that you could bring out [on tour]. I thought they had the sort of intensity that would be great. A Geils audience is a very tough audience . . . you had to work! We had a conviction behind what we did and we put our energy behind it — there was no way you could just sort of go through the moves. I think that's the element that U2 could respond to, and the element our audience could respond to when they saw U2 — they had that same sort of primal drive."

The J. Geils/U2 package played halls ranging from 2,500 seats at Jacksonville University to Los Angeles's Sports Arena with a capacity of over 12,000. The headlining band was at the top of its game, and although no one knew it at the time, in its final series of tour dates, as Wolf would announce his departure from the group later that year. Allegations were made by Eamon Dunphy in his 1987 biography of U2, *Unforgettable Fire*, that J. Geils sought to sabotage its warm-up band's best efforts onstage as U2 grabbed more and more attention with every tour stop. Peter Wolf vigorously denied those suggestions. "What's disturbing," he told me, "is that the Geils Band is painted [in the book] as a band that was envious and tried to prevent in any way possible the success of U2. There was never any feeling of being threatened, even if U2 got nine encores! We felt great that there was a band [on the bill] that we thought had a certain integrity; we respected them."

Still virtually unknown, U2 bravely met the Geils audience on fifteen occasions, even though most people in the crowd were more interested in finding their seats than paying attention to the band's set. The band's effort was clearly not wasted, however, because at every show at least a few surprised J. Geils fans would be intrigued by this unknown group. U2 also reached some younger U.S. fans for the first time in the arenas, since most of its career had been spent rising up through a circuit of bars where no one under twenty-one was admitted.

While U2 crossed the South, a new single recorded during the Christmas break was released in Europe. Since there were no plans for "A Celebration" to be pressed in America, U2's record was imported and eagerly gobbled up by Stateside collectors. "It was an attempt on our part to go into the studio with nothing, and come out with a single," Edge informed me during a 1985 interview for WBCN. "We recorded and mixed a version with our assistant engineer at the time, Paul Thomas, but it was definitely not there. I think at that stage we needed someone who would fight us, get the best take out of us; so we called Steve [Lillywhite] over."

"Why didn't the song appear on the next U2 album?" I asked.

"We felt it wasn't really connected with any of the albums. When we go into the studio to produce an album, there has to be a continuity — a feeling that all of the songs make some kind of statement or are related in some way. 'A Celebration' just didn't fit into that."

The B-side of the new single was "Trash, Trampoline, and the Party Girl," an odd assemblage of Bono's cracking vocals, vibrantly strummed acoustic guitar, wispy piano, and ghostly drums. Edge greatly enjoyed recording this song. "We finished 'A Celebration' and had, literally, two hours left [of studio time] to do a B-side. I kind of relish the moments where we have the clock against us — you gotta do it, you gotta do it now, and it's gonna be made eternal so it has to not be embarrassing!" The band set a limit of only two takes per musician and tried to build a song from the ground up. "Larry didn't have to play because we took an old drum track, slowed it down, and gave it some treatment so it was unrecognizable . . . in fact, it was the drums from 'A Celebration.' I went in with an acoustic guitar and out of thin air, this chord sequence arrived with a rather unique, disjointed rhythm. Bono did some really weird synthesizer stuff, then we did the vocal in two takes. To do the lyrics and melodies in two takes is unbelievable because I think it's one of Bono's strongest lyrics."

"A Celebration," U2's only record release of 1982, was not a spectacular chart success in England, although it did make the singles survey, thereby qualifying as something of a hit. The band briefly kept the song alive by playing it during the remainder of its *October* tour dates before dropping it from future set lists. Ironically, it was the rough and unpolished B-side that would live on in U2's concert legacy: "Trash, Trampoline, and the Party Girl" evolved during the *War* support tours into an encore song simply entitled "Party Girl."

U2 squeezed some New England and New York headlining club

dates into a ten-day break from the Geils tour before rejoining the arena swing in Arizona. At the end of March, the band left America for European concerts, some well-deserved vacation time, and the task of writing and recording a third album. With the hurried creation of *October* painfully in everyone's mind, a wealth of time from late summer through the fall was set aside for the upcoming studio project. U2 was quietly under much pressure to deliver a blockbuster and leave the mediocre sales response to its second album firmly behind. Far from being poised for American success at this point, U2 was in danger of passing into rock and roll history as a merely promising band that had introduced some exciting possibilities on two albums, its demise scarcely arousing attention. Although the band members and a fiercely loyal circle of fans considered *October* an important and satisfying creative step, the question remained: could U2 combine its artistic desires with an effective commercial appeal? The recorded answer was due early in the new year.

5
WAR STORIES

A S THE SUMMER of 1982 passed into fall and then winter, U2's dedicated American fans waited for any word from the band. When New Year's Day 1983 came and went, even the hardiest supporters began to wonder if the band had broken up. If and when U2 returned, there were still doubts in the music industry about the group's chances for success. *October* certainly hadn't attracted many more listeners to the fold since U2's debut, and a similar experience with the third album could be disastrous. Record company executives regarded the situation in cold business terms as a sophomore sales slump. That U2 had crafted a record that advanced the band artistically was beside the point to those concerned with balance sheets and profit quotas.

Fortunately, Chris Blackwell decided to stick by his discovery, who were quite active, laboring diligently on their new album back in Dublin's Windmill Lane Studios. The band had once again engaged Steve Lillywhite to produce the session, with help from engineer Paul Thomas and also Kevin Killen, an assistant engineer who would later become a respected producer in his own right. During an interview for this book, Killen recalled that U2 wasted little time getting started. "Usually the first day [of a recording project] is a sort of relaxed session because you're going to be there for three months, but we started at midday and left at seven in the morning. I didn't mind working eighteen hours a day because it was great to always hear something new — Bono getting the lyrics together or Edge coming out with some great guitar lines. They were better prepared than they were for *October*; I knew very early on that it would be a special album; you could tell because there was a lot of magic happening in the studio."

The first fruit of these labors was exposed on "New Year's Day," a single released to Europe in January 1983 and then issued to American album rock stations the first week of February. The imported seven-inch single, in a simple white sleeve with gray and black lettering, featured a picture of Peter, the boy who had graced the U.K. cover of U2's debut album. This time, however, his previous expression of wonder had been replaced by fear. Grounded in the same punk-edged energy that had powered U2's earlier rockers, "New Year's Day" was musically far more ambitious. The piano melody was anchored firmly in U2's powerful driving beat with guitar relegated to a rhythmic role, though Edge did showcase a brief but superb guitar solo in the middle. The turbulent power of the music framed lyrics about the human price of conflict, the agonizing separation of lovers and friends, and the resignation that another passing year would bring no change.

The single's B-side, "Treasure (Whatever Happened to Pete the Chop)," a relatively undistinguished rock and roll exercise assembled from U2's pile of spare parts, was of note to fans since it would not appear on the album. Initial copies of the U.K. single package were also stuffed with an additional seven-inch disc containing tracks from a 1982 Belgian concert recorded for European television. In America, the label released only a seven-inch disc with no picture sleeve and just "Treasure" as the B-side. The cheaper packaging for the U.S. market was economically sensible; although Island could be assured that its U.K. package would sell briskly, the success of the U.S. single was in question. By January 1983, U2 had amassed three British chart hits ("Fire," "Gloria," and "A Celebration") and could boast of headlining massive European outdoor music festivals, while its profile in America was still lagging far behind with no hit singles and mainly club and theater appearances under its belt.

The release of "New Year's Day" caused an immediate sensation in England, where the song powered its way into the Top Ten singles chart. In America, it was a constant struggle to build U2's airplay base beyond the small number of radio stations already familiar with the group. Michael Abramson, Island Records' newly installed vice president of promotion, was a fiercely energetic and determined businessman who loved music and became passionate about U2. In an interview he told me, "U2 [at the time] was still at an underground status — 75,000 units average for *Boy* and *October*. I felt [that] U2 was not a fluke, that these kids were going to be around a long time. They weren't ready to take America by storm with the 'big single,' but I knew I could get this album played on any AOR station in the free world."

Abramson hired several independent record promoters to supplement his own company's resources, helping to ensure that U2 wouldn't be lost in the crush of competing releases. Once the advance copies of "New Year's Day" had been mailed, Abramson and his staff got on the phone, pressuring radio stations to give the single a shot. Their efforts prompted an immediate reaction as the song climbed onto the *Radio and Records* AOR chart (compiling the amount of national airplay for new releases) on February 18. A stunning video clip of the song was added to MTV's list of promising acquisitions, soon making significant airplay gains at the television channel. Many album radio programmers who had been reluctant to play "New Year's Day" were heartened by MTV's decision to feature the clip and became convinced of the single's potential. By April, Abramson and his staff had won the battle at America's rock stations. "New Year's Day" peaked at number two on the *Radio and Records* AOR chart.

Just as album radio programmers utilized the list of MTV's newly added and hit video clips, which was printed openly in music industry trade journals such as *Billboard*, to help make choices about playing songs, CHR programmers used the same information, as well as AOR playlists featured in magazines like *Radio and Records*, in making their decisions. Even college radio stations coast to coast were now linked in a network reporting playlists to *College Media Journal*, which compiled and reprinted the information in a national chart. In this way the data from college stations could also be used by commercial radio programmers to indicate future airplay picks.

The album radio success of "New Year's Day" impressed some CHR programmers, who added the single to their playlists. As a result, the song debuted on the *Billboard* Top 100 singles chart on April 2. Island tried to turn its promotional attention to the undecided CHR programmers, asking them to take note of the success beginning to happen in their own format. Unfortunately, the label wasn't able to focus the needed amount of attention, as Michael Abramson related: "We couldn't get a cohesive handle on [promoting to] Top 40 as we did with AOR. It took all the energy everyone had just to establish and solidify the album radio play, and convince everyone that U2 was for real." Island wasn't able to sustain interest in the single at CHR and as airplay fell off, so did sales. "New Year's Day" peaked at a disappointing fifty-three and then dropped quickly off the *Billboard* chart.

Since 1981, MTV's airplay of videos had reaped immediate benefits for the groups that rushed to produce visual clips for their songs. New careers were built overnight as television exposure promoted the bands' images, boosting record and concert sales. This could only benefit a group, especially when, as in U2's case, radio airplay was not a guaranteed factor. Wisely gauging the medium's potential, U2 had entered the video fray early with its "Gloria" clip and then followed in 1982 with "A Celebration," seldom seen in America because the companion single wasn't released domestically. The dramatic video clip that accompanied "New Year's Day" was the most successful yet for U2, with heavy airplay at MTV continuing throughout the spring of 1983.

The video's powerful testament to the horror of war incorporated battle footage from the bloody German invasion of Russia during World War II, adding additional scenes of the band members performing in a snowy meadow and riding horses across a bleak, wintery landscape. Edge talked about U2's strong commitment to the medium during the band's live interview at WBCN in May 1983. "We get involved very much with our videos. I think credit should go to the director, Meiert Avis, who's part of the Windmill Lane complex where we record our albums. We're all involved in the same way we work with Steve Lillywhite — he becomes a member of the band. A lot of the ideas come from us originally — which is the best way, ultimately, because we know what we're trying to portray. It's too easy for a director to come in and overrule the lyric or the whole idea of the song, and come up with some TV-style commercial video, which is really not what we want."

"Where was the video for 'New Year's Day' filmed?" I asked.

"We happened to be in Sweden doing a few shows, and we had this idea to do a video in the snow . . . [we] just felt that it portrayed the mood we wanted. So, off we went in a couple of small planes and we ended up in a place called Salen, which is four hundred miles north of Stockholm. We shot on the side of a mountain . . . it was actually twelve degrees below zero, so you notice certain extremities are being frozen! Unfortunately, I couldn't actually ride the horse [provided for a scene], so there was a girl that replaced me."

"Edge, that's not you on the horse?"

"No, that's not me — that's why they've got those masks on. I just couldn't get it together with my particular steed."

In March, Island released U2's new album *War* in Europe and

America. Pete's face, with its haunted, streetwise stare and torn lip, occupied the entire front cover of the album. The boy's hands were clasped behind his head, as if he were about to be marched off in surrender. Angry red letters superimposed over the black-and-white photo shouted out U2's name and the album title. Beginning as powerfully as the artwork implied, a sobering military cadence introduced "Sunday Bloody Sunday." The drumwork was actually recorded under the front staircase beyond the receptionist's desk at Windmill Lane, an unusual but ideal location to obtain the natural echo Lillywhite and U2 desired. A haunting violin note provided by guest Steve Wickham (who was recording with the Irish band In Tua Nua and would eventually join the Waterboys) darted in from above, embellishing Edge's visceral guitar work. The track soon became album radio's second favorite selection from the album following the success of "New Year's Day."

U2 took the title "Sunday Bloody Sunday" from two infamous occasions of violence in Ireland — when British soldiers fired into the crowd at a Dublin football match in 1920, and when twelve civilians were killed in a 1972 skirmish with British troops in Northern Ireland. Edge explained the inspiration during the May 1983 WBCN interview: "Though we have picked the two incidents by the same name, that is really not what we're getting at. We're using [the name of the incidents] as the medium by which to get across the power of the song. For a lot of people that sentence, 'Sunday Bloody Sunday,' just means so much. We're using that, to a certain extent, out of context. It's the atmosphere of the song [and] the other lyrics that really qualify it. We felt that we should stand up and be counted on this very volatile but personal topic [of] Northern Ireland without actually coming through on any political stance. [Our songs] deal with real issues, but they're not partisan either way."

"Has the war in Northern Ireland affected you personally?" I asked.

The guitarist continued, "I would personally feel, not that much directly, there's much more of an undertone to the way of life in Dublin. We've said in interviews that the bombs don't go off in Dublin, but some of them are certainly made there. There is that sort of backdrop to your life, it doesn't ever come to a head as such — you very rarely get into fights."

"It affects us when we see Northern Ireland people getting shot because they're either one religion or the other," Larry interjected angrily.

After the opening rage of "Sunday Bloody Sunday," *War* continued with the bouncing, acoustic-flavored "Seconds." The lyrics (lead vocals by Edge — a U2 first) all but failed to reflect the cheery, shuffling mood of the music, however, as U2 used the song to comment on the nuclear arms race. Halfway through, the music died away to be replaced with the sound of marching troops. In the WBCN interview, Edge elaborated about the excerpt, which was taken from the movie *Soldier Girls*, a story about women in the U.S. Army. "The whole spectacle of these girls going through this incredible torture of training seemed perfect to slip there in the middle." The excerpt caught the action of young female recruits on the march, shouting, "I want to live a life of danger!" "It's not obvious, but if you listen close you can hear [it] . . . it's very disturbing," Edge observed.

One of Edge's personal favorites from *War* was the song "Drowning Man," as he told me during an interview for WBCN in 1985. "It was one of those songs that we almost took for granted — we knew that we were going to enjoy recording it and that it would present no major problems, although most of the work still hadn't been done on it. There was the root of a very strong piece somewhere in there, so we left it for quite a while before we worked on it." Knifing acoustic and shimmering electric guitars entwined with Steve Wickham's exquisite violin textures as Bono traveled confidently into a breathtaking arena of hushed words, leaping falsetto, and emotional cries. Edge related that once the band actually began recording "Drowning Man," the sessions were delightful. "It was so inspiring — it just got better and better and better, and Bono produced one of his best vocal performances. Whereas I know some of the songs on the *War* album could be re-recorded and improved on, with 'Drowning Man' — it's perfection for that song. It's one of the most successful pieces of recording that we've ever done."

On the other hand, "Refugee" was left relatively unfinished. The song was actually one of the group's demo tapes, a rough recording quickly laid down in the studio to help the band members decide which tracks they would later re-record and finish for an album. U2 ended up liking the demo as it was, so Steve Lillywhite salvaged the tape from the scrap heap and dusted it off with a gleaming remix. Larry took an aggressive role on "Refugee," launching the track with percussive sound effects, counting out the beat with a steady crash, and piling up a solo section of colliding drum blocks answered by jagged vibrato guitar and Bono's shouts.

Flirting with funk and soul music on "Red Light," U2 asked the

Coconuts, an accomplished female trio that usually backed up popular dance singer August Darnell (a.k.a. Kid Creole), to help out on vocals. Bono's convincing falsetto and a striking trumpet solo from guest Kenny Fradley added two more musical textures that were new for U2. On "Surrender," Edge produced a wave of spatial slide guitar sounds from his newly acquired lap steel instrument, which lay flat on a stand and was played from a sitting position. Edge utilized the guitar, most often heard adding bright leads above twangy country-western melodies, for a highly unconventional, frightening solo of leaping and plummeting metallic shrieks.

The pulsing dance track entitled "Two Hearts Beat as One" was released in June as the album's second CHR single in America. An accompanying video, filmed in Paris among white marble facades under gray March skies, with colorful circus characters added to shots of the band members themselves, was introduced on MTV. The television exposure didn't appear to assist Michael Abramson in his quest to move the single onto CHR radio, however. He related: "By the time we got to 'Two Hearts Beat as One,' the phenomenon of [*War*] was over. CHR, more than anything, is based on the domino theory — it takes forever to start a record, but you can't stop a hit! There wasn't enough action on 'Two Hearts Beat as One' for it to really take hold." The single was indispensable to U2 collectors because of its B-side, a song not found on the *War* album entitled "Endless Deep." This curio was a foretaste of the band's later experimental recordings with Brian Eno in the way it sounded like a band rehearsal with its false start, Bono's disjointed vocals, and excessively echoed guitar.

U2 also released special extended and remixed dance versions of "Two Hearts Beat as One" for nightclub deejays. During the 1983 WBCN interview Larry recalled, "[I] put some new drums on [the track] and then [Francois] Kevorkian did the mixing on it."

"Who is Kevorkian?" I asked.

"I don't know. I haven't even met the chap. I just play drums," he admitted with a laugh.

Edge came to Larry's rescue. "We met him in London — Larry was obviously somewhere else at the time. He is from New York and primarily works with dance music. It was a project we were approached on by Chris Blackwell, who thought it might be an interesting experiment to hand over the multitracks to Francois who would then do his own interpretation."

Since the disco-crazed days of 1976, twelve-inch remixes of

rhythmic songs had become popular as yet another method of exposing a band's music to an audience. Club deejays concentrated on holding their audiences on the dance floor by mixing smoothly from one record to the next during extended sets of energizing dance music. The "club" or "twelve-inch" mixes (so called because they were usually pressed on album-sized singles to pack as much audio information into the vinyl grooves as possible) were created by producers who took the master tapes of conventional singles back into the studio to remix them. New musical sections were created from the tapes to lengthen the track, and a beefier rhythm with more drums or bass was usually added for extra punch when played through high-powered club sound systems. Creating a hit record in this alternative format often introduced a band's music to an audience it might have never "crossed over" to from radio.

Francois Kevorkian's remix added more depth to the rhythm of "Two Hearts Beat as One" and exposed Edge's backing vocals and some disguised guitar sections. An English twelve-inch single released in March 1983 included the remix along with Kevorkian's reworked version of "New Year's Day," which recovered a verse that had been cut from the final album track. Steve Lillywhite had a go at remixing and extending "Two Hearts" as well, and his effort appeared on the B-side. The twelve-inch was a hit in European discos, prompting Island to release a promotional version for the American market. Its subsequent Stateside success in dance clubs made up somewhat for the failure of the single on CHR. When the twelve-inch discs went out of print after a few years, they became one of U2's most sought-after collector's items.

Christian belief once again permeated U2's lyrics on *War*, but not as obviously as it had throughout *October*. In some cases, the spiritual messages could be interpreted as more general philanthropic statements or love songs, but elsewhere the Christian content was obvious. "Surrender" spoke of hope for personal salvation, "Drowning Man" emerged as a prayer for spiritual rejuvenation, and "40" incorporated actual phrases from the Fortieth Psalm. On the last of these, U2 borrowed the chorus from a verse of its own "Sunday Bloody Sunday" ("How long to sing this song?"). With Adam absent from the "40" session, Edge plucked the melody out on bass guitar and added distant-sounding, delicate wisps of electric guitar.

In April 1983, U2 began a three-month U.S. tour with shows in North Carolina, Virginia, and New York, before reaching Brown University in Providence, Rhode Island. At Brown, George Skaubitis, the ebullient representative from Warner Brothers, gave up his comfortable seat halfway back in the hall to search for a closer vantage point in the crowded area up front. He waved from his new location, painfully kneeling in the narrow walkway between the stage and a wooden security barrier holding back the crowd, just as the houselights died and the members of U2 walked onstage. Larry and Adam swung into the introductory beat of "Out of Control," Edge blasting out the first three monstrous chords, while Bono, with neatly cropped hair, black corduroy shirt, and matching dark jeans, danced across the stage and slapped hands with those in the first row. Instantly, the auditorium floor turned into a sea of bouncing heads. U2's latest music made a strong impression, too, with "New Year's Day" and "Sunday Bloody Sunday" receiving as much applause as any song in the set. When the group left the stage eighty minutes later, clumps of fans slumped wearily against the front barrier, grabbing a quick breather and leaving sweaty outlines on the wood before the rising din of shouts announced U2's return for an encore.

Bono's broad smile made it obvious that he was delighted to be back in America. The singer's unbridled enthusiasm, however, lured him into overreaching during the Brown University performance, straining his voice past its limits and reducing it frequently to a cracked whisper. The situation failed to dampen Bono's composure, however; he maintained his usual eloquence while speaking to the audience. "When we came here three years ago, we thought that the music business would be all machinery. But we found that everywhere there are special people. We'd like to say hello and thanks to George from Warner Brothers, because he was there when we started — and still is. This song is for him." The band then eased into "40" as George stood in shock, slowly swaying with the rest of the crowd.

Bono exhorted the audience to join in singing the chorus of "40" as Edge propelled the melody on bass and Adam took his only spotlight as lead guitar player. With the lyrics done, Bono waved goodbye and slowly walked offstage as the band played on. After a few moments, Adam finished his electric guitar wanderings and also disappeared. Edge thumped along with Larry's steady rhythm, then allowed a last note to trail off into silence before nodding to the cheering crowd and following his companions. The stage now belonged to Larry, U2's timekeeper. Naked drum reports echoed through the auditorium as the assembled throng sang the song's chorus, "How long to sing this song," over and over. After a final mighty crash, Larry waved goodbye and left the stage as dreamy Irish music welled up in the speakers and bright houselights snapped on. Minutes later, even after the college security team had urged the audience to leave, loud chanting continued to echo throughout the hall and out into the streets—"How long . . . to sing this song!"

Afterward, those lucky enough to have backstage passes waited patiently in a concrete tunnel leading to the dressing room. Ellen Darst appeared, telling everyone to relax because the band members needed at least a half hour "to decompress." I expected Bono to skip the backstage gathering to rest his ragged vocal cords, but he was the first to appear and all he wanted to do was talk. Although freshly showered and dressed in a clean T-shirt, Bono hadn't cooled down yet and a clammy sweat glistened on his skin. "I really need to rest my legs," he apologized, with a raspy voice, then slid to the floor and signed autographs for a court of fans who reverently arranged themselves in a semicircle around him. Adam soon appeared, his recently trimmed curls still falling down around his eyes and a contented smile on his face as he greeted everyone in the tunnel. After twenty minutes, Larry also emerged from the dressing room — much to the delight of several young ladies who rushed over for autographs.

A few days later, U2 reached Boston for a pair of shows at the Orpheum Theater. Ellen arranged to bring the entire group over to WBCN's studios for what turned out to be a two-hour interview on my weeknight show. When the band arrived, however, Bono was absent. Once Larry, Adam, and Edge were comfortably seated, I asked where the singer was.

"He went to a specialist—Tom Jones's doctor." Edge replied.

"Tom Jones? Now, we're talking *the* Tom Jones?"

"Absolutely!" the guitarist affirmed.

I roughly sang a few scraps of 'It's Not Unusual,' adding, "The 'It's Not Unusual' Tom Jones?"

Edge laughed, "That Tom Jones! He's been told to go to bed and shut up."

Adam broke in, "Well, we've been telling him to shut up for ages, but he finally needed to pay someone to tell him!"

After the laughter subsided, I announced: "We're getting a lot of calls from ladies about Bono. [They're] asking whether or not Bono is really married, [and we're receiving] lots of telephone numbers as well! But let's get the straight story. Bono has gotten married, hasn't he?"

The guitarist hedged, "Uhhhhhhmmmmm . . . "

Adam pounced, "Yeah! But you can give *me* the telephone numbers."

Later, continuing their pattern as comedian and straight man, Adam and Edge pondered a question about U2's involvement scoring a ballet for the Dublin theater. "This is the other face of U2," Edge answered with mock seriousness. "Though we may be impersonating a rock and roll band at the moment, Adam has been practicing ballet for the last ten years—very conscientiously."

"I'm still working on my thighs," the bass player continued unabashed, "but they just don't look right."

Attempting to steer the interview back to slightly more serious matters, I asked Edge if he feared being labeled a "guitar hero" as a result of his highly original style. Before he could reply, Adam interrupted, "I don't think guitar players are heroes really, it's drummers and bass players. [You've] got it all wrong."

I played along. "Yes . . . it is a myth, the guitar hero is a myth." Remembering that Adam and Edge switched instruments to perform a song in concert, I added, "Actually, Adam, you're playing guitar now on '40.' "

"Uh . . . I'm a guitar hero when I play that," Adam replied. "I pretend I'm playing guitar. There's someone behind the curtain doing all the work!"

"Bono just picked up the guitar. I believe last tour he had just started playing it," I ventured.

Larry piped in from the corner microphone, "He's been trying for ages and he still hasn't gotten it right!"

"Bono has a sort of love-hate relationship with the guitar," Edge observed. "I think he feels somewhat inferior because he's only got five fingers and it's got six strings."

The band members revealed much about what inspired U2's ideology and unique musical style when they chose records to play during the interview. Without hesitation, Edge picked "Love Will Tear Us Apart" by Joy Division. The layered sonic depth of the song mirrored U2's own instrumental attack and production. Larry's choice of the 1964 Bob Dylan song, "With God on Our Side," displayed a knowledge of the antiwar songwriting tradition. Adam's love for aggressive rock and roll roots was exposed when he selected "Shadow Play" by Irish blues and rock guitarist Rory Gallagher. I asked him, "[Would you] basically call yourselves, first and foremost, a rock and roll band?"

"Yeah I think so . . . if you want to bring it down to categories. I think U2 is, in that way, slightly subversive because the whole structure of radio and music these days is to 'pin them down, get a name there, then we know where they're at, they're safe.' I think that because we, as U2, transcend those barriers, it upsets people because they can't pigeonhole us in any particular place. That's a great place to be — to have the range to go from one side of the spectrum to the other."

Curious about how U2's growing popularity was affecting them, I asked Adam: "For the first time in America, you have to deal with success. You've only done a few American dates [on this tour], but has it become a problem?"

"Well," Adam replied, "we're still practicing dealing [with it] so we'll tell you in a few months' time."

"We're not that good at being rock stars," Edge mentioned, adding facetiously, "we'll have to practice a lot and get the hang of it."

"You have to get the walk right," Adam put in. "If you get the walk right, you're halfway there."

Edge then turned serious: "I think what a lot of people are seeing is a band that has suddenly had success. [But] in fact, we've been working hard for the past four years, so this level has been fought for. I don't think it has the same earth-shattering effect as it would if this was our first record and we were still wet behind the ears."

"It also depends on the way your fans see you," Adam explained. "Whereas somebody like Rob Halford [lead singer of Judas Priest] would be seen very much as a rock star, somebody like Bruce Springsteen is not perceived in the same way at all — he's actually taken seriously for his music. I think, particularly with our fans, that they don't see us [as rock stars] at all. I don't think they ever will see us as that."

Edge and Adam also commented during the interview on the band's attitude about performing. Edge observed: "People say that playing live is stunting — you get bored, you get bogged down. But for us, every time we go on stage there is a real atmosphere of anticipation within the band. There are no two nights which could be said to be the same — the set may be the same, but the audience is different and our approach to each audience varies. There's a lot of improvisation from Bono and from all of us."

Adam clarified further: "There's no use going out there trying to repeat the night before. You really have to believe it's gonna be better. As long as you go out there with that attitude, it *is* better than the night before."

6

THE WHITE FLAG

THE SALES breakthrough established by *War* hadn't yet occurred as U2's American tour to support the album began.
Paul McGuinness had obtained tour support funds from Island's new distributor, Atco Records, but strict attention to a
shoestring budget would be necessary to parcel that money out over the
planned three-month visit. The situation was humorously illustrated after the May 1983 interview at WBCN when McGuinness, Ellen Darst
(who had left the record label to work directly for U2 as media liaison),
and the band members (minus Bono) agreed to eat dinner with the station's general manager Tony Berardini, Oedipus, and me. On Tony's
suggestion, we all met at a Newbury Street restaurant within view of the
Boston Common. "Can I have the wine list?" asked WBCN's manager
after everyone had been seated. The establishment was strictly upper
crust and highly priced, as one glance at the menu quickly confirmed.
U2's manager rolled his eyes; traditionally the band and record label
paid the tab on promotional dinners, and this one was bound to blow
his budget for a week.

McGuinness hadn't realized that the U2 entourage was being
treated to a fine meal to celebrate the pair of sold-out shows at the
Orpheum. Tony, who planned to foot the bill, now wanted a suitably
fine vintage to inaugurate a round of toasts. "How about this white?" he
suggested, pointing to an especially tasteful, expensive selection.

U2's manager, also a proud connoisseur, paled slightly at the
price and gestured at a less costly brand. "I think I'd prefer this one."

"You like that one? How about something a little dry?"

"Actually I'd like a red."

"A red? For a toast? Well, this red is wonderful here," Tony replied, indicating another one of the restaurant's most expensive vintages.

McGuinness deflected again, "Perhaps this one would be better?"

"A white now!" The slightest hint of irritation colored his voice, but Tony remained unperturbed. "I have an idea, we'll get a bottle of both white and red!"

"Umm, umm," was all McGuinness could offer.

"I don't mind paying for a couple of extra bottles, let's celebrate."

McGuinness's features relaxed and he broke out in a broad smile, chuckling to himself. No one else picked up on the meaning of the exchange until later when Ellen said, "Paul was quite touched by Tony's gesture of buying dinner . . . and relieved because he really couldn't have afforded it!"

Edge had discovered during the afternoon that a friend of his, former Public Image Limited bassist Jah Wobble, was performing in town with his new band, Invaders of the Heart. Edge had lent his own slide and lead guitar work to Wobble's just-released EP on Island Records entitled *Snake Charmer*. After dinner, Edge and I drove down to the Boston Harbor area, where the nightclub perched by an oily waterway. Inside, a small crowd watched the eight-piece ensemble work through its funky jazz selections, briefly noting two new additions to the audience but failing to recognize U2's guitarist. After the show, Wobble greeted Edge enthusiastically and led us out the back door to his band's small van. "You haven't heard the finished record," he said to Edge while jamming a cassette into the dash. "Listen to this!"

An electronic drum pattern in sinuous disco beat with keyboard jabbings and Wobble's chanting loudly punctuated the silence. The sound of Edge's distinct atmospheric guitar eased in from above for a cascading solo similar to the wild slide riffing he'd played in U2's "Surrender." Wobble played the entire tape, and Edge smiled broadly. Featured on three of the five cuts, Edge handled a chunky rhythm on the next selection along with ringing guitar chimes that complemented Wobble's electronic effects. As his first departure from U2, this flight into mostly instrumental dance music and jazz-rock fusion seemed to be as far as Edge could get from the more traditional rock stylings of U2. *Snake Charmer* marked a giant step for the guitarist, as his involvement in the project revealed a musical hunger and a questing instrumental imagination that would inspire much of U2's future evolution.

After Wobble and his entourage stuffed themselves into the van for their long overnight drive to Buffalo, Edge suggested we return to his hotel. Within seconds of our arrival, a knock at the door brought Paul McGuinness and a silent Bono, who carried three pizzas. The latter was under strict orders not to talk while recovering from his hoarseness, an effort that was clearly difficult for the loquacious singer. Any attempt by Bono to speak a word was met with a sharp glance from McGuinness. The two played out an inadvertent comedy routine all night as Bono tried to sneak bits of conversation past his watchful manager. Adam and Larry soon arrived with Elliot Easton, guitarist for the Cars, in tow. The pizzas quickly disappeared and I left, desperately seeking sleep. Edge, however, remained wide awake on another musical bender as he launched into a marathon session with Easton, excitedly discussing guitars until dawn.

The pair of U2 concerts at the Orpheum had been selected by the D.I.R. Broadcasting Company for an in-concert taping. The recordings would be assembled into an edition of "King Biscuit Flower Hour," the popular syndicated concert program then played coast to coast on subscribing stations. D.I.R. hired engineer Randy Ezratty and his New York City–based Effanel Mobile recording studio for the occasion. Even by U2's own high standards, the concerts turned out to be thorough successes. Racing to the studio in New York, the band members mixed the raw tapes into a master recording, creating an hour-long program that aired a few weeks later and remains one of the series' most popular shows ever.

As a crowd of disappointed ticket seekers wandered outside the Orpheum, Bono, Edge, Larry, and Adam were led from their dressing room to the stage's side curtains, then took their positions on stage. Bright lights flashed on, revealing a huge picture of the boy from the cover of *War* at stage center and three white flags on gleaming silver poles standing a few feet to the left of the drum kit. As Larry thundered into "Out of Control" to start the concert, the flagpoles began rocking in time with the force of his spirited blows. Bono screamed into the microphone, "You may leave your seats now, Boston!" The security team put up no resistance, allowing the throng to spill into the aisles and up front, instantly transforming the theater into a massive dance hall.

Larry's leaden drum thump inflamed "Two Hearts Beat as One," which featured an unexpected interlude as Bono bridled the band's raging thrust to bring the music down to a whisper. Then he urged the crowd to sing a few lines of Chubby Checker's "Let's Twist Again." The fans responded enthusiastically on the first line of the song, but faltered and began laughing when Bono confessed that he didn't know the rest of the words and couldn't lead them any further. As Larry fired up the rhythm and Edge brought back the melody of "Two Hearts Beat as One," the emboldened Bono suddenly surprised the audience by strolling off the stage and dropping into their midst. He was safely borne aloft and passed above and around the crowd for two minutes before finding himself rolled gently back onstage.

That frenzied emotional peak was maintained as U2 delved back into its first album for "The Electric Co." Bono vanished when Edge launched into his guitar break, only to reappear a few seconds later perched on top of the left column of P.A. speakers. Spotlights caught him as he seated himself twenty-five feet above the audience and dangled his legs over the precipice. Bono waited until Edge's solo had simmered down, then used the hushed section of the song to ease into a verse of the classic "Send in the Clowns," once again surprising the crowd by switching over to an unexpected cover tune. This was not a selection one might expect from an Irish rock and roll band, after all—it had last been a hit in 1975 for folksinger Judy Collins. Bono offered a few lines of the song before Edge reasserted himself with a monstrous guitar swipe and accelerated the group back into a sweaty climax.

Although Bono constantly roved about, attracting most of the audience's attention, Edge too generated excitement and covered a lot of ground as he moved between several instruments. On "Surrender," he acted first as a rhythm player measuring out an urgent pattern of notes, then seated himself at a horizontally mounted steel guitar to play a ghostly lead break of sobbing metallic tones. During "Seconds," he strapped on an acoustic guitar and strolled to the center microphone to take over on lead vocals. On "New Year's Day," Edge played piano throughout much of the tune, but a black Stratocaster guitar sat in his lap for easy access on a series of whooping rhythmic melodies that he later referred to as "helicoptering." When he stood up and played the song's signature guitar solo while advancing toward the front of the stage, the Orpheum crowd's excitement boiled over into a frenzy of shouting and applause.

The emotional charge from the crowd carried on to the next song from *War*, which Bono introduced by slowly intoning, "There's been a lot of talk about this next song, maybe too much talk. This is not a rebel song . . . this is 'Sunday Bloody Sunday'!" As Larry's martial beat kicked off the song, the audience shouted in recognition and raised its fists toward the ceiling, waving them in time to the rhythm. When Bono yelled for everyone to scream "no more" in support of his plea for no more fighting, the response was instantly deafening. A casual observer arriving through the doors at that very moment might have been alarmed at the explosive chant filling the theater, but considering its sentiment, the crowd's earsplitting response was completely positive and quite reassuring.

U2's next tour stop was an outdoor gig at the State University of New York in Albany. Glorious blue skies rendered the protective green and white canopy over the stage unnecessary. While one of the warm-up artists, David Johansen, wrestled playfully backstage with two women from the university's concert committee, most of the road crew lazed about in the grass enjoying the warm day. Fresh scents borne by a brisk wind contrasted sharply with the stale beer smell of U2's customary venues. Since the spring weekend celebration was expected to draw a student crowd in the thousands, the sound company had placed its bulky P.A. speakers high above ground in scaffolding located on either side of the stage to boost volume over a wide area of the campus common. The field was deserted when Philadelphia rock and roll performer Robert Hazard stepped up to play, but soon the music summoned the students from their surrounding dormitories. By the time David Johansen had finished rocking out a set of solo tunes and favorites from his former band the New York Dolls, the entire area was filled with a sea of faces squinting up through the bright sunlight toward the stage.

The outdoor show gave U2 more opportunity than ever to connect with the audience. Bono was a striking figure dressed in a dark military-style shirt with the sleeves cut out, black jeans, and black boots. He raced back and forth on the stage, making the eye-to-eye contact with fans that bright spotlights and surrounding darkness usually prevented during indoor shows. He reached out, literally, to the audience by walking out on a metal ramp that had been placed from the stage over the wooden security barrier and into the crowd. He grabbed and shook a flurry of hands, knelt down close to sing directly to the people nearby, and allowed himself to be hoisted onto the shoulders of one burly student and paraded about, with the microphone cord his only connection to the stage.

Later, when Edge attacked his solo guitar centerpiece on "The Electric Co.," Bono grabbed one of the white flags and raced to the left scaffold. Eyeing the tower's pinnacle, he promptly began to clamber up the steel rigging. Behind the column of black speakers, U2's road manager Dennis Sheehan shot a worried glance at the same spot and duly followed to play out the singer's microphone cable and prevent it from snagging. Bono quickly reached the top of the scaffolding, with Sheehan struggling along behind, and triumphantly wedged the flagpole deep into an open pipe. When the white material unfolded fully in the wind, the Albany audience let go a collective breath and erupted in applause. The lone figure wrapped his arm around a metal support and softly sang the verse from "Send in the Clowns." The crowd fell silent, and the moment seemed frozen as Bono peered down with the flag flapping loudly overhead. Then, Edge's twin-note scream blew away the precious moment, the thunderous pace of "The Electric Co." returned, and Bono shouted out the remaining lyrics from his precarious pulpit. After double-timing his way down the tubing while Dennis scurried out of the way and retreated behind the speakers, Bono leapfrogged across the band's monitor cabinets and onto the center stage as Edge signaled the song to a crunching halt.

It took a long time for the audience to settle down after that. Bono used the time to catch his breath. The security barrier in front was now embattled as students inched forward trying to get closer to the stage. Despite the turmoil, Bono once again stepped confidently onto the ramp and walked into the excited mass to signal a female fan sitting on someone's shoulders. He motioned for the young lady to come to him. "Who, me?" she said. Bono nodded and helped the surprised but very willing fan onto the ramp. Then he took her hand and led her onstage where, to everyone's amazement, he bowed politely and asked for a dance. After doing more than a few turns with his thoroughly charmed partner, Bono leaned over and planted an appreciative kiss on her cheek before helping her back down the ramp and into the crowd.

The next day, a frazzled campus phone operator at Trinity College in Hartford, Connecticut, grew weary of the onslaught of callers. "There's no U2 concert here today!" she complained over and over again. Boston fans, freshly inspired by the Orpheum shows, had heard rumors of a performance at Trinity, but needed some assurance before embarking on the hundred-mile drive to the college. School officials, wanting to maintain a students-only policy for their annual spring festival, decided to deny knowledge of U2's scheduled performance. But there were no security measures to prevent curious onlookers and nonstudent U2 fans from entering the campus; the handful of spectators from off campus who wandered onto the school's spacious grassy fields were welcomed into a crowd of five hundred who waited in front of a small stage, soaking up the afternoon sun.

The band members walked out of the four-story student union building directly behind the stage and stepped onto a platform barely three feet high to claim their instruments and take positions. The order of songs was nearly identical with the last few shows, and by the time U2 reached the opening chords of "The Electric Co.," I found myself wondering what sort of stunt Bono would pull this time. As Edge moved up front to bang out his solo, U2's rambunctious singer raced off the side of the stage with white flag in hand and disappeared. One minute passed . . . then another, but he failed to reappear. Framed by the huge building behind them, Edge and Adam faced each other, concentrating on their guitars while Larry pounded out a steady pace behind his kit. Five minutes passed and it was clear that something was amiss when Edge looked questioningly at Adam and the bass player shrugged and shook his head. The two turned and glanced at the top of the student union, betraying their knowledge of where Bono had intended to be, but after another minute he still hadn't shown himself.

Suddenly, from behind the stage, Bono raced into view with the white flag of surrender trailing behind him. His cheeks were deeply flushed while he panted into the microphone, "I've been to every room in that building to show them this flag!" The crowd cheered, few realizing that anything had gone wrong, but Edge, Adam, and Larry knew something was up as they ended their instrumental tirade with a mixture of relief and fatigue. After the concert, I found Bono surveying several platters of food that the concert committee had provided. "That must have been the longest version of 'The Electric Co.' in U2 history," I ventured.

Bono laughed, "Yes, that it was. Before the show, I decided I wanted to run onto the roof, so all the doors were supposed to be left open. I got all the way up to the final door that leads onto the roof and it was locked. There was a man standing there who said he couldn't open it, so I left. Then I had to think of something to say to everyone when I got back!"

"I think it was a pretty clever comeback."

"You know," he wondered aloud, "why was that man standing up there in the dark by a locked door anyway?"

Bono's attempted ascent in Hartford was quite a bit safer than his daredevil antics two days later, which frightened even his own road crew and bandmates. Yale University's Woolsey Hall had been completely sold out; U2's audience filled the floor seats while the Los Angeles band Dream Syndicate opened the show. Faces filled the balcony, which ran around the back of the hall and down front almost to the stack of P.A. speakers on each side of the stage. Many of those present knew that during the May 10 show Bono would be celebrating his twenty-third birthday, so from the very beginning of U2's set, the concert was one huge party.

Bono had requested that a small square of staging be arranged, like the metal ramp in Albany, to provide him access across the security barrier to the front rows. The innovation might have allowed Bono the direct audience contact he desired, but it also opened up a quick and easy return route onto the stage for his fans. As the performance unfolded, a veritable rush of star-struck fans flooded into the band's domain, most women heading directly for Bono to give him a birthday peck on the cheek and the men shaking hands or dancing alongside the singer. One zealous female flanked the group and ambushed from Adam's speaker area, running into Bono from behind and nearly pitching him headlong into the audience. Later, when four young women converged on him simultaneously, one holding out a camera, Bono directed them to sit on a monitor cabinet by his microphone so he could snap their picture. As Bono fumbled with the lens cap, the usually serious Edge abandoned his guitar and lounged on another speaker while yawning and slowly paging through a photo magazine that someone had tossed up. Dennis then appeared onstage with a large cake, inspiring the audience to sing "Happy Birthday." Bono joked, "Just throw money," and was deluged (painfully) by a shower of flying change.

After U2 had sliced halfway into "The Electric Co.," Bono grabbed the white flag and ascended the left P.A. stack, as Dennis trailed dutifully behind. The road manager had seen this move a few times before, but his eyes widened in alarm as Bono abruptly leapt across the three-foot gulf onto the balcony. Performing a similar jump did not appeal to Dennis or U2's younger production manager, Steve Iredale; both remained on the speakers and played out microphone cord. Bono paraded along the foot-wide balcony ledge between astonished fans and a thirty-foot drop to the crowd below. "He's crazy!" someone yelled as all eyes riveted on Bono. When he knelt on the narrow ledge and began singing, fans held onto him to prevent a possible fall. Bono stood up, pivoted, and returned the way he had come—not an easy task in his leather boots and with a spotlight beam in the face. After

Bono completed a jump back onto the speaker stack, which wobbled somewhat under the impact, Dennis visibly relaxed. "I wish he wouldn't do that," he admitted later backstage. "One of these days there's going to be an accident." The road manager, as well as Bono's bandmates, had voiced their concern about his reckless risk-taking, but so far Bono's penchant for losing control during performance had been unchecked. Dennis shrugged his shoulders before moving off to direct the breaking down of the stage, adding, "With someone like Bono, though, what are you gonna do?"

The anxiety growing in the U2 camp over Bono's stunts was joined by another mounting concern: the need for improved security during concerts and afterward in the backstage area. U2's audience, for the most part, was remarkably well-behaved, but even the best intentions of individual fans could produce disastrous results when fifty or a few hundred others were attempting to crowd into the same front seats or bolt onstage to dance. The worsening situation became obvious when the group reached New York City a few days after the Yale show. U2 had graduated from its usual stand at the Ritz, easily selling out the Palladium, a more spacious theater in Manhattan. The audience sat in assigned seats, which could have prevented overcrowding up front, but as soon as U2 came onstage, the first few rows were hopelessly overrun by determined fans pouring forward seeking better vantage points. The show lacked Bono's usual control, and U2 was twice forced to stop playing so that people who had been pushed onto the stage could be cleared off. The chaos in the audience pushed Bono for the first time to a visible breaking point when his poignant speech about the antiwar stance of "Sunday Bloody Sunday" was made inaudible by the shouts and screams. Angrily answering the tumult, he shot back, "Some guy is over here yelling 'fuck the British.' I think you're missing the point!"

After the show, U2's backstage scene also degenerated into a frustrating debacle. A small army jammed the entrance to the band's hospitality suite, impatiently waiting for admittance. While surveying the grubby basement room, Ellen Darst fumed over the exorbitant number of backstage passes that had been handed out by the record company and promoter. She grabbed a can from the tub of sodas but abstained from the bowls of soggy pretzels and chips. "This isn't a hospitality suite, it's a hostility suite," she remarked, disgusted. "In fact, it's worse than that — it's a snake pit!" Ellen instructed the security team to open the door and the room instantly boiled with bodies. Like a school of piranha, they reached the party food table and quickly picked it clean. Most of these guests didn't seem to care whether they met the members of U2; they jabbered excitedly to their friends, ate and drank as much as they could, and soon left. "These aren't fans, they just want to crash backstage," Ellen muttered before fleeing upstairs past two security guards to the band's dressing room.

An atmosphere of gloom hung over the room, where U2's members huddled on and around a couch talking disconsolately about the concert. Someone had sent Bono a birthday cake, which sat untouched by the doorway. "Hello . . . have some cake," he greeted me halfheartedly before pointing to a pretty dark-haired woman next to him. He introduced her as his wife Alison. Then the singer quietly continued: "I am so angry with myself. After the show, after that mess, Ali and I were walking around on the back of the stage and this guy on the security force grabbed her — really grabbed her! He tried to throw her out. All I wanted to do was smash the guy's face. That's all I could think about! I mean, he was rude, but I should have been able to control myself."

"You are allowed to get mad sometimes," I offered.

But Bono could not be consoled. "I'm supposed to know better."

It got better the following night when U2 moved a few miles west to Passaic, a bustling concrete jungle in suburban New Jersey. The band's performance at the Capitol Theater was an aggressive masterpiece during which Bono exorcised his previous night's frustration and anger. Ellen concentrated on improving the backstage arrangements and tightly controlled the distribution of passes, ensuring that nearly everyone gathered to meet the band members after the show was either an ardent fan or a representative of the media. Most were so excited at the prospect of meeting U2 that they failed to recognize the figure lounging in a chair behind them in the backstage room. Sting had arrived fresh from recording in the Caribbean with the Police, his deep tan a striking contrast to his casual white outfit. In many ways, U2's career had followed in the footsteps of the Police, a group which had also fought its way out of the new wave underground (in 1978) and did not taste success in the mainstream until the release of its third album. Adam showed up and began signing autographs, then excused himself to greet his fellow bassist. While Edge diverted the autograph seekers, Adam and Sting were able to carry on a spirited and uninterrupted conversation. When John Entwistle of the Who made an unexpected appearance a few moments later and joined the pair in their tête-à-tête, backstage fans witnessed a true bass players' summit.

At their next stop, in Philadelphia, the group received a visit from another important new fan. U2 was scheduled to perform two nights at the Tower, an aging theater that commanded recognition in rock and roll circles as the location where David Bowie had recorded his *David Live* album in 1974. Even if it was the hall's reputation that inspired U2 to churn out two powerful performances rivaling any on its tour, the overwhelming excitement in the audience was as important as ever in encouraging the band's best effort. Bono insisted on adding to the momentum with a spectacle of his own during one show, as he abruptly climbed off the stage and jumped into the chairs directly in front of the left P.A. column. While the audience sang along to "Surrender," Bono pointed his microphone into the small group of fans clustered by the speakers, urging them to add their off-key voices to the chorus. The private sing-along lasted about five seconds before the area swarmed with people who had raced down the aisles and poured over seats to touch the singer. Dennis Sheehan unceremoniously reeled Bono back to the stage by his microphone cable. During the second concert, Bono crawled on top of the speaker column and suggested with a mischievous look in his eyes that he might try a twenty-five-foot plunge into the audience. To Dennis's relief, Bono chose to stay perched on the speaker column and sing.

After the second show, the appearance of a figure in a cut-off denim shirt and faded blue jeans sent everyone backstage buzzing with excitement. Smiling and looking every bit like a muscular gas station attendant about to begin his night shift was Bruce Springsteen, who had driven in from Asbury Park, New Jersey, to see U2's show. An admitted U2 fan, Springsteen had stood quietly on the side of the stage all evening. Paul McGuinness decided to take the party back to U2's hotel, where he reserved the restaurant for a celebration. Bono and Alison accepted Springsteen's offer of a ride and walked into the alley next to the theater where his car was poised for a quick getaway. The rest of the band members strolled out to the chain link fence shielding the alley from a large crowd and began signing autographs. The size of the gathering and its somewhat restless nature made Dennis uneasy, so he hurried the group through its greetings and formed a wedge of security personnel around the members. When the gate was opened, it took all the muscle of the road manager's crew, plus the Tower's security team, to move Adam, Edge, and Larry a few feet forward into their bus idling on the street.

"Where's Bono?" a pretty blond girl shouted at me.

"He's in that car with Bruce Springsteen," I replied as the dark shape glided past the commotion. Looking back skeptically, she laughed. I shrugged in reply and smiled — I wouldn't have believed it either.

Following the band members through the screen of security personnel, I entered the tour bus. Larry sat up front across from the driver while Dennis returned down the alley to attend to some minor problem. The drummer, whose figure was hidden by curtains in the window, began to fidget as the minutes dragged and the crowd outside milled about hopefully. Finally he turned around, whipped the curtains aside, and slid open a window. Larry's attempt to console the fans caused a small riot instead as people desperately tried to get within earshot or even close enough to touch him. Dennis returned, loudly warning everyone to stand back as the bus pulled out, but several people remained dangerously close to the wheels. "Let me tell them!" Larry yelled. Dennis cautiously opened the door and Larry stuck his body halfway out to urge everyone back. Almost immediately, however, he began to slip through the doorway as hands clutched his leather jacket and began pulling. Dennis and I dove to grab the arm remaining inside, but Larry continued to be slowly dragged from the bus. When the driver engaged the emergency brake and reached over to help, our combined strength finally pulled Larry inside. He lay back, his face pale, while the driver put the bus in gear and carefully eased away from the curb. Larry might have thought it was just an isolated incident, but Dennis knew better; U2 hysteria had begun.

The growing intensity of U2's crowd situations distressed the members, who still wanted to believe that a natural bond existing between them and their fans would intuitively inform and control each fan's behavior. Perhaps that unspoken communication had succeeded in the past, when U2's audience barely filled small clubs, allowing an intimate relationship to develop between the musicians and their supporters. But now, with the audience size growing on every concert date and contact between the band members and their fans becoming rare and coveted, it was far more difficult to control these encounters. The pressure of greater competition among U2's followers — in obtaining concert tickets, getting close to the stage, and trying to meet the band members — only made the resulting crowd situations more susceptible to mob behavior. U2's members were reluctant to make security concessions that would reduce affinity with their supporters; the last thing they wanted to do was hide behind a battalion of police or security. But Larry's incident was just the latest example of how failure to recognize and deal with the problem could only lead to further danger — for both the band members and their fans.

At the hotel restaurant, in an area roped off for the privacy of the band members and their guests, Ellen Darst held court with a few Philadelphia record company reps while a ring of fans that had shadowed the tour bus from the Tower observed from the other side of the bar. Edge arrived with Aislinn, his fiancée, but Larry came and went almost immediately, admitting that his experience after the show had pretty much ruined the evening for him. Springsteen, Bono, and Alison walked in together, gathered around a table, and began talking animatedly. Bono was impressed with the star, as he told me in a phone interview for WBCN in 1984. "It's the spirit of Bruce Springsteen that interests me. I don't think we share a lot in common musically, but it's the spirit. He is a performer and a soul singer, and I would aspire to being a soul singer. The commitment from his band is hopefully the commitment that comes off from U2. He's real . . . he is who he says he is."

With stardom beckoning at this important stage in U2's career, Springsteen's example was reassuring. As one of rock music's leading poets, and a highly successful one as well (*Born in the U.S.A.* would take him even higher the following year), he maintained an open working-class identity in his songs and performance, sharing a close affinity and trust with his legion of fans. Bruce Springsteen was living proof to the members of U2 that fame need not destroy their own honorable intentions and desire for direct communication with their supporters (although Larry had found that there could be some danger in getting too close). As U2 became more popular, the group could remain devoted to its following in a relationship of mutual respect, rather than become increasingly aloof, as did many stars in rock music's hierarchy. Perhaps their devotion to the audience could help carry the group through the distasteful but necessary task of administering additional security measures.

As U2's soirée broke up, Bono, somewhat tipsy from a couple of glasses of wine, ambled toward the entrance of the bar where a few admirers had been waiting patiently all night. Tired and wobbly in Alison's steadying arms, he nevertheless stopped to speak with the fans before disappearing into the elevator. Springsteen, laughing as he watched the couple hobble off, got up and signed autographs for the remaining fans, then reclaimed his car and vanished into the night.

7

A CROWD HAS GATHERED

EDGE TELEPHONED me at WBCN on May 30, 1983, for an impromptu on-air interview. He jabbered excitedly: "I'll tell you, he made us so scared. He didn't tell us he was going to do it, maybe he didn't know he was going to do it himself! Myself, Adam, and Larry were down there, mouths open, just waiting to see what was going to happen." Edge was speaking about Bono's latest stunt, accomplished during U2's just-completed performance at the US Festival in Devore, California. The massive commercial event combined a high-tech computer and electronics fair with three days of rock and roll concerts, followed by a day-long lineup of country-western acts. Not only dwarfed by the huge stage that looked out over a reported half-million people, U2 was viewed as a minor combatant next to the stars booked to perform on that day: David Bowie, the Pretenders, Stevie Nicks, and John (Cougar) Mellencamp.

The hundreds of stagelights that were attached to an immense riot of steel tubing far above the members of U2 were not needed during the band's performance in the withering afternoon sun. Tight and well-honed from weeks on the road, the group hit its stride early and began to connect with many in the gigantic sea of faces. The reaction obviously wasn't enough for Bono, though; during "The Electric Co." he raced to the side of the stage and reached for a rope ladder leading up the tall scaffold that held up the titanic equipment truss and canvas canopy. Even talking about the experience on the phone sent U2's normally unflappable guitarist into near-hysterics. "It was the biggest festival we've ever played to—the crowd was good and we just had an incredible show. Bono, as usual, was up to his antics. He ended up climbing four hundred feet to the very top of the stage and ceremonially planted the Irish flag and a white flag at the very top. Everyone went bananas! It was incredible!"

The actual height Bono climbed was probably closer to 150 feet, but the sight of his tiny figure clambering up a series of ladders to finally emerge on top of the huge orange US Festival banner capping the stage mesmerized the entire crowd. Delirious applause greeted Bono when he waved from the heights while a microphone was passed to him by a member of U2's crew, now well practiced at following the singer during his frequent offstage excursions. With the white flag in one hand and the mike in the other, Bono sat with a huge television monitor behind him that projected his every move in enormous detail. Even the most disinterested members of the crowd couldn't help but notice all the activity. After finishing his vocal section, Bono tossed the light aluminum pole into the audience far below (not a good idea, but it was caught without injury) and retraced the hazardous path to rejoin his astonished bandmates.

Bono's climb made U2 one of the most talked-about items from the most talked-about concert of the year. Television coverage of the incident carried U2's name and reputation across the country. However, the debate about Bono's antics raged even stronger backstage, where his bandmates and U2's management staff severely questioned the wisdom of his move. Interviewed for this book, Ellen Darst told me she agreed with Bono's critics, but understood why he felt compelled to continue the dangerous activities. "There was pressure on him; he had to feel that he could play these places [arenas, stadiums, and festivals] and still reach people. He kept feeling pushed to do these grand moves to be seen. There was an ongoing disagreement about whether or not this was what should be happening. Everybody felt it was dangerous, wasn't necessary, or worth the risk."

For the moment, though, this conflict was tabled as plans moved swiftly ahead for U2's next major project. Paul McGuinness had become fascinated with the prospect of filming a full-length U2 concert video. His idea was not without precedent, since MTV's acceptance of the "New Year's Day" clip was an enormous promotional success for the band, and the experience of creating the video had been artistically satisfying as well. U2's reputation as a terrific live act was unquestioned by the growing cult audience that came to its concerts — why not record that display of intense energy and direct communication between band and audience, making it easily accessible to everyone? U2 had only recently climbed out of debt, but McGuinness and the band members decided to risk every cent accrued on their first financially successful U.S. tour to make arrangements for the filming. Still, when the potential costs were tallied, the group's resources fell far short of the amount required. Seeking financial help, McGuinness soon welcomed Island Records and promoter Barry Fey as U2's partners in the project.

Barry Fey was an entrepreneur who handled concert bookings for a large area of the southwest and who had once collaborated with Frank Barsalona to bring Led Zeppelin to America in 1968. He suggested Red Rocks, an outdoor concert facility near his home base of Denver, as an ideal site for filming U2's performance. Fey often booked the location, a natural amphitheater wedged between towering Rocky Mountain cliffs and equipped to handle crowds of nine thousand people. McGuinness agreed with the suggestion and set June 5 as target date for the special concert. Accepting the added expenses of flying personnel and equipment across the Atlantic, he decided to import a crack film crew from "The Tube," a popular English television show that presented bands in concert. The members of U2 had been so pleased with Randy Ezratty and his Effanel Music unit at the Orpheum in May that he was invited to return with his equipment to record the audio portion of the concert. The group once again called on its longtime associate Steve Lillywhite to handle the production. Rights were sold to NBC Radio to create a syndicated radio program from the raw tapes as part of its live concert series, "The Source."

"It was a big gamble," Ellen recalled. "That's one thing about Paul: he's a terrific gambler. It was . . . like $250,000. It seemed like a fortune because it was everything they [U2] had. This would have been nerve-racking enough, but for the fact that it poured!" Normally, bringing the equipment necessary to mount a concert at Red Rocks up along the mountain road was difficult enough, but the rain that fell steadily at the site for days beforehand made the task appear impossible. Even after the sound and film gear had been manhandled through the thick mud into position, it was a major chore just to keep the equipment dry during the steady downpour. Edge's guitar technician Steve Rainford related: "I was more worried about people getting electrical shocks than anything. Just before the show, Bob Morbeck, the chief lighting guy, got one from the netting. We hung netting in front of the *Boy* picture and the lighting truss. There were extra lights there that day for the filming and there was a ground fault problem, so this netting was 'live' because of the rain." Morbeck's shock raised further worries that a stray electrical fault might endanger the performers or crew during the show.

The rain continued the night before the concert, raising questions about U2's ability to perform in the deplorable conditions and whether an audience would even show up. The band members huddled with their manager and decided it would only be fair to give a free concert at an indoor arena the night after the Red Rocks appearance for anyone who had an original ticket or stub. Those driven back by the elements would still get a chance to see U2 and anyone who did brave the weather up in the mountains could experience the band again under less extreme conditions. Meanwhile, the pressure on Paul McGuinness to cancel the outdoor extravaganza became enormous. He bided his time, though, holding to the original schedule throughout a long night of rain and into the foggy morning of the concert.

By midday, to the amazement of everyone working at the site, figures in bright raincoats and hooded sweatshirts began to appear out of the mist to find their seats in the amphitheater. The fans' spirits were high, everyone confident that the show would go on as planned, and cameras dutifully recorded footage of the optimistic fans for possible inclusion in the video. McGuinness was assured by his crew that the band members would be safe onstage during their performance, but the final decision as to whether the concert would proceed had not yet been made. Ellen recalled the tension of that moment: "[At] 3:00, maybe 2:00 in the afternoon, Barry Fey, who had been out of town, came back. As much as he wanted the gig to happen, [he] was saying that we had to cancel. Paul was saying, 'We're not canceling the gig!' Of course, [if they did cancel] they were going to lose all the money they had put into pre-production for the shoot. I just marveled at the sheer nerve of the guy, he was just standing his ground ferociously, even with Barry pressuring us like mad to pull out."

Fey argued for U2 to cut its losses in the face of a potential rain-out and production disaster. Even though much of the money spent on setting up Red Rocks for the video shoot would be lost, the options of filming the free indoor show or another outdoor concert were much safer. Paul McGuinness, however, counted on something that Fey didn't yet understand about U2, as Ellen remembered: "I'll tell you something about this band—the more screwed up things are, the worse the odds are, the better they will be. The more adversity there is, the more to overcome, the bigger the challenge — the better they'll come through!"

Randy Ezratty recalled that he was amazed at Paul McGuinness's determination. "A lot of people wanted to pull out — they said the equipment was at risk. Downstairs from the stage was this big communal area where we ate our meals; it was the only place that was dry. McGuinness called everyone down there. He was a guy that nobody knew — just a band manager who had no track record — and he called together all these television guys, our team, the lighting team, and Clair Brothers [sound]. He said, 'Look, this show is going to happen! This band has put every cent on the line, it's our money, it's our future, and it will be a major setback if this show doesn't go on. It's going to happen, so don't listen to anybody else!' Paul took charge, he made it clear that there was no questioning his decision — a lesser guy would have backed down."

Paul McGuinness proved his tenacity before the concert, but it was still up to the group to deliver its typical punch despite the discouraging conditions. Fortunately, the sheets of rain slicing through the amphitheater had not deterred the faithful, so when the band members walked onstage, it was to a deafening tumult from thousands of voices. U2 launched into its set while Bono constantly prowled the stage, a black T-shirt barely warding off the cold damp that had settled on every surface. When he reached for notes, steam poured out of his mouth, enveloping the microphone in a ghostly cloud. Island Records' Michael Abramson stood on stage looking up at the torches that had been placed on the surrounding rocky crags, surveying the mysterious, medieval atmosphere. He told me: "You could see it in the audience's faces — people were getting into the mysticism, the magical qualities of U2. Despite the horrible conditions, it turned out to be an unbelievable performance."

U2 fans who attended the Red Rocks concert have to be praised for their incredible devotion amid the soggy conditions that night. Prominently featured in the eventual video, the singing and dancing crowd clearly inspired the members of U2 to forget the weather, focus on their music, and present perhaps the most inspiring show of the entire tour. The group's seventeen-song set drew heavily from its first album and introduced six new songs from *War*. Refined steadily from concert to concert, U2's songs had evolved into sturdy live versions: "Two Hearts Beat as One," with its Chubby Checker jam in the middle, a coda added to the beefier attack of "Sunday Bloody Sunday," and the festive "Party Girl" encore. U2 concluded its success in the rain with an especially moving version of "40." The song officially ended with Bono waving goodnight, but cries of "how long to sing this song!" welled up so strongly from the crowd that the singer was recalled to lead another chorus before the band members finally quit the stage.

In July, while the group toured Europe, "The Source" program became the first fruit of U2's Red Rocks performance. A boxed two-record set of the concert entitled *War Is Declared* (which became an instant collector's item) was mailed out to NBC Radio's network of affiliate stations and was broadcast nationwide on the weekend of July 8. "The Tube" completed its video production and televised the concert in America on the cable pay channel Showtime. U2's choice of *Under a Blood Red Sky* for the title (from a line in "New Year's Day") aptly captured the vivid image of flaming torches high in the cliffs at Red Rocks casting an eerie crimson glow onto the low clouds. The initial televised appearance of the concert incorporated a dozen songs with Steve Lillywhite's audio production. A second version screened soon after as an MTV special only used nine tracks, some of them different from the earlier broadcast, with audio remixed by Los Angeles-based producer Jimmy Iovine and engineer Shelly Yakus. The duo's talents were also used on the commercially released videocassette of *Under a Blood Red Sky* — a third version of the concert that offered a different selection of twelve tracks in altered arrangement from the previous TV specials. *Rolling Stone* quickly lauded U2's video effort and *Billboard* eventually nominated the release for "Best Long Form Music Video of the Year" in its annual awards.

Jimmy Iovine was a tireless music enthusiast whose studio skills with Patti Smith, Tom Petty, and Stevie Nicks had earned him considerable fame. Yakus's engineering credits dated back to such stars as John Lennon and the Band. Randy Ezratty recalled: "Iovine loved that band [U2], from day number one of the *War* album. He wanted nothing more than to produce them, so he got on a plane to Ireland to pitch himself, with Shelly, to do the next studio record."

"How many times do you find a band that you *really* like?" Iovine asked passionately when I questioned him about why he had pursued U2 so fervently. "I loved them, so I just flew over and told them face-to-face that I really wanted to work with them." Even though the band members were already thinking seriously about a production relationship with Brian Eno for their next studio effort, Iovine's enthusiasm compelled them to give the L.A.-based team an audition of sorts. U2 handed over a set of live tapes, including the Red Rocks recording and concerts in Europe later that summer, and asked Iovine and Yakus to come up with usable stereo mixes of the songs. Impressed with the results, McGuinness and the band members began thinking of assembling a live record.

As concert tracks for the audio *Under a Blood Red Sky* were being selected, U2's members decided they liked the later interpretations of their songs recorded at "Rockpalast 83," a concert in Lorelei, Germany, in August better than the Red Rocks tapes from June. Interviewed for WBCN in 1985, Edge explained why their selections included some later versions. "Evolution is really what happens when we start playing a song live. Adam and Bono tend to do an awful lot of improvisation. The songs become pulled about and changed: almost every night there's a new twist to a song. The good things that happen, we keep; and the things that fail, we just forget about. After a tour, a song becomes a collection of successfully improvised parts—it's a great process. Steve Lillywhite used to say to us, 'I wish you would play your albums for about six months before you record them!' "

Five fresh tracks from Rockpalast 83 were substituted for Red Rocks recordings previously used in the *Under a Blood Red Sky* videos. The Colorado versions of "Gloria" and "Party Girl" survived the cut, the former deserving preservation on vinyl if only for the intense audience response that threatened to drown out Edge's guitar solo in the middle. Mike Abramson admitted that he fought "like mad" with McGuinness and Iovine to eliminate the latter song because of a weird note that Edge accidently hit during his solo. Bono made the mistake even more obvious when he facetiously introduced his bandmate a moment later as a "guitar hero." The group favored preserving the lighthearted moment though, so Abramson was overruled. The band also wanted to include "11 O'Clock Tick Tock," which had never appeared in any form on an American U2 record. Believing that the Boston recording for the "King Biscuit Flower Hour" was the best version of the song, U2 retrieved the tape and added it to the album.

Abramson described McGuinness's plan for the live record: "They wanted to do something that had never before been done. You know, at Christmastime there's that 'Give the Gift of Music' thing? Well, what U2 wanted to do was give the gift of music by doing an eight-song record at a $4.98 list price. It was something that everyone could afford, as opposed to the eight- or nine-dollar price tag that was then on records.

Discounted, the thing would go for three dollars." Island went along with the plan, releasing the mini-LP, as it was called, in October 1983. Two months later, the label put out a seven-inch single of "I Will Follow" from the mini-LP with an edit of Francois Kevorkian's "Two Hearts Beat as One" remix on the B-side. Some comments from radio programmers about the intense crowd noise on "I Will Follow" prompted Iovine and Yakus to mix a special radio version of the single that virtually eliminated the obscuring cheers. The single failed to chart appreciably, peaking at number eighty-one on the *Billboard* chart, but by then *Under a Blood Red Sky* was already streaking toward gold.

U2 did not consider the live mini-LP a throwaway release, but viewed it as an artistic bonus born from the video project. Adam Clayton was particularly proud of the record, as he said to me in a 1985 interview for WBCN: "I think *Under a Blood Red Sky* has to be the simplest idea that was executed in the most competent way. It was ideal that we actually had the stuff on tape. We didn't [have to] spend too much money on it, which meant that we could actually put it out at a low price and the guy on the street ultimately benefited. It was representative of that *War* tour and, I think in many manys, was the record we should feel proudest of." The band demanded its usual high standards for the record package, which was illustrated with appropriately murky stills from the video, including an arresting front cover shot of Bono poised in silhouette onstage.

The new live version of "The Electric Co.," recorded at Rockpalast 83 in August, vastly improved on the original studio version on *Boy*. Bono's penchant for adding a verse of "Send in the Clowns" to the song's middle section was represented along with a sung snippet of "America" from *West Side Story*. Ultimately the use of the former song, written by Stephen Sondheim for the Broadway musical *A Little Night Music*, brought more trouble than it was worth when publishing copyright lawyers came looking for U2. The band had neglected to obtain legal permission to add the song portion to its live album, believing that Bono merely acknowledged the melody and some words briefly without fully interpreting them. The lawyers disagreed, and U2 was forced to remit a hefty payment for incorporating "Send in the Clowns" on the record. Subsequent pressings of *Under a Blood Red Sky* omitted Bono's unauthorized vocal passage, noticeably chopping twenty-seven seconds from the middle of "The Electric Co." — and thereby creating a collector's demand for original unedited copies.

While performing in the States in 1983, U2's members had already been thinking about their next studio album, a project that would be deeply influenced by an experience in America's heartland during the *War* tour. In Chicago, U2 was introduced to the Peace Museum, a venue launched by activists dedicated to educating people about non-violence through contact with the arts. In this museum, the first of its kind in the world, volunteers assembled collections of antiwar placards and posters, a display about civil rights advances made by Martin Luther King, Jr., and an exhibit of chilling personal views of the atomic bomb blasts created by survivors of Hiroshima and Nagasaki entitled "The Unforgettable Fire." Far from the museum's humble, barely noticed beginnings in 1981, the opening night attendance of "The Unforgettable Fire" exhibit one year later numbered over a thousand patrons.

Marianne Philbin, a free-lance writer who had become involved when the museum was only a dream, served as curator of exhibits and helped steer the institution's artistic course. In 1982, Philbin and her associates began planning a major display designed to spotlight artists who had promoted peace through their music. Early attempts to launch the project were given a tremendous boost when Yoko Ono agreed to contribute several items of memorabilia recalling her own consciousness-raising efforts with John Lennon in the seventies. Entitled "Give Peace a Chance," the exhibit would also focus attention on the ex-Beatle's lengthy immigration battle with the U.S. government. Terri Hemmert, a radio personality at WXRT–FM in Chicago, was brought to the project as a consulting expert on the Beatles and Lennon, but she also counted herself a loyal U2 fan. In an interview for this book, Hemmert mentioned that *War* appeared while she was hard at work on the "Give Peace a Chance" project. "I remember reading the lyric sheet from *War* and thinking, 'This is perfect for our exhibit.' I thought of how terrific it would be to get their involvement in the museum and help them make a comment on the issues they were addressing."

Although U2 was not an overtly political band, throwing support to the right or left, or endorsing specific parties, its members had always been outspoken in condemning violence created by political friction. Disillusioned by the destructive tactics employed by the I.R.A. in Northern Ireland, U2 had made a significant statement for peace by never supporting the organization. Although unfortunately misinterpreted at times as an I.R.A. anthem, "Sunday Bloody Sunday" was U2's brave castigation of the hatred and violence inherent in the tragic religious and political Irish struggle. The band members' long-standing willingness to confront the conflict, expressed as far back as 1981's "Tomorrow," made them proponents of peace whom Hemmert felt were more than appropriate for inclusion in "Give Peace a Chance."

Philbin agreed to incorporate U2 into the exhibit, but would the band be interested? Hemmert wanted to obtain a handwritten manuscript of one song from *War* plus a promotional white U2 flag from Island Records. "Someone finally gave me Ellen Darst's phone number and we talked," Hemmert recalled. "Ellen was really receptive to the idea of sending something to the museum, but had to check with the boys, who were on the road at that point. Then she called me at home and said that they were so excited about it that they wanted to do more! They wanted to meet with us to find out what the museum was about." With U2 scheduled to perform in Chicago only two days later a meeting was quickly set up. The band's itinerary was tight — they had driven in, taken a day room at a hotel, and would leave town immediately following the show. The brief conference would have to be held in the hotel coffee shop before soundcheck.

Terri Hemmert remembers the gathering fondly. "I got Marianne [Philbin] and a couple of other representatives from the Peace Museum and we went down to meet them. I thought maybe one or two would show up, but all four of them were there. It was a real grind tour for them — you could tell they were ready to drop — but they were so enthusiastic to talk about what we were up to. We told them about past exhibits like 'The Unforgettable Fire' and gave them a catalogue from that one." The graphic paintings and drawings which made up the exhibit stunned the band members. Philbin and Hemmert also informed them of the museum's devotion to the life of Martin Luther King, Jr., and about plans for the upcoming "Give Peace a Chance" exhibit.

Marianne Philbin, also interviewed for this book, recalled the meeting. "We ended up sitting there for a couple of hours just brainstorming and they had some wonderful ideas about the show. I told Bono that if he ever wanted to be a curator, he could drop by. The way his mind works!" One suggestion from the band members was to recreate a stage set at the museum that visitors could actually step up onto, then sit at the drums or stand behind the microphone. Philbin explained: "The idea was to demystify the notion of a rock star being different from you and therefore having more power to make a statement and get involved. They wanted to suggest that, yes, these people [the artists represented in 'Give Peace a Chance'] have made a difference through their own contributions because they happen to be incredibly talented musicians and writers, but that every person has some talent and ability to make a contribution as well." Before Bono, Edge, Larry, and Adam left the coffee shop, they agreed to provide the requested items and do what they could to promote the museum's ideals. Eventually the exhibit would grow too large to incorporate U2's idea for a complete stage mock-up, but the band did donate its large concert backdrop picturing the cover of *War*, one of the white flags that Bono regularly carried to the heights, and the original handwritten manuscript for "New Year's Day."

"Give Peace a Chance" was unveiled to the public on September 11, 1983. Along with John Lennon and U2, the exhibit featured the art of Woody Guthrie, Pete Seeger, Bob Dylan, Stevie Wonder, George Harrison, and many others. "Each artist had a small room, arranged in a sort of maze pattern," Philbin explained. "You moved through a history of popular music and culture to see how things had been woven together and how one musician's work influenced another's. Bono told us later that for him — being from over there [Ireland] — there was a sense of isolation, and that the show helped give him a sense of the tradition and history out of which some of U2's music was coming."

The band's experience with the Peace Museum profoundly influenced its next studio album, which would be released in the fall of 1984. Its title was taken from the "Unforgettable Fire" exhibit, and the memory of Martin Luther King, Jr., directly inspired two songs. The members continued an active relationship with the museum by providing funds to duplicate both the King and atomic bomb exhibits and convert them into traveling shows for visitors to witness across America. During U2's concert stop in Chicago the following year, the band would dedicate its encore of "New Year's Day" to the museum and visit the institution the following afternoon. That encounter resulted in plans to bring "The Unforgettable Fire" and "Martin Luther King— Peacemaker" exhibits to Dublin for a special dual showing in June 1985. Ireland's *Hot Press* wrote about the poignant scenes depicted in the exhibition: "The message was stunningly clear . . . and it amplified the message at the heart of U2's music — that we must wrestle with the demons of violence and hatred and aggression and that we must win. Peacefully."

Much later, in 1987, Bono would contribute a poem to the Peace Museum that was regularly displayed in exhibits and also intended for a never-completed book by Chicago writer Don McLeese about the history of the peace movement. Written in a hotel suite in Phoenix, "Dreams in a Box" summed up Bono's feelings for a simple brick build-

ing in Chicago that contained worlds of inspiration for him and many
others.

Dreams in a Box

The Chicago Peace Museum is dreams in a box
Some come true, some to be realized
Yet . . . we know that peace is a living thing
That it cannot be put in a place, contained
That it is not the absence of war
That it does not bow down to Marx or Lenin, Reagan or Thatcher
That it is not infected by hypodermic needles
And yet it must infect us with a cure, contagious.

Peace will not prosper while the poor are controlled in ghettos
Cornered by color or greed,
From Watts to Harlem, Belfast to Beirut
We must find new solutions to new problems.

The Chicago Peace Museum is a building
put up and run by men and women who believe
that peace does not exist by itself
That it is/will be brought into being by people
That it must be taught in classrooms as well as churches
At street level as well as at the negotiating table
By businessmen as well as artists.

I am a word writer . . . but it is actions
man-made and concrete
that we need . . .

We see love torn down
Begin the rebuilding.

—— Bono

(Reprinted by permission of the Peace Museum and Don McLeese.)

Boy reaches the New World—U2 at the Paradise Theater, Boston, December 13, 1980. (PHIL IN PHLASH)

Edge, Larry, and Bono in full flight—Paradise Theater, December 13, 1980.
(PHIL IN PHLASH)

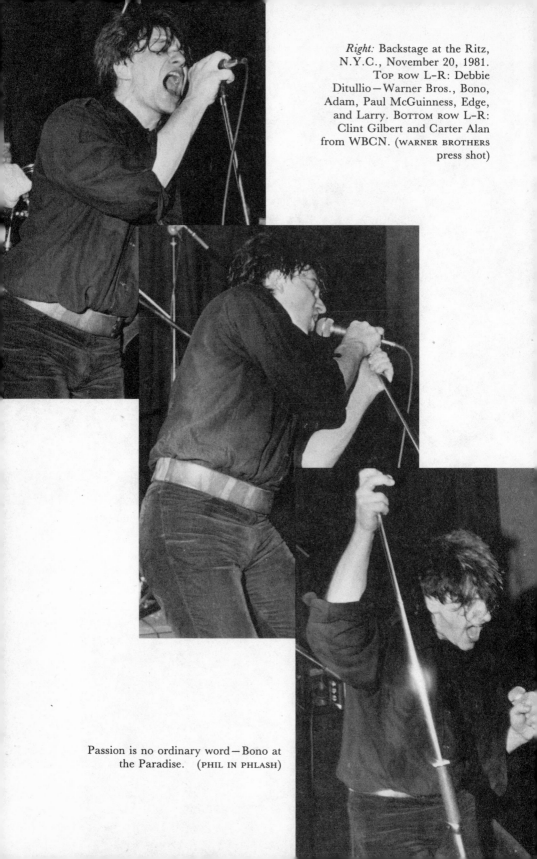

Right: Backstage at the Ritz, N.Y.C., November 20, 1981. TOP ROW L–R: Debbie Ditullio—Warner Bros., Bono, Adam, Paul McGuinness, Edge, and Larry. BOTTOM ROW L–R: Clint Gilbert and Carter Alan from WBCN. (WARNER BROTHERS press shot)

Passion is no ordinary word—Bono at the Paradise. (PHIL IN PHLASH)

Below: Boston radio meets the band in New York City March 1982.
L–R: Bono, Jane Richter—WLYN, Edge, Adam, Carter Alan—
WBCN. (WARNER BROTHERS press shot)

The Cross of Light—U2 at Brown
University, Providence, March 20,
1982. (DERRIL BAZZY, courtesy New
Sound, Inc.)

Bono in the trenches — Tower Theater,
Philadelphia, May 1983. (DEBORAH PADOVA)

The Unforgettable Fire — the Peace Museum
collection of Japanese atom bomb drawings
inspires U2. (THE PEACE MUSEUM)

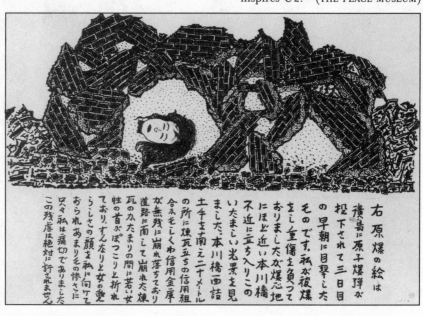

右原爆の絵は

横島に原子爆弾が
投下されて三日目
の早朝に目撃した
ものです。私が被爆
をし重傷を負って
おりましたが爆心地
にほど近い本川橋
不近に立ち入りこの
いたましい光景を見
ました。本川橋西詰
土手を南え二十メートル
の所に煉瓦五ちの信用組
合みをしくや信用金庫
が無残に崩れ落ちており
道路に而して崩れた煉
瓦の九たまりの間に若い女
性の首がぽつこりと折れ
ており、すんなりと女の愛
らしさの顔を私に向けて
おられあまりもの惨さに
只々私は痛切でありました。
この残虐は絶対に許されません

Flying the white flag — Bono and Dennis Sheehan in Albany, May 7, 1983.
(CARTER ALAN)

Edge with double duties on "New Year's Day"—Fox Theater, Detroit, December 1984. (KURT ITIL)

Delivering *The Unforgettable Fire*—Bono onstage at Radio City Music Hall, N.Y.C., in December 1984. (DEBORAH PADOVA)

8

ONE MORE IN THE NAME OF LOVE

LARRY EASED back in a comfortable seat that vibrated as U2's tour bus navigated through the choked streets of central Philadelphia. On his way to the opening show of a U.S. tour in December 1984, he had time to reflect on U2's new album, recorded during the past summer. He leaned forward so I could hear his words over the engine. "This album — we had to do it for ourselves, instead of doing another *War*. You know, *October* was an album about the band, and people called it self-indulgent the way they call *The Unforgettable Fire* self-indulgent. I guess they're right . . . but we still had to do it for us. We grew on this album . . . a lot."

For *The Unforgettable Fire*, U2 had decided to take the bold step of working in an altered environment under a completely different set of rules to cast off its songwriting and recording habits. The attempt at change was not unlike what U2 had done at the beginning of sessions for its previous album, as Edge elaborated in an interview I conducted for Island Records in December 1984. "On *War*, our original idea was to find an alternative to Steve Lillywhite — not because we weren't satisfied with his work, but simply [because] we felt in order to keep our enjoyment of the recording sessions to their utmost that it would be beneficial to get some new blood into the recording. It was an attempt to break away from a sort of idea of the band that had been previously held. In the same way, *The Unforgettable Fire* is an album like that. If we had worked [again] with Steve, I think he knows us too well — knows the direction that we natually go — it would have all been a little bit too easy."

Bono elaborated during an on-air phone call to me at WBCN a few days before the December tour began: "There was a danger where we were being seen as the vanguard of a movement, and I'm really not into movements, myself. I'm into a movement of one . . . you know, the individual. I think if we had made another *War*, [people would have said] 'ahh, that's the group U2, they make records which sound like "Sunday Bloody Sunday" and "New Year's Day," that's all they do.' If *War* was a black-and-white record, this is much more in color . . . this is a reading between the lines of *War*. I really believe that the band is only being born. At the end of the *War* tour, after the release of *Under a Blood Red Sky*, we felt we'd finished a complete cycle. We really broke up the band and formed it again with the same name and the same people — but there were no rules. *The Unforgettable Fire* is the first step."

Although the team of Iovine and Yakus was close at hand, the band members knew they required a different sort of producer for the project they had in mind. Edge told *International Musician & Recording World* about the group's realization that Brian Eno might be able to help take U2 where it wanted to go. "There's one particular track on [Eno's] *Before and After Science* which impressed me a lot. He had some echoed drums on it, so when we were putting together 'I Threw a Brick Through a Window' for the *October* lp, I brought down the record and we stayed up very late one night with Steve Lillywhite and got out some rototoms and started working on that. When we were deciding on a producer for this record, [Eno's] name just kept coming up."

Brian Eno had initially received acclaim as the outrageous synthesizer player for the English rock group Roxy Music, but later solo efforts extended his reputation as an artist and producer. A series of albums using traditional song styles culminated in *Before and After Science*, but with the 1975 release of *Discreet Music* Eno threw pop convention out the window in favor of minimalist music structures either played by the synthesizer or gathered in magnetic tape loops of recurring sounds. Even though he began to create instrumental records such as *Music for Films*, designed to serve as unobtrusive background music, no single project could categorize the efforts of this daring, inventive artist. Eno's methods expressed his belief that nothing was constant and creativity would be compromised if it fell into routine. The procedures he followed often broke new ground, inspiring artists and critics alike. Eno's collaborations included work with Robert Fripp of King Crimson, David Bowie, Talking Heads and David Byrne, the German group Cluster, and

Harold Budd. Recently, Eno had collaborated on a series of albums with Daniel Lanois, a musician, producer, and studio owner in Canada.

Edge outlined U2's game plan for the new album and found he was speaking Eno's language. In the December 1984 Island interview, he elaborated: "Instead of recording in an acoustically dead environment and trying to revitalize the sound using technology, we would record in a situation which offered very alive acoustics. We would try to control that natural ambience using the technology that we would bring in." U2 invited Eno, plus Lanois as his engineer, to Dublin for face-to-face talks. Edge continued: "Neither Brian Eno or Danny Lanois were particularly familiar with our previous work. It was, in some ways, as much a part of our determination to do something new as well as the band ourselves that made Brian Eno want to work on the record. Both Danny and Brian were very intent on challenging some of the preconceptions that we had toward recording. It was a very challenging session from beginning to end and it was one where we all gained a lot of insight into how other people work. They never worked with a band like U2 before, [so] it was quite unique for them as well."

The group decided to record at Slane Castle, a two-hundred-year-old stone fortress thirty miles northwest of Dublin. Owned by Lord Henry Mountcharles, the castle overlooked the River Boyne and a huge green meadow that had once been filled with thousands of fans when U2 and Thin Lizzy co-headlined a show there in 1982. The site would continue to be a popular concert location, with Bob Dylan performing there and Bruce Springsteen drawing an audience of over 70,000 for his first-ever Irish performance in 1985. Steve Rainford, U2's guitar and keyboard technician, and Steve Iredale, the production manager, had gone ahead to set up the castle for a month-long stay. It wasn't all work, as Rainford mentioned to me in an interview. "After we loaded some equipment in, we wanted to see what this historic castle was all about. On the second floor, we found unbelievable stuff, hundreds of years of junk! There were these old angular hats that, you know, naval officers would have worn, and some old sabers. We were fighting up and down the staircase, having battles from the second floor down to the disco in the basement." Eventually, the pair would have plenty to keep them busy as technical problems cropped up daily. The ancient diesel generator in the yard turned out to be unable to power a modern rock and roll band; one day it burst into flames that had to be doused by the local fire brigade. Suspicious of Slane's alternate source of power—a dubious looking watermill — U2's technical team acquired its own diesel to solve the problem.

U2 required a mobile studio, and Randy Ezratty's setup from Red Rocks was the first one that came to mind. In May, the New York engineer arrived at the castle with his portable twenty-four-track studio carefully packed in twenty flight cases. The sessions struggled to a shaky start, however, when Brian Eno and Daniel Lanois arrived. Certain that U2 would select Jimmy Iovine and Shelly Yakus to produce the album, Paul McGuinness had begun business dialogues with the team. Randy Ezratty recalled: "I cut a deal with McGuinness and we were all excited — I was talking to Shelly [about technical considerations], then all of a sudden I find out that Shelly Yakus and Iovine aren't doing the album. So I figured that maybe I wasn't doing it either. But then they [U2] called to say I was still on, with Eno and this guy Dan Lanois." After Ezratty arrived in Ireland, he discovered that the technical situation was strained. "It was very awkward," he admitted. "They [Eno and Lanois] had no say in what the [recording] system would be. They wanted so much more than my portable system, which was designed for recording live shows, could offer. When Brian and Danny saw it, they sort of went, 'Omigod!' "

Kevin Killen, the young Irish engineer who had helped out on *War*, quickly proved adept at helping Ezratty with his portable studio, which calmed Eno and Lanois somewhat. But equipment breakdowns constantly plagued the production. Killen recalled: "The generator would break down every day, there were cows in the way — it was mayhem. It was difficult for Daniel because he came from his own studio where everything worked. Here, hardly anything ever worked!" Lanois, unknown to everyone except Eno at the beginning of the session, soon showed himself to be a tremendous asset.

"It was weird in the beginning," Ezratty explained. "The band didn't know who this Dan Lanois was, and no one responded to him. But he was an amazing musician — whatever he picked up. After a while he really established himself."

The band members eyed the main ballroom, which echoed loudly under a high ceiling, as the location for their "live" sound recording sessions. But there were many rooms in the castle, each with its own size, shape, and acoustics. Ezratty elaborated: "We set up the equipment in this beautiful library and that became the control room. We ran cables into the ballroom and a study for 'live' sound and 'dead' sound respectively." The band members arrived on May 7 and occupied the ballroom immediately. Later, though, they moved gear in and out of the other rooms almost daily, using myriad equipment combinations, microphone placements, and recording techniques.

Steve Rainford revealed: "Most of Edge's guitar was recorded with his amplifier outside on the balcony with a plastic bag over it so the rain wouldn't get in. We just put the amp outside with a mike on it. I'm sure if you could listen to the [guitar] track by itself you'd hear birds in the background."

Eno's presence and his philosophy ordered the session; his prime directive was for U2 to experiment freely. Edge found the environment inspiring, as he related to *Boston Rock* magazine: "Everything around us was really stimulating. There was an open, diffused sense of creativity there. The casual approach proved to be a real benefit. In the first couple of weeks, while working on songs like 'A Sort of Homecoming,' 'Indian Summer Sky,' 'Pride,' and 'Unforgettable Fire,' we wrote about ten new pieces, improvising and challenging our accepted ways of writing."

In our 1984 interview for Island, Adam mentioned: "The making of the record was totally different. With Steve [Lillywhite] we were a lot more strict about a song and what it should be; if it did veer off to the right or to the left we would pull it back as opposed to chasing it. Brian and Danny were definitely interested in watching where a song went and chasing it."

But recording in Eno's environment could be as disquieting as it was inspiring, as Adam explained in the interview. "It was definitely the most difficult record to get through, no doubt in my mind. I found particularly the time taken, almost three months, to be an excruciatingly long time to be in the studio. You just end up running up the walls! Also, [when] doing a lot of the backing tracks on location in a live situation, there's an incredible feeling of not ever having finished anything. At the eleventh hour you can say, 'I don't like that backing track, let's do another one.' You may think that your work is done [but] two weeks after the event, you're going in there to do it again. There's a lot of uncertainty in that situation."

Eno and Lanois shepherded the potentially chaotic recording process to completion, planning each day's work around the breakfast table by using a blackboard to chart progress on various pieces of music. U2 quickly grasped the reasons why Eno and Lanois made such a great team, as Bono remarked to me in a 1984 phone interview on WBCN. "Batman and Robin — one had what the other hadn't. Whereas Dan was a musician in his own right, I suppose for Brian Eno the studio is his instrument. The balance is that we developed our arrangements musically with Daniel Lanois, but atmospherically with Brian Eno."

Edge told *Boston Rock* magazine: "Eno got Bono to change his approach to recording. Where previously, seven or eight different tracks would be collaged into one vocal, Brian started insisting, as much as was practical, on doing one take." During one experimental session, Lanois slowed down the instrumental tracks of the song "A Sort of Homecoming" and recorded Bono ad-libbing some lyrical ideas on top. Eno heard the murky and sometimes unintelligible vocals, which Bono had not considered an official take, and declared that the track had captured a valuable moment in the recording of the album. Despite its rough form, the vocal track became the basis for another song — the released version of "Elvis Presley in America." In the WBCN phone interview, Bono maintained that the words had just poured out and even he didn't know all of their meaning.

"I suppose, as a singer, I approached that [vocal track] the way a jazzman would approach his instrument. I just let my voice take the song and I followed it. It was left in its unfinished form on the record, and I think it's an important statement of the way U2 work."

The moody instrumental entitled "4th of July" was another piece of improvisation that made it onto *The Unforgettable Fire*. "We weren't even aware that it was being recorded," Edge revealed in the December 1984 Island interview. "We'd just done a version of 'Bad' and Adam struck up this little bass figure. I started playing along, totally unaware that Brian was listening in the other room. He happened to have some treatments set up for the vocal Bono had been doing and he applied those to the guitar. He thought it was really nice, so without bothering to put it on multitrack, which is the twenty-four-track tape machine, he just recorded it straight down to stereo tape. It was very much a live performance, there was no way we could mix it or redo any of the instruments."

On June 6, the band moved out of Slane and into the comparatively cramped quarters of Windmill Lane for additional recording and mixdown. Kevin Killen recalled: "When we went back into the studio, things definitely got more stressful." The arduous task of selecting and mixing material from the previous month of recording took much longer than anyone anticipated. In particular, the group and its producers labored over a jewel entitled "Pride." Killen, whose familiarity with the equipment at Windmill was now being utilized to the utmost, remembered the struggle with that song, which was recorded over and over again, slowed down, speeded up, and overdubbed interminably. "Certain things weren't jelling, like 'Pride' just wasn't coming together. But then one day [U2] came in, tried it a couple of times, broke for lunch, and then came back and just nailed it. The version of 'Pride' on the album was cut at Windmill, the Slane tapes were never used."

Running past its deadlines in July, the band kept booking additional studio time until the entire project suddenly reached a crisis stage. With an Australian tour looming in September, the band members realized that they might not finish the album on time. "When we got into the overdub stage it began to get quite elaborate," Killen remembered. "Edge wanted things to sound different and Danny and Brian were getting into their instrumental treatments. Meanwhile, Bono was furiously trying to write lyrics for the songs. He'd obviously come up with ideas but hadn't settled upon them. Twelve days before the album was due to be finished, Bono walked in and said, 'I can't finish it.' Everybody's heart sank." Once again, as Killen related, it was the band's manager who used his enormous force of will to propel the band members out of their slump. "Paul pulled everybody into a room and said, 'Okay, you guys are going on tour in Australia and we're not waiting until you get back—so you better finish it now!' We'd been working pretty hard anyway, but for the next two weeks we went into overdrive mode and worked twenty hours a day. The last three days of the album, I remember going into Windmill on Friday at ten A.M. and not coming out until Monday at noon!" U2 delivered the *Unforgettable Fire* tapes to eager hands at Island Records in August, but by then the exhausted band members were weeks late for critical tour rehearsals.

Island released "Pride (In the Name of Love)" as a single in advance of the album. For all the experimentation of the *Unforgettable Fire* sessions, this track would have sounded right at home on *War*. Both Larry's martial beat and Edge's choppy guitar rhythm drove the song along a familiar musical road for U2, with Eno's influence not at all obvious. The message delivered by Marianne Philbin and Terri Hemmert at the Peace Museum had rung loud and clear, inspiring the band to create a moving tribute to Martin Luther King, Jr. When the U.K. single appeared in September, the seven-inch version featured a white and black gatefold sleeve with printed lyrics and a back cover photo of King. In complete contrast, the "4th of July" B-side offered an early glimpse at the Eno-influenced qualities of the album. Initial copies of the single also included a bonus seven-inch disc with two tracks entitled "Boomerang I" and "Boomerang II," which did not appear on the album. Both were U2's variations on a rhythmic piece that Bono had developed by himself on the drum machine. In addition to a twelve-inch single release, Island issued a special seven-inch picture disc with the group's photo on the front and individual band member shots on the flip. When "Pride (In the Name of Love)" was released in America the first week of October, the seven-inch single was issued with "Boomerang II" as the B-side.

As U2's single enjoyed top-ten status on the English charts and American radio began to embrace the song, *The Unforgettable Fire* was shipped to stores. The album's front cover photo showed the ancient ivy-covered remains of a castle under sunny skies; the back cover pictured U2's members gazing toward the ruins through an angry, gray storm. Stunning gold lettering adorned the rich scarlet color of the entire package. By sharp contrast, U2's previous studio albums had each been dominated by white, with black, gray, and/or brown embellishing tones. The basic appearance of *The Unforgettable Fire* announced a change — it was an album with new colors and passions to explore. Edge explained to Tristram Lozaw in *Boston Rock* why the haunting Peace Museum exhibit title seemed to express the album's central theme: "Painting was a part of the therapy to help these people [the victims of Hiroshima and Nagasaki] purge themselves of some of their internalized emotions. The image of that purging quality, coupled with the insight into the horror of the nuclear holocaust, stuck in Bono's mind. Later we found that the title fit the new record in many ways, especially in reflecting its multicolored textures."

Eno and Lanois's influence was apparent on the opening track, "A Sort of Homecoming." Larry's drums rolled out with an almost muffled quality, unlike his usual forceful punch. Edge swathed the beat in thick layers of lush guitar and keyboards, and Adam lowered an inventive bass figure into place. Bono offered a typical pattern of verses and chorus, but then led the band into a beautiful rhythmic chant. Through the song's dense web of keyboards and string sounds, Edge's familiar guitar rang like a beacon as U2 tempered its usual assault for a sonorous and more subtle approach.

The band plotted a similar course for the lilting title track with its layers of instruments blended into a complex but harmonious whole. Occasionally, Edge would step out with strangely echoed guitar notes to lead the way into another chorus, but, for the most part, "The Unforgettable Fire" was a homogenous work given dynamics from Bono's vocals alone. The singer pushed out of his usual element by singing some parts falsetto. Edge considered the track his favorite on the album, as he related to me in a 1985 interview for WBCN. "It's classical . . . almost; I see it as a music piece rather than a song. Bono, in a very unconventional way, explored numerous melodies over sections. Instead of repeating melodies—you know, verses and choruses, which is what everyone does—we've got three chorus melodies and two verse melodies. It has a certain symphonic feel for me because there are so many intertwining themes. I know we could have recorded it slightly better but I think, for all its flaws, I just see a great piece of music."

"Bad" would evolve from its moody form on *The Unforgettable Fire* into one of U2's most exciting concert statements. Built from a simple repeating keyboard pattern with the band in close formation, the dark tale of heroin abuse was a prime test for Bono, whose flexible, passionate singing drove the song's dramatic tension for over six minutes. In an interview for Island Records in 1987, Edge told me: "It was really an improvisation started by myself, with all the other guys in the room joining in with parts they thought of. We did two or three takes and that was our basic track, so it's almost live. Certainly, Larry's drum part is a product of the environment of that moment. You can hear Larry putting down the brushes and taking up the sticks, with this sort of pause which has a great dramatic effect."

The visceral "Wire" punched behind an odd guitar figure and wild echoed blasts; the energetic melody of "Indian Summer Sky" shifted down into airy choruses with ghostly background vocals; and the delicate "Promenade" became U2's most obvious love song, with romantic lyrics gently touched by soft guitar tones. Delivered a cappella with a synthesizer drone in the background, "MLK" was a companion piece to "Pride" that also eulogized Martin Luther King, Jr. A bedtime prayer for rejuvenation and courage through King's (and our) trials, "MLK" was another expression of U2's continuing spiritual commitment and closed the album with a peaceful benediction.

The first major American review of the album appeared that October in *Rolling Stone*. Kurt Loder was fairly disappointed, subtitling his review, "Alliance with Eno yields flawed album." He wrote, "U2 flickers and nearly fades, its fire banked by a misconceived production strategy and occasional interludes of soggy, songless self-indulgence." Loder still gave the album a rating of three stars on a scale of five, but mentioned, "*The Unforgettable Fire* seems to drone on and on, an endless flurry of chinkety guitar scratchings, state-of-the-art sound processing, and the most mundane sort of lyrical imagery." Writing in the December issue of *Hi Fidelity*, Wayne King agreed. "[Edge's] scorching riffs, which dominated *War*, are doused on most of *The Unforgettable Fire*; while that leaves ample room for his subtler side, the result is that too many tracks lack the solid base he once provided." At the end of the review, though, King had to admit, "U2 remains, on the strength of Side 1, the most instrumentally articulate outfit operating in rock." Anthony DeCurtis's review in *Record* pointed out some problems, calling "4th of July" "laughable," but gave the new album a resounding thumbs up anyway: "*The Unforgettable Fire* may well be the most stunning outing to date by these always ambitious Celtic soul brothers."

The negative comments stung the band members, but they were heartened to read, often in the same reviews, that most critics at least honored U2's risky attempt at change. During the 1984 Island Records interview, Edge mentioned that the band had expected criticism for its bold move—at first. "In North America, the record is less in keeping with the sort of trend in music over here. I really believe that this album is European in essence, so I have sort of anticipated some of the difficulty in relating to it—as we've seen in some of the press reviews. But I think it's just a question of time. It's been the case in our experience that the songs we felt strongly about didn't necessarily have a favorable reaction at first; they became influential and important songs after people got to know them and came to terms with them."

While critics scratched their heads, though, *The Unforgettable Fire* flew out of stores in greater quantities than any of the band's previous works. Initial album radio airplay of "Pride" spread out to include the finicky CHR stations, paving the way for the single to storm onto *Billboard*'s Hot 100 sales chart. "Pride (In the Name of Love)" would spend fifteen weeks on the singles survey, peaking at number thirty-three to become U2's deepest penetration into commercial territory yet. Meanwhile, album radio and noncommercial college stations ventured further into *The Unforgettable Fire*, playing "A Sort of Homecoming," "Wire," and the title track. This airplay would spearhead the album's march to platinum as *The Unforgettable Fire* became U2's first American million-seller.

U2's aggressive campaign to maintain its video exposure continued when the clip for "Pride (In the Name of Love)," directed by Donald Cammell and filmed at St. Francis Xavier Hall in Dublin, debuted on MTV in September 1984. Featuring the band onstage in rehearsal with a young boy jigging about in response to Bono's own spirited step, Cammell's video was one of three versions produced. Barry

Devlin, former bassist for the seventies Irish rock band Horslips and now a video director, created a second clip for "Pride." Filmed during sessions for the album, Devlin's version compiled various recording scenes and was featured in "The Making of *The Unforgettable Fire*" documentary. Shown on MTV in the fall, this half-hour special reappeared in December 1985 as part of *The Unforgettable Fire Collection*, a commercially released compilation of U2 videos. Few viewers saw version three of "Pride," a clip directed by Anton Corbijn that was quickly withdrawn. On U2's fall concert swing through Europe, Barry Devlin filmed a collage of views from the tour bus and stage for videos of "A Sort of Homecoming" and "Bad," the former receiving generous MTV airplay after November 1984. Using fresh shots and old footage from the *War* period, Meiert Avis assembled a clip for the album's title cut, which appeared on *The Unforgettable Fire Collection*.

The murky, experimental nature of *The Unforgettable Fire* raised a serious question about what sort of band U2 would be onstage — how could the group replicate in concert the album's complex textures and lush Eno/Lanois production? Reports from the September tour of Australia and New Zealand offered no clues. With the album completed only days before the band members had to depart for the Pacific, there was not enough time to sufficiently rehearse new material for the stage. Edge, in particular, had thrown himself so completely into the long months of recording that, in order to relearn U2's older songs, he had to purchase some of his own band's albums and study the guitar parts. Edge's equipment technician Steve Rainford related: "U2 didn't do anything with electronics in it [on the Australian tour]; it was just the *War* tour again including 'Pride.' By the time we got back from there, they were fairly panic-stricken. They couldn't go out and perform *The Unforgettable Fire* live because they hadn't had any time to rehearse anything. So we spent two weeks in this tiny little theater in Dublin rehearsing the stuff. The band had some Oberheim synthesizers, a sequencer, and a drum machine; they'd used the synthesizer on "MLK" and the sequencer on "Bad." I knew nothing about them, [but] they knew even less, so [we held] a rapid crash course in Oberheim programming."

"I was a bit nervous going into rehearsal," Edge mentioned in the 1985 interview for WBCN. "We toyed around with the idea of a keyboard player, but we thought that one of the unique qualities about this group is seeing just four people on stage. With Danny and Brian's help, we [had] played everything on the album, so it would have been a shame to bring in extra musicians." So U2 set about adapting its studio arrangements to fit the concert setting, as Edge explained: "We've always felt [that's] legitimate because the things you are looking for in a song in a live context are very different from the things you look for a song to provide on an album. We wouldn't think twice about, for instance [on] 'The Unforgettable Fire,' using string sections to enhance the production of the song in the studio and [then] not have a string section on the road."

The new electronic keyboards solved U2's dilemma, as Edge explained in the same interview: "I use [a sequencer] on 'The Unforgettable Fire' mainly because there was a choice—I could either play guitar or keyboards. I started off playing keyboards, but everyone thought that it needed the extra textures of the guitar. So I programmed [on the sequencer] what I'd been formerly playing [on keyboards]. In 'Bad,' I programmed a repeating sequence that I use almost like a drone—a held note. It's a different approach, it leaves us all the capabilities to improvise and change the structure of the song, to lengthen it or shorten it."

U2 built a new live show from the ground up during the two-week hiatus, then headed out for its European tour beginning in France on October 18. By all accounts, the concerts were a grueling test as the band struggled to master its new material with the still alien presence of Edge's added equipment. The sequencer, in particular, was prone to malfunction during the weeks of damp and cold weather. Through the rainy conditions and performance snarls, however, U2's members remained proud of their latest endeavor. That optimism helped sustain them even when the complete entourage came down with colds soon after arriving for the first show in Lyons. "It never stopped raining," Rainford recalled. "Everyone was sick for months. Then we headed right to America for that pre-Christmas tour."

U2 had arranged a ten-date visit to America for the beginning of December 1984. Designed as a brief, tantalizing taste to announce that U2 had returned, the jaunt preceded a much longer domestic concert swing through America in the spring. Accordingly, the December tour utilized hit-and-run tactics as the band moved quickly across the country in a two-week period. U2 was booked into 3,000- to 5,000-seat theaters, even though it could easily sell out larger venues. The exceptions were the Centrum in the Boston area and L.A.'s Long Beach Arena, both of which could both hold over 12,000 people. Opting for the relative intimacy of the theaters, which sold out almost instantly, the band and its agent Frank Barsalona temporarily forgot about the troubles they had experienced in the small halls during the *War* tour. That U2 had only become more popular since that period, threatening even greater crowd control problems this time around, made the upcoming visit potentially troublesome.

9

WIDE AWAKE
AT THE
BULLETPROOF
DELI

AS SOON AS U2 touched down in New York City a few days before its December 1984 tour opener in Philadelphia, the band
members became aware that their popularity in America had
increased dramatically. Word spread quickly that the group
was staying at Manhattan's Parker Meridien hotel, and the building's
entrances were soon besieged with fans. Holed up in his room high
above the street, Bono called WBCN to give an enlightening interview,
but finished on a pensive note. "I'm in the twenty-second floor of the Parker Meridien hotel, there's a lot of people downstairs, I can't walk out
on the street because people are pushing up against us. So, as I say, I'm
in the twenty-second floor, in this hotel room, and I wish I was onstage.
I don't like this waiting around." We said good-bye and hung up. Within
moments, Bono received a frantic call from the Meridien's management, loudly complaining that its phone lines were hopelessly jammed.
He realized that without thinking he'd given out the hotel's name over
the air and now the Meridien was under a massive long-distance telephone assault from Boston.

A few days later, in Philadelphia, Ellen Darst emerged from an
elevator into the Hershey Hotel's opulent lobby, scanning the area for
possible troublemakers among the regular guests. I rose to meet her,
glancing at the parade of fashionable clientele and expensive furnish-
ings; U2 had obviously left its budget motel days behind. The afternoon
rendezvous at the hotel would allow me to accompany the group to its
first American concert soundcheck in a year and a half. The last time
U2 had been in Philadelphia they had performed two nights at the Tow-

er; this time, with the pre-Christmas tour a two-week rush across the States, there would be only one concert at the theater.

Ellen's greeting was interrupted by a small sneeze. "Europe was awful—everyone's sick," she complained before managing a smile. Three of the band members soon appeared, sniffling and sneezing occasionally as everyone boarded the tour bus; Bono was still fielding interviews in the hotel and would join the rest of the group later at soundcheck. Larry, Edge, and Adam sat down slowly, faces somewhat sullen from their colds, but everyone brightened immediately when Anne Marie Foley bounded into the bus, weighed down by a grocery bag filled with assorted music cassettes she'd brought for the group.

As Larry dug through the treasure, he announced, "There must be sixty or seventy tapes here, just enough for me!" Edge and Adam swiftly appeared to stake a claim, and soon the three were battling over their prizes like schoolboys trading baseball cards. ZZ Top's *Eliminator* and a Nona Hendryx tape were among the most sought-after prizes.

"Hey! You guys have to leave something for Bono," Anne Marie scolded. The three pretended they were innocent, then reluctantly returned a share for their bandmate.

Edge, Adam, and Larry stepped off the bus when it reached the Tower, eagerly wading into a group of fans gathered by the theater's backstage entrance. Inside, head soundman Joe O'Herlihy and his crew had been assembling U2's stage equipment for hours; now it was time to fine-tune the sound and volume of each instrument. After signing autographs and chatting, the band members disengaged from their admirers and filed inside the old brick building. Adam sauntered onto the quiet stage and strapped on his bass equipped with a new wireless transmitter unit that eliminated the long cord from his instrument to the amplifier. He also had a foot pedal array that activated a booming bass synthesizer. Larry slipped behind his kit and Edge tinkered with an assortment of metal cases filled with new musical hardware. These items included the sequencer which provided the repeating notes in "Bad" and synthesizers to form the murky foundations of "MLK" and "The Unforgettable Fire." After twenty minutes of isolated notes, crashes, and assorted screeches from the three players, Bono arrived and vaulted onstage, long hair now spilling onto his shoulders from under a black hat.

There was only a brief warning of loud shouts in the outside hallway before the two main doors leading into the room suddenly burst open to admit about fifty excited fans, shattering the peaceful and methodical mood of soundcheck. The fans stopped dead in their tracks, wide-eyed and completely taken aback that they had actually penetrated all the way into this hallowed chamber. A critical door leading past the box office and into the building had been carelessly left unlocked. A beefy security team quickly showed up to force the crowd back outside. "Wait!" Bono yelled. Everyone froze and turned around to look at the singer onstage. "If they promise not to run in here again, can we keep the doors open so they can listen?" The bouncers and trespassers stared at each other and back at Bono, considering. A silent agreement was struck at that moment and the fans filed peacefully out to the main entrance where they obediently waited by the open door to hear an early sampling of U2's new live show.

The band lashed out with a cacophony of amplified blasts that eventually coalesced into "A Sort of Homecoming." This melody demanded some particularly high notes from Bono which, despite his cold, he hit perfectly. When U2 finished the number, wild applause from its impromptu audience could be heard outside. Easing into "Bad," Edge's brow furrowed in concentration as the sequencer spit out a basic rhythm pattern which he embroidered upon with guitar. Larry donned headphones for his new high-tech role, listening in on a succession of electronic clicks that cued his drumming and triggered the sequencer at the same time. For over eight minutes, Bono's anguishing tale of heroin addiction and death unfolded with such clarity that it raised goosebumps. As U2 continued its soundcheck with snippets of "Pride" and "New Year's Day," the listeners outside had heard more than enough to spark intense expectations for the band's return to the American stage that night.

The Waterboys opened the Philadelphia show, as they would for the entire minitour, with an appealing blend of folk and rock and roll. However, the Scottish group received only polite, scattered applause from an audience obviously preoccupied with seeing the night's headliners. Once the theater plunged into darkness and the members of U2 walked onstage, the sedate crowd erupted into frantic action. Before the band had even hit its first note, the entire audience rose to its feet, aisles boiled with impatient figures spilling out of their seats to get a closer vantage point, and the pit area directly in front of the stage was completely overrun.

U2 began in familiar *War* tour fashion, firing an opening salvo of "11 O'Clock Tick Tock" into "I Will Follow." The veins bulged on Bono's neck while he belted out the words and moved up and down the lip of the stage, pumping hands and slapping palms with the entire front line pasted against the barricade. Intoxicated with being onstage in America again, would the singer lose control and leap into the crowded audience or attempt a hair-raising climb up to the balcony? The temptation was probably greatest when U2 blazed into "The Electric Co.," since Bono had usually chosen this song as his opportunity to roam the heights and wings of each venue. But Bono resisted whatever impulses of that nature he felt, rooted himself at stage center for the entire song, and concentrated on his singing.

A few days later in Cleveland, during an interview for Island Records, Edge revealed that the band had consciously adopted a fresh idea for Bono's live performance. "The broad strokes, the high points [of our show] are the things that people remember, [and] it has been Bono's persona onstage that people have carried away with them. The unfortunate side of that is not that he has the ability to lose control, but that it is all [the fans] remember. That's a very one-dimensional view of the band, [which] is really so complex, so full of subtleties."

"How do you counter the problem?" I asked.

"At this stage, we're trying to let the music speak. You really can't ask him to go on stage and perform like Ian McCulloch [of Echo and the Bunnymen], who basically just stands there in front of the microphone and sneers at the crowd. He can't do that—it's not natural for him. But, at the same time, it becomes a problem when people start seeing you as a sort of caricature, a cartoon of yourself." Eliminating the singer's now infamous stage stunts was a bold move, since many fans had come to expect them. The band members would have to test their more subdued approach in front of each audience, not knowing until the encore if they'd managed to deliver the high-intensity experience that fans were accustomed to.

It was time for U2 to introduce its latest music to the Philadelphia crowd, beginning with "A Sort of Homecoming." At first, Bono glided elegantly above the lush instrumental melody, but his voice faltered halfway through. In his excitement, he had pushed past his limit on the opening numbers, straining his voice, which was already bothered by the stubborn cold. Bono eased back on "MLK" and skipped the falsetto parts during "The Unforgettable Fire." Frustrated, he apologized to the audience and asked if everyone would sing the words for him when he couldn't. The plea was unexpected, since Bono could have said nothing and most people wouldn't have minded, but the crowd burst into cheers at his display of candor. Bono called on the people to support him on the high choruses of "Bad" and the Tower audience responded with a roar.

At the end of the set, during "Pride," Bono pointed the microphone away from himself and toward the audience, silently asking everyone to add their voices to the chorus. Once again, his request was rewarded with a deafening sing-along that continued on into steady applause as U2 left the stage. For an encore, the group offered its whimsical "Party Girl," an unsteady "Two Hearts Beat as One" (with Edge making the rare, but humorous, mistake of beginning another song), and "40." Bono remained silent during most of the last song, but his arms conducted a match-lit audience that eagerly provided every word.

Bono barely spoke while the band packed for an overnight drive to Massachusetts. "I let that audience down," he said miserably to no one in particular while retreating into a sulk. He brightened slightly when Anne Marie reminded him that everyone in the theater had been joyously screaming their lungs out. Then Adam pointed out with his usual optimism, "It's only the first show, it'll get better from here on."

The following afternoon, Ellen relieved Bono from promotional duties and pressed Adam into service for a few phone interviews. He was happy to comply, but later at soundcheck he wasn't at all pleased with the calls. "No one even mentioned the new album," he complained. "They all wanted to know if Bono would walk off the stage or something." Bono appeared next, miming with exaggerated gestures to demonstrate that he wasn't supposed to talk. Despite this effort to be amusing, he confided in an apprehensive whisper, "I have absolutely no idea how my voice will be tonight." Joe O'Herlihy had to be content with a mostly instrumental soundcheck, but Bono's voice was strong on a rendition of Neil Young's "Southern Man," perhaps offering a positive omen for that evening's sold-out Worcester Centrum concert.

Sure enough, that night U2 tore into a triumphant performance that blasted away the day's anxiety. The group repeated its Philadelphia set with only a few adjustments — most notably moving "Sunday Bloody Sunday" and "The Electric Co." into the middle of its suite from *The Unforgettable Fire*. The change helped maintain U2's crisp intensity through material that was still mostly unfamiliar to the crowd. Bono had regained much of his vocal strength and versatility, generously charging "Bad" with raw emotion and firing up "Wire" with a chain of chilling war whoops. Afterward, the obviously relieved singer joined in on the backstage celebration before taking time with the rest of the band to offer encouragement to a young cancer patient. Perhaps the abused condition of his own vocal cords reminded Bono of just how fragile the human body is: after the band members all signed the boy's sneaker, Bono whispered into his ear for a few minutes until Dennis Sheehan loudly demanded, for the third time, that the entourage board the bus.

After a wearying overnight drive to New York City, U2 checked into a Manhattan hotel before dawn. The band members grabbed some sleep before their important show that night. Radio City Music Hall was the crown jewel of the entire tour, a prestigious gig that many of U2's most powerful critics and supporters would attend. A successful night in the world-famous theater would send a definitive signal to the American media that not only had U2 officially "arrived," but the band was here to stay. The concert easily sold out well in advance to become one of New York's hottest tickets, but organizing the whole affair strained Ellen's talents to the limits. The normally placid promotion manager disappeared for hours of frantic telephone combat, jamming together a ponderous interview schedule, dispensing tickets, and adding to the overflowing backstage guest list. The after-show hospitality suite had to be arranged as well as a traditional late night/early morning celebration at some Manhattan restaurant. Ellen hired Keryn Kaplan, her former assistant at Warner Brothers, to help with the workload. While both toiled to satisfy the requirements of the band and the demands of the media, troublesome memories of U2's debacle at the Palladium a year before persisted. A return bout of crowd violence in New York City would hopelessly mar the band's personal triumph and, in addition to being physically dangerous, could destroy any inspiration the band members managed to spread through the audience during the concert.

The show began with expected fury as U2 blasted into its set underneath Radio City's gracefully arching walls. Behind Larry's drums hung a giant Christmas wreath with smaller companions off to each side. Colored lights dotted the stage backdrop, spreading a festive glow over the band's equipment and forward into the ocean of bouncing heads. With everyone in the front rows standing on the armrests of their seats by the second number, it was difficult at first to see why the booming cannonade powering "I Will Follow" abruptly halted. Larry stood up and pointed into the crowd, which had surged forward to engulf the front of the stage. Two grappling figures had caused a ragged hole to open up in the audience around them. Bono barked at the combatants, "No . . . none of that," but they ignored him. Edge flew into motion, whipping his guitar off over his head and diving across stage toward the scuffle. The guitarist screamed at the pair to stop fighting as his instrument hit the stage heavily behind him. Security personnel rushed to the scene and sorted out the problem, but the restless crowd began to heave forward and backward in frightening waves. Bono pleaded with the mob, "This could be a great show . . . we had problems last time we were in New York . . . we want it to be a beautiful show!"

Tempers cooled and the jostling subsided after a few moments, so Edge turned to recover his guitar, discovering that it had broken into two pieces. Anger pulled his normally imperturbable features into a strange mask while he strapped on another guitar and the band resumed playing "I Will Follow." Although bouts of shoving occasionally flared, the concert proceeded peacefully until the band slammed into a rousing encore of "Party Girl" and "Gloria." Suddenly the audience pushed forward, forcing people up onto the stage itself. A photographer was dragged into the melee and had to roll all the way up to Bono's microphone to escape the crush. U2 abandoned its attempt to finish "Gloria" and Bono lost his temper. "I said last time that I didn't want people to be on this stage! The barrier that's to be broken between the audience and the band tonight is a mental barrier, not this physical barrier." He pointed into the crowd of sweating and disheveled people, yelling, "If you want to be on this stage, then you must do what I'm doing!" Bono's challenge, which echoed loudly through the theater, seemed to wake everyone up. The fans sitting on stage, both those who had been forced there and those who had instigated the trouble in the first place, began returning to their seats. Even with the help of Radio City's ushers and security personnel, it took ten minutes to clear up the knotted confusion. Bono walked along the stage's lip offering encouragement and adding, "We feel as close to the people back there as the ones up here!" The audience in the rear and those in the balconies threw out a frustrated shout in return.

When the situation once again seemed under control, the band eased tentatively back into "Gloria" and then directly to "40" before eagerly abandoning the stage. Edge, who was chagrined about his broken guitar, told me backstage: "I saw some bouncer, I guess, beating up this guy right in front of me. I just lost control." The after-show "meet and greet" session was crowded, as expected, but the U2 support team had learned from previous mistakes, ensuring that this situation, unlike the concert, was firmly in control. Securely guarded and curtained areas were limited to those guests who possessed a proper pass, eliminating a repeat of the backstage anarchy that had plagued the band's Palladium visit.

With much relief U2 left New York, arriving in Toronto for a small theater show at Massey Hall three nights later. There seemed to be more fans outside trying to score tickets in the cold December night than actually in the building. Already seated before the Waterboys' set was even half-finished, the audience remained peaceful and attentive as U2 walked onstage, indicating, it was hoped, that the Radio City chaos had been just a fluke. With U2's first note, however, the Canadian crowd started moving. People rushed to the front and danced in the aisles while the remainder stepped up onto their armrests for a better view. A few hardier souls attempted to balance even higher, on the backs of their chairs, many plunging out of sight when they lost their balance. Within moments, everyone had peeled off their winter leathers, wool coats, or down parkas, stripping in response to the steadily rising heat being thrown out by the dancing mass.

I noticed a gaunt and frail-looking gentleman with his lady companion struggling into the row to claim two empty seats next to mine. With a shock I realized the figure was Brian Eno. He had surmised, with visible distaste, that his view would be completely blocked if he didn't climb up onto the seat, which bounced in rhythm as everyone in the row danced on their armrests. After struggling ignominiously into position and observing the action for only a few moments, Eno decided that his jerking platform was not the best option, so he stepped back down and led his friend into the aisle for a better view. What awaited them out there was far more intense — a riot of bouncing bodies, some dancing fervently and others threading their slow course down to the front rows. I soon lost sight of Eno and his friend as they were absorbed in the commotion.

Onstage, Bono observed with a laugh, "I never considered myself a pop star!" as he dodged the females who struggled to embrace him. Edge, limited in range by the length of his guitar cord and unable to use his hands to resist, was a much easier target, receiving more than a few kisses on the cheek. He blushed noticeably when a pretty young woman darted up during "Party Girl" to wrap her arms firmly around his body and guitar, strangling his solo cold. During "40," Bono prevented a pair of stagehands from escorting an exhausted woman off the stage; instead he embraced her in a dreamy slow dance while the crowd roared. This simple act capped the concert with a powerful symbol, unifying band and audience with a bond far stronger than what Bono could have achieved even if he had climbed all the way into Massey Hall's rafters.

Replacing mere sensationalism with some honest emotion, he tapped into and displayed the feeling at the core of U2's music.

As Bono was trying a new approach to performance, the band confronted another problem. Addressing the increased crowd control difficulties at concerts as well as worries about the personal safety of U2's members, Dennis Sheehan had added security specialist Ron McGilvray to the traveling entourage. They had worked together for Led Zeppelin, but Ron had also cut his teeth guarding the members of Bad Company and Kiss. Despite his easygoing, friendly nature, Ron's eyes were constantly on alert, and even though he had reached middle age, muscles bulged on his frame. As U2's bus rolled up to the entrance of the Hyatt-Regency hotel in Dearborn, Michigan, the security chief noted with satisfaction that there was no crowd waiting for them. Their base of operations still undetected, the road-weary travelers got some desperately needed sleep before the concert at Detroit's Fox Theater that night.

After a few hours, the groggy band members and their staff reassembled in the hotel lobby, then disappeared into several limousines for the half-hour drive to the theater. The caravan glided through Detroit's suburbs and then past sobering views of vacant trash-filled lots, ramshackle tenements, and broken sidewalks. Camouflaged perfectly by its cracked and tired concrete surroundings, the Fox went unnoticed by Ellen and the band members even as the cars pulled up at the backstage entrance. Ron got out first, quickly hustling his passengers into the ancient building while I went across the street to a deli blazing with white fluorescent light. Hot coffee was dispensed from behind a counter protected by floor-to-ceiling bulletproof glass. The bored cashier gave up his tiny styrofoam cups of thick java only after money had been pushed around the slug-resistant revolving tray to his side. The place was a haven of sorts, with people loitering in the aisles to warm their hands while calling out for possible concert tickets. Since the theater's seats had sold out in less than an hour, only those who were willing to pay a scalper's price were getting in off the street.

Once a proud playhouse, the Fox Theater now begged for a refit. Its faded red rugs led past crumbling statues and edifices coated with peeling gold paint. The bathroom was the worst: dirty pools of water on the floor and only a few naked yellow light bulbs dimly lighting the area. The dreary atmosphere couldn't dampen the spirits of Detroit's jubilant audience, however, once U2 hit the stage for one of the strongest sets of its tour. The greatest applause greeted Bono's soliloquy during "MLK," though a flashbulb barrage from the audience overwhelmed the dramatic effect of one spotlight trained on the singer from below. During "Pride" a chilling effect was created by drenching the band in blood-red lights while a slide of Martin Luther King, Jr., slowly materialized on the movie screen behind Larry's kit.

Unfortunately, trouble flared as people began to aggravate each other in the close quarters up front. Bono eyed the pushing and shoving mass until he could tolerate no more, suddenly shouting above "Sunday Bloody Sunday," "Listen to the words of this song . . . it is not about violence!" Bono's appeal had little effect; the situation grew steadily worse as U2 hurried through the last two songs of its set. The group quit the stage with relief, but wild applause made the band members hesitate in their dressing room. To return for an encore could dangerously escalate the energy of the audience, but not responding at all would be an insult to the majority of the crowd that had nothing to do with the disturbances up front. The members decided to chance an encore and returned to tear into "Gloria," inspiring the unnerving sight of the Fox balcony bouncing up and down several inches at a time to the simultaneous dancing of the entire upstairs audience. The open adulation, however, was marred by more shoving matches and fistfights during the quick encore. Afterward, a solemn Ellen Darst informed her backstage guests that U2's members were too upset by the violence to see any visitors.

U2 had more trouble at its next stop, where an army of determined fans easily overflowed the band's still fledgling security measures. Even as the band's tour bus rounded Lake Erie on its way to Cleveland, fans had already staked out the city's hotels. Most people concentrated on the Boncourt, located across the street from the Music Hall, where U2 would perform that evening. Unfortunately for Dennis, on this occasion he had chosen convenience over stealth, so the Boncourt was indeed U2's destination. The lobby, resplendent with elegant rugs, crystal chandeliers, and fine furniture concealed a sizable greeting committee which rushed out to engulf the group once it arrived. The surprised band members complied with the autograph requests as a shocked hotel staff looked on at all the unexpected commotion.

Within moments, news about U2's arrival brought fans running from all over the city. Soon after the band members disappeared into their rooms upstairs, the Boncourt lobby was completely overrun. Although well behaved, the fans began to interfere with the hotel's operation—occupying all available chairs on the first floor, monopolizing the telephones, and getting in the way of regular guests. Fans hung out nonchalantly on the stairs leading down to the hotel restaurant and bar, some tried to blend in by roving the upstairs hallways, and others simply rode endlessly on the elevators. Finally tired of the extra "guests," the Boncourt management rooted them out of the building with security personnel before two entrances were closed and city police staked out the others.

Upstairs, in the relative calm of a hotel room, I was involved in an interview with Adam and Edge. Concerned that the lightning progress of their minitour allowed no time to visit the college radio stations where they had received much of their earliest airplay, U2's members had conceived the idea of producing a radio program that would be sent free to these stations as a next-best option. Recognizing that I'd been involved with U2 as a representative of both college and commercial radio since the beginning of the band's American career, Ellen invited me to conduct the interview, which would be dubbed onto cassette and sent to over four hundred stations in North America. We had a rare, full hour in which to conduct the interview before it would be time for the soundcheck.

The guitarist sipped from his cup of tea and Adam lit another cigarette in front of a large rain-streaked windowpane as I opened by asking about the new musical direction staked out on *The Unforgettable Fire*. Beginning seriously enough, the interview soon degenerated into a silly, but nevertheless enlightening roast. Edge offered: "I'm very much into this new record. I think [it] displays the variety of what we're capable of doing musically. The other albums each overemphasized one aspect of what we do. It's very easy for one album to be off-center for a group and you are judged by that record, but really, that can be affected by so many things: the mood you were in the morning you did the vocal or whether there was a good guitar amp around . . . "

Adam jumped in: "It's obvious with *The Unforgettable Fire* who's important. I mean, Edge doesn't really play any guitar on it and it's the rhythm section that made that record. In fact, we're thinking of losing a member for the next couple of records!"

"What I like about the bass playing on that album is that it exists where it should be—in the bottom," Edge retaliated.

Adam laughed, "Like where you can't hear it?"

Edge pressed his attack. "There's no exursions by the bass player into the mid and high frequencies."

"Aw, c'mon! What about 'Wire,' that's [got] a pretty filthy bass sound on that!"

"Yeah, that's a highlight actually," Edge agreed. "The bass sound on 'Wire' is one of *the* highlights of that album."

I asked if either of the two had time to work with or produce groups other than U2, and Adam admitted: "Possibly if time permits, but our schedule has really been too busy. There actually hasn't been any time to get bored and find things to do."

Edge continued: "We've been on the road for a long time in a sense, because the way we record and the way we tour means that for most of the year we're doing either one of those two things. There hasn't been a great deal of time to follow solo projects."

"Like buying furniture?" Adam interjected.

"If you got up early in the morning you could buy bleedin' furniture [too]! This man doesn't get up until three in the afternoon most days," Edge laughed.

Adam clarified: "Edge's solo project for the past few months has been buying furniture. Whenever Edge is missing, [we say] 'he's buying furniture.' "

"It's just jealousy because his house is in such a shambles!"

I asked, "Adam, do you own a house?"

"No, I live in a squat, that's why it looks so bad."

Edge quickly added, "Adam actually lives in an upturned Land Rover."

"With a hole cut in the roof so the smoke gets out," Adam finished with a chuckle.

Attempting to steer the discussion back to more serious matters, I asked, "Does the image of being considered by many to be a political band bother you?"

"I think most of our audience probably don't see us as a political band, but an aware band — which is what we really are," Adam replied. "I don't think we want to take part in the U.S. elections or anything like that."

"Some people have described us as a band that soar above reality and we're hanging in the air somewhere," Edge continued slowly, apparently lost in thought. "I think this band refuses to admit the existence of ordinariness. In a sense, every person has a sort of individuality and potential." He delved deeper into the concept: "We're fighting with that realization that nothing is ordinary. Simple Minds have that approach; they are a band that see through the superficial layer . . . there's something beyond that, a magic to the industrial landscape. A lot of people don't credit that, they think that this band refuses to see things that are going on in the street and that's not true at all . . . " Edge's stream of words halted and he appeared momentarily lost, "Uhhmmm . . . "

"No, not true at all," Adam repeated with a smile at his confused bandmate.

"Where do we go from here?" Edge asked the bassist.

"You were talking about soaring above everyone. We can roll the tape back and figure it out."

I piped in; "We were talking about how the band can be considered to be partisan in its views, at times."

"What the fuck does that have to do with what I was talking about?" While we roared with laughter, Edge looked bewildered and more than a bit embarrassed. "Politically aware . . . let's just scrub that!"

Bono had actually answered the question about U2's political stance more clearly during the WBCN phone interview with me a few days before. "It's no fun being seen as a political group if you don't know that much about politics, or don't particularly want to. I'm not really that much into politics, but I know a little about people. There is a battle and everybody's got to fight in that battle, whether it's on the factory floor, in an office, or making music. You've got to find your place . . . and my place is doing what I'm best at, which is making music. That's the best way I can challenge a system or inspire people. I've never pointed a finger at anyone other than myself in my songs. We don't write songs about 'you' or 'they,' it's always about 'we' or 'I' with U2."

While searching for political messages and affiliations in U2's music, observers were perhaps blind to the band's more universal message of peace and the idea of sharing as a way of attaining it. Bono concocted an impromptu but elaborate demonstration of sharing from a minor incident during the Cleveland concert. While leaning into the audience to grasp a white flag someone offered, he had to struggle with a woman grabbing earnestly at the towel around his neck. Instead of merely tossing the towel as a souvenir to her, though, Bono disappeared offstage for some time and returned with a large pair of scissors. While the band played on, he sat down by his microphone stand and methodically cut the towel in half. The audience looked on with growing curiosity as Bono found the woman again and gave her one piece. Then the purpose of the act became clear when he strode to the opposite end of the stage to give his remaining half to someone else.

There was no noticeable violence at the Cleveland show since the security force prevented anyone from even standing up until the encore, but Bono was mobbed by some fifty fans as he returned to the Boncourt. Ron McGilvray and several escorts tried to sweep him away, but the exhausted singer refused. Bono backed into a doorway to address questions and autograph requests in an orderly fashion for nearly fifteen minutes. Inside the hotel some determined fans had penetrated the security barriers and were roaming about, but their presence was benign. A group of young female admirers detained an uncomplaining Adam Clayton before he retired to the bar for a nightcap. After a few quiet hours of work, the Boncourt bartender must have been surprised by the sudden surge of patrons who rolled in to his establishment on the heels of the blond Irish bassist who sat on a stool sipping his beer.

Early in the December tour, a holiday single involving Bono and Adam began to appear on the U.S. airwaves while an accompanying video clip was introduced on MTV. Bob Geldof of the Boomtown Rats and Midge Ure of Ultravox had written and recorded "Do They Know It's Christmas?" weeks earlier to benefit the millions of starving people in Ethiopia. They had invited a variety of significant musical guests to participate in the daylong recording session in London, then pressed and released the single and video in record time. By the time U2 hit the West Coast of the United States for its final shows in San Francisco and at Long Beach Arena near Los Angeles, "Do They Know It's Christmas?" was a runaway success on U.K. and American radio, selling thousands of copies a day. As the peaceful finale to U2's often riotous tour, Bono wished everyone at Long Beach Arena a happy holiday before sliding from the lyrics of "40" into the chorus of "Do They Know It's Christmas?" The warmth of the crowd chanting "Feed the world! Let them know it's Christmastime!" over and over again, then back into "How long . . . to sing this song!" eliminated, at least temporarily, some of the band's more troubling memories of this December minitour. For the moment, Bono, Edge, Larry, and Adam could fully enjoy the positive spirit they had inspired in an audience that held thousands of flickering matches and candles aloft. It was the best possible way for U2's American concert swing to finish.

10

UNFORGETTABLE AMERICA

AFTER THE U2 entourage scattered to celebrate Christmas at home, the New Year's Eve edition of *Newsweek* confirmed the group's soaring reputation. An article entitled "Stop in the Name of Love" introduced U2 to mainstream readers outside the rock and roll realm, claiming that the band had become "one of the most influential acts of the decade." The article acknowledged the band members' spiritual beliefs, noting that it is difficult to promote "the hocus-pocus of Christian enlightenment." Bono clarified that his was a "very personal" faith, and U2's music was not intended to preach Christian sermons, but that its spiritual leanings perhaps inspired a message of hope. "I'm very wary of people who bring the 'message to the masses,' " he said. As Bono was himself a preacher of sorts in front of a growing and increasingly unwieldy audience, he could expect at least some distrust and a lot of misinterpretation of U2's simplest intentions. It was a problem that would only intensify as the band's popularity grew.

Raw sales data indicated that the number of U2 supporters was indeed increasing. By the end of February 1985, auditors at the Recording Industry Association of America had certified *The Unforgettable Fire* for sales of one million copies, earning U2 a platinum award. The surging interest in the band had doubled the sales figures of *War* and it was certified platinum at the same time. *Under a Blood Red Sky* attained gold record status in February and breezed past the million sales mark that summer. While the group toured in Europe after the first of the year, an extended U.S. visit set to begin in Texas on February 25 was announced. To accommodate the increasing demand for tickets, U2's road trip would last more than two months and hit twenty-nine cities, and the band would leave theaters behind to enter the country's much larger sports arenas.

U2 was now joining the elite of rock and pop groups that had outgrown smaller venues to step up into the hockey arenas, sports complexes, and eventually the football stadiums that doubled as concert facilities. Rather than perform several dates in each city, interminably lengthening a tour, playing the larger venues allowed a band to reach its supporters with far fewer appearances. Aside from being a more efficient manner of exposure in front of the greatest possible number of fans, the larger capacity locations also made touring far more lucrative. Not only would fewer shows mean lower attendant costs for each concert — from catering and security to hall rental and hiring of the stage crew — but less time on the road meant fewer days a band manager had to pay the enormous overhead costs of moving a tour entourage across the country.

Playing the arenas would also enable U2 to cover the demand for tickets in each city, removing another undesirable result of the group's increasing popularity. Each of the band members was disgusted to find that scalpers, lured by quick sellouts on U2's December theater tour, had made huge profits by hawking high-priced tickets to desperate fans. One huckster in front of the Tower was seen openly strolling up and down past the marquee calling out his sale price of $150 for a single ticket and backstage pass. In simple economic terms, if U2 could oversupply, then everyone would be able to find a fair-priced ticket, reducing the demand for black market alternatives. As Bono emphatically stated during his December 1984 phone interview on WBCN: "It's the people that are more important than the place. If we play these small venues all the time, the people [will continue to be] ripped off by these gangsters that are hanging outside of the gigs. [In this] way, I hope we'll cater [to] the demand for tickets."

But the decision to move into the larger concert settings was still not an easy one to make. Would the cavernous spaces swallow the energy of a typical U2 show, with the audience too far away to feel the band's passion, or, in turn, the crowd too removed to inspire the band members' performance? Bono continued: "The whole band, and I especially, were very wary of playing these large arena-type venues — we'd grown up in the smaller, more intimate venues. It was two things that changed our minds on this: one was seeing Bruce Springsteen [successfully] play Wembley Arena in London and the other was playing Worcester Centrum ourselves on the *War* tour. Because of the reaction to that, we feel that yes, we belong here. We make big music and we can make it in these big places, these tin boxes."

The energizing, catalytic effect that U2 had on its audience was rare in rock and roll, and had led to frequently explosive effects on the last tour. Most groups experienced few or none of the in-concert disturbances that U2 found to be common because they simply failed to generate such a vibrant physical reaction in their fans. But U2 could look to the examples of other seventies and eighties megabands, like the Who, the Rolling Stones, and the J. Geils Band, who thrived on delivering a similar ecstatic energy in concert. These groups had also experienced crowd control problems in theaters, but greatly alleviated their difficulties when they made the jump into larger concert settings where the more spacious area reduced audience pressure just by providing more elbow-room up front. During my April 1985 interview with Adam and Edge for WBCN, the bass player talked about U2's new attitude toward the larger facilities. "I think we're a lot more relaxed onstage because the arenas contain the sort of energy that is generated better than some of the four- or five-thousand-seaters. The Orpheum shows were legendary — but we couldn't go back into the Orpheum now because that energy just can't be contained anymore in that size building."

For the new tour U2 adopted some of the security enhancements that the Who, the Stones, J. Geils, and others had established in the seventies to make their arena shows safer for all concerned. An efficient barrier system in front ensured that there was always a space between the band and its audience that would discourage access to the stage, and through which security personnel could easily be brought in to remove troublemakers. If an audience pushed forward, threatening the safety of those in the front rows, they could be pulled quickly over the barrier into the safety zone to avoid injury. U2's crew also used the strategic space to keep a watchful eye on the band members, jumping up to intercept those from the audience who did make it onto the stage and then escorting them to the wings from which they would be returned to the seating area.

As the *Unforgettable Fire* tour began, however, it became clear that U2's crowd control problems were far from over. After witnessing the fourth show of the tour, an outdoor gig for 20,000 people at Phoenix's Compton Terrace, Eric Levin reported in *People*, "The area down front was a cauldron of faces — people wild eyed, bobbing, waving banners, so crushed that simply craning one's neck could trigger a jostling chain reaction." After the show, an exhausted Bono whispered to Levin, "When the energy of the crowd is so brutal, the spirit of the music flees and all you're left with is crashing drums and clanging guitars."

U2's sincerity and the emotional attachment of its fans combined in a potentially combustible mix as each side strived to get closer to the other. While the band aimed for that immediacy in a musical and emotional sense, many in the crowd pursued a dangerous physical course. In the *People* article, Bono noted the futility of forcing physical contact. "I always thought passion was like a clenched fist, but when I relaxed it, it flowed in a fuller way. I've learned that if I'm close to the music, and the audience is close to the music, we are close to each other. It doesn't depend on physical proximity." On stage, with memories of Radio City Music Hall and the Fox Theater all too recent, he would have to reaffirm that view time and time again.

The sight of fans climbing over the threshold and rushing on-stage to embrace the band was still routine. The group, especially Bono, usually returned these embraces and then passed the fans off to a helpful stagehand. There was always potential, however, for this simple act to become more threatening, as Bono discovered at the Los Angeles Sports Arena the night after the difficult Phoenix concert. A young man bolted up and ringed the singer in a tight bear hug. It seemed there was nothing unusual about the display of affection. Bono soon realized, though, that the fan had no intention of letting go. He motioned back his stage assistants who had immediately dashed forward to help. After a long thirty seconds, Bono finally kneeled down on the floor and rolled over, breaking the boy's grasp and stepping back while the fan was gently escorted offstage. Bono mentioned to me later that certainly he had been concerned, but this situation had been handled without force. "Hopefully, meeting violence with nonviolence can solve the problem," he finished, echoing some of the philosophy he sang about in "Pride."

Bono had to restate the philosophy at Joe Louis Arena in Detroit three weeks later. In front of 19,000 fans, he nearly lost his temper after completing a symbolic gesture to illustrate his hope for peace in Northern Ireland. When an Irish tricolor was heaved onstage at his feet, Bono scooped it up and draped the flag over his microphone stand. The audience responded with a chorus of screams and yells. This sent him into a determined search through the assorted stage debris that had been tossed up from the crowd until he finally located a square of white material. Taking the symbol of surrender solemnly into his hands, Bono slowly and carefully placed it over the Irish flag and left it for a few moments.

Then he handed each piece back to the audience, one on either side, and returned to his microphone. When he turned to face the crowd, however, a group of people were scuffling over the tricolor. "Stop fighting!" he bellowed. "Don't you know, that's what the problem is all about."

U2 continued to emphasize the music over stage antics, as it had since beginning its December tour, with Bono remaining onstage and not journeying into the crowd or up onto the lighting truss. Even with these restrictions, however, the singer still had more than enough territory to cover on U2's larger and mostly barren stage. As Adam elaborated in the April 1985 interview, "What we needed was absolutely no clutter to distract from what was going on onstage." The band now played "three-sixty," concert promotion slang to describe a performance set-up which eliminated the backdrop and slide show screen to allow seating behind the stage with 360 degrees of unobstructed viewing. The audience was now literally surrounding the band. Adam continued: "It's quite nice playing to those people because they're seeing the same thing you're seeing from stage. In a way, they've ended up with the best seats in the house."

Edge piped in, "It's like the people have become our backdrop; it's more intimate."

U2's latest live set resembled the one presented on the pre-Christmas swing, with much more self-assured execution of songs from *The Unforgettable Fire*. The new material was also more familiar to the audience, especially "A Sort of Homecoming," documented by Barry Devlin's video which was now receiving steady MTV exposure. "MLK" had become an important moment in the show — recognized by wild applause and a thousand lit matches when the hall darkened and Edge's synthesizer drone entered. "Bad" asserted itself as the centerpiece for the entire set, even stealing the spotlight from U2's earlier anthems. The band was now adept at playing along with the sequenced keyboard pattern, and Bono frequently added extra vocal melodies and bits of other songs to the extended piece. In Los Angeles he used snatches of the Rolling Stones' "Ruby Tuesday" and Lou Reed's "Waiting for My Man" to embellish the basic lyric. The beautiful mystery of "The Unforgettable Fire" was retained in its concert re-creation, and on "Wire," the latest album's most fiery entry, Bono's wild war cries split the air.

U2 changed its set list each night, altering the song order and replacing selections, to comprise a ninety-minute set. Two new additions were played nearly every concert: a verse of the venerable eighteenth-century hymn "Amazing Grace" replaced "Send in the Clowns" during the middle break of "The Electric Co.," and, with Bono and Edge on acoustic guitars, U2 interpreted Bob Dylan's classic "Knockin' on Heaven's Door." One of the group's proven standards and the oldest song in the set, "11 O'Clock Tick Tock" remained as the opening number. Previously, the 1980 import single was familiar only to the band's most ardent fans; upgraded on *Under a Blood Red Sky*, it had become a recognized standard.

Now that U2's latest material had jelled onstage, the band members were able to relax enough for their often-hidden sense of humor to reemerge. One particularly amusing moment occurred during a March 1985 show at the Los Angeles Sports Arena when U2 began playing "October." Usually, while Edge performed the opening piano section, the other members used the minute for a hurried break out of the spotlights — Adam would grab a smoke, Bono and Larry guzzled water. Edge would finish the melody and pause for dramatic effect as the final note rang through the arena and applause welled up from the darkness. Then Larry would ease behind his kit and gently tap on a woodblock as Bono sang the brief set of lyrics. On this occasion, however, echoes of Edge's final note hung on and on . . . for too long, slowly dying out in the cavernous hall without the answering taps. Edge glanced over his back and was surprised to see an empty drum set. Suddenly Larry raced into the stagelights, recklessly leaping over assorted stage gear and into position while deftly grabbing a drumstick. If he hit the woodblock quickly, the song could be saved. Larry brought the stick squarely down on its target, but with too much force. The woodblock recoiled, bouncing off its stand to the floor. He began convulsing with laughter while his stage assistant, Tom Mullally, groped around in the semidarkness. Locating the woodblock, Tom held it out steadily for Larry to hit while Edge, Bono, and Adam just stared. With all pretense of covering up the situation long gone, the laughing drummer finally found his mark and timed out a beat. Bono, smiling widely, faced the audience and valiantly tried to return some semblance of seriousness to a song about spiritual awakening.

Behind the scenes, Ellen was run ragged by Los Angeles, which matched the overwhelming media demands of New York City in every way. Suddenly, it seemed, the whole world wanted to know about this "new" band from Dublin. She hired another assistant to hold down the Manhattan management office and brought Keryn Kaplan out on the road with her. The pair found themselves on the phone at 9:00 A.M. most days, and worked until two or three the next morning on performance nights. In Detroit three weeks later, Ellen looked over at me as the limo pulled out of Joe Louis Arena and said wearily: "It's starting to happen . . . in a big way for this band. I expected it to be crazy in L.A., but here we are in the heartland and the pressure just hasn't quit." As she spoke, Bono, who was in the car in front of ours, opened his door to greet some fans and was instantly stampeded back into his seat.

The next day, U2's caravan of limousines whisked the band to the airport for a short flight to Cleveland. Larry bounced up and down in the rear seat of one car, listening to a soul tape I'd compiled for him. The tunes by Al Green, Sam and Dave, Staple Singers, and Ann Peebles had him singing along in ecstasy. "I can't stand the rain!" he bellowed while gazing out at endless storefronts under a depressing gray sky. "They really knew how to make these records. I love the drum sound on Al Green . . . Hey! Look at that!"

Keryn roused herself. "What's that, Larry?"

"Bikes!" Two members of a Detroit motorcycle gang, the Scorpions, were wheeling by the limo on two shiny Harley-Davidsons. "All right!" Larry lowered the window, hanging half his body outside the door while yelling approval to the pair, who stared in disbelief. The long black car flashed by when the riders pulled over to turn left. The bikers glanced back at the strange fellow in the black leather policeman's jacket who waved his arms crazily out the window and shouted at them until he was out of view.

The three cars avoided the main airport terminal and turned into a private traffic area about a mile away. There, parked on the concrete apron, was U2's latest acquisition, a rented four-engine Vickers Viscount passenger plane. Admittedly a hefty additional expense to the tour, the plane allowed U2 the luxury of setting its own schedule and avoiding the time constraints of commercial airlines. No longer would the band members lounge restlessly for hours while a canceled or late flight trapped them at the airport. Dennis Sheehan and Ron McGilvray were more confident of the band members' safety now that they didn't have to drag them through overcrowded concourses filled with fans greeting the band or sending them off. Because the Viscount picked up and discharged its passengers at each airport's separate private facility, the group could now avoid the airline terminal buildings completely.

The airplane certainly added tremendous comfort and convenience to U2's traveling plans, but also represented another troubling concession for the band members, who had always been uncomfortable avoiding fans. While Dennis and Ron figured out ways to sidestep potentially dangerous crowd situations, the four musicians were often uneasy following the very instructions designed for their own safety. But the band's staff was persuasive and firm on the matter: U2 was and ought to be invariably accommodating when individuals or small groups of people were involved, but larger crowds had to be treated more carefully. Those groups of fans could easily overcrowd an area, growing into a mob that posed as much danger to itself as it did to U2. In time, the band members began to accept that walking blithely into these situations was not only risky for them, but could be a disservice to their supporters as well.

At the Stouffer in Cleveland, the members of U2 with Ellen, Paul McGuinness, and Keryn enjoyed a quiet dinner in the hotel restaurant during their day off. The waiter, in his early twenties, knew who they were and was extremely nervous. He announced the evening's specials and then in a loud, wavering voice continued, "I also want to add that I love *The Unforgettable Fire*."

Larry jumped up and exclaimed, "Then dinner is on the house!" As everyone laughed, the waiter looked uncomfortable, not quite grasping that Larry was joking.

Paul came to his rescue while perusing the wine list. "Look, how would you like a couple of tickets to tomorrow night's show?"

"Sure!" the waiter croaked in disbelief.

"This is Ellen. She'll take your name and set you up," he said.

"Thanks!"

"By the way, do you have a bottle of this handy?" Paul indicated a selection on the list.

"I'm sorry sir, we're out of that particular vintage. This *is* Cleveland," he replied in embarrassment.

Bono looked the waiter in the eye, stating with perfect seriousness, "Well, we *love* Cleveland and we *love* playing here." The waiter flushed, then smiled as he turned and walked back to the kitchen, probably a foot off the floor. It took him a while before he realized he had forgotten to take Paul's new wine order and came rushing back.

Bono's words to the waiter were perfectly sincere; Cleveland was one of the best U2 audiences in the country. The crowd that gathered in the Richfield Coliseum the next night had a reputation to live up to — U2 was accustomed to an enormous audience response every time the group played the city. The band wouldn't be disappointed; this concert was one of the biggest events of the year in the mainly blue-collar town, so the audience was too excited to hold itself back.

Backstage, Bono introduced me to Greg Carroll, his new stage assistant, who spent each night in the pit directly in front of the singer, rushing onstage to clear the microphone cord when it snagged during long onstage journeys. He also kept an eye out for objects thrown onto the stage that might trip or injure Bono, as well as troublesome audience members who struggled over the threshold. Greg was a Maori Indian whom the band had met the previous September while touring New Zealand. "He does a very good job, but I'm getting upset now because he gets all the attention," Bono laughed. Greg, or "G-Dub" as he was nicknamed, was already much loved by the group for his warm good nature and steady stream of jokes.

Bono, G-Dub, and I were escorted to a press box high above the crowd to watch Lone Justice, U2's new warm-up group from Los Angeles, work the crowd. During the first month of the tour, shows were opened by the Red Rockers, an energetic young group featuring members from New Orleans, San Francisco, and Northern Ireland whose song "China" was a video hit on MTV. Now Lone Justice would take care of the remainder. Fronted by a gutsy country music–influenced singer named Maria McKee, the group had released a debut album, produced by Jimmy Iovine, which Bono greatly enjoyed. Onstage, though, McKee and her bandmates were having a difficult time getting their show together. To make matters worse, the audience was virtually ignoring the band's efforts by walking about, chattering loudly over the music, and barely applauding. After the concert, when U2 had returned to the Stouffer, Bono would spend over an hour cheering the despondent McKee by telling her his own horror stories about warming up for J. Geils and offering advice learned from U2's own years of hard touring.

It didn't help that the sound had been awful during Lone Justice's set. Once U2 took the stage, however, Joe O'Herlihy had the challenging acoustics figured out by the second song and the coliseum began to sound less like the hockey arena it was and more like a concert hall. The highlight of the band's set was "Knockin' on Heaven's Door," which featured some unique audience participation. During the past few shows, Bono had been introducing the number as a simple song that required knowledge of only three chords to play. He would then invite a member of the audience onstage to "sit in" on acoustic guitar. The guests were understandably shocked to be the lucky volunteers, but tonight's participant was going to experience much more than he could have imagined.

After the young man was hauled over the security barrier and stood nervously onstage, Bono greeted him with a reassuring embrace, handed over his own guitar, and helped the volunteer work out the chord progression. In a matter of moments, the new, fifth member of U2 was happily strumming along with the band while Bono ambled out of the spotlights and listened. The roar of the crowd as its representative led the group was what counted; again, U2 had discovered a way to get closer to its audience. When Bono reappeared to reclaim the guitar, he suddenly changed his mind and motioned for Edge and Adam to stop playing and join him on the sidelines. The pair removed their instruments and waved to the amazed fan before vanishing behind Bono. As the new front man repeated the chords over and over with Larry beating steadily behind him, the roar from the crowd grew steadily louder and louder. After two minutes, when U2's delinquent trio finally strolled back into view, to the volunteer's visible relief, the noise in the coliseum was deafening.

U2's arena tour jumped up to Canada for dates in Montreal, Toronto, and Ottawa before returning to New York City on April 1. While still in Cleveland, Paul had explained to me that the band's first-ever appearance at Madison Square Garden in New York was to be a momentous occasion for the group. "You have to understand that to an Irishman, Madison Square Garden is an important symbol—it means that you've made it. We can play larger venues—in fact we've booked three nights in Meadowlands [in New Jersey just outside of Manhattan] and that room is much larger—but Madison Square Garden is special. All the band's families are flying in, plus half the journalists and media from Ireland will be there." What Paul neglected to mention was that U2 was picking up the tab to bring most of these friends across the Atlantic for the celebration.

With its latest album a platinum success and four of its five records on the *Billboard* Top 200 album sales chart, U2 marched triumphantly into Madison Square Garden. There, in front of their families and friends, as well as nearly 16,000 faithful fans, the members of U2 carried away their trophy in a blazing rock and roll tour de force. Tremendous waves of passion swept through the arena as the audience thundered its approval and recharged the band's every move with even more energy. Bono quietly mentioned backstage afterward: "For an Irishman to be standing on that stage just means so much, not just for us, but for all Irishmen. Famine . . . war . . . emigration—there's been so much. I feel we have not let them down . . . I feel good about that."

The next morning's *Wall Street Journal* featured a glowing article on the band. Pam Lambert managed to telescope the entire history of U2 into a half-page story while describing the explosive energy of the show she'd witnessed (in Detroit), and picking up some choice quotes from the band. Bono mentioned: "To me a rock and roll concert is 3-D, it's a physical thing — it's rhythm for the body. It's a mental thing in that it should be intellectually challenging. But it's also a spiritual thing, because it's a community, it's people agreeing on something, even if it's only for an hour and a half." Edge observed that U2's audience was particularly attentive: "People tell us during our shows we sell very little in the way of hot dogs."

The thumbs up from *The Wall Street Journal* was preceded by a hallmark March 14 issue of *Rolling Stone* that placed the band on the cover and effectively retracted its highly critical October 1984 review of *The Unforgettable Fire* by lauding U2 as "Our Choice: Band of the 80's." In the March 14 article, Christopher Connelly reassessed the latest album. "Eno and Lanois kept U2 from harnessing its talents into compact, concise rock and roll songs and instead encouraged the group to preserve its more inchoate creations just as they were." Bono had the story's closing quote. "People are interested in bridges, I guess I've always been more interested in what goes on beneath bridges." The triumvirate of important press reviews was completed by an April 13 article in *Billboard* which mentioned that U2 would have played to a half-million people on this American tour by the time it finished in Florida on May 4.

In New England, hysteria greeted the announcement of upcoming U2 dates for the Providence Civic Center on April 2 and the Worcester Centrum on April 16 and 18. U2 supporters immediately packed essentials and camped at local ticket outlets to wait for the seats to go on sale. At one Ticketron located in the Orpheum theater, a determined pair of female fans showed up three days in advance to stake out the front of the line. Behind them, a motley assortment of lumps and bundles were scattered on the sidewalk as people wrapped themselves in layers of blankets and sleeping bags to ward off the bitter January cold that plunged to eighteen degrees.

When the ticket windows opened and a third Centrum show on April 19 was added, all 38,000 seats were gone in five hours. Neil Jacobsen, second in command for local concert promoter Don Law, told me the tickets were sold "as fast as we could pull them from the computers." Jacobsen had reserved a fourth date that U2 could have easily sold out, he lamented, but the band had balked at the proposal. Ellen mentioned in her interview for this book that the band members had discovered that performing a long series of concerts in one place impaired their later shows. "It's not true for every band, but they found it deadly. They feel that it blows their performance — they lose their spark." Accordingly, three nights in one venue had been the most that was booked for the band on the entire tour. Also, U2 never played more than three nights in a row — good news for Bono, who could become hoarse if too many concerts were strung together.

During the first Centrum concert, U2 exhibited extreme grace under pressure as a technical mishap threatened the safety of its audience. Edge told the story the following day in his interview for WBCN. "I saw our lighting truss — it's like a T shape with one section going out over the audience — start lowering slowly [on] the left side, which is Adam's side. It was only going about an inch every five seconds and went down, I should imagine, about three or four feet. It meant that the T was lopsided and hanging at what looked like a precarious angle." The truss framed an area as large as the stage and hung over the band from anchor points in the arena ceiling. From this platform, U2's stage crew always fastened down a multitude of stagelights, including regular stationary lights and follow spotlights with live operators, who were now perched diagonally in their chairs.

"We had been told time and time again by our rigger, whose job it is to make sure everything is safe, that there was no chance of anything falling out of the ceiling," Edge continued. "But when Bono saw what was going on, he decided that the only responsible thing he could do was quietly and calmly get the people to move out from beneath it. In fact, nothing could have fallen; the worst thing that could have happened is that people could have panicked and started some sort of stampede." But that potential danger was threatening enough, and Bono's cool instructions to the audience cleared the rows of seats directly in front of the stage with a minimum of fuss. There were no injuries and only a minor delay while U2's crew found the renegade electric motor which had lowered the truss and hoisted that side back into place. Then Bono reassured the worried members of the audience that there was no danger and they returned to their seats.

Edge's comments about the incident were culled from my interview with him and Adam in an elegant and inconspicuous hotel by Boston's waterfront. The location permitted easy access for city sightseeing during U2's four-day stay and would also afford some degree of privacy since it was fifty miles away from the Centrum. The situation could only be temporary though, since the band's hiding place would inevitably be discovered, prompting a twenty-four-hour stakeout of the hotel by fans. In one of the band's suites, Bono reveled in the knowledge that he had an afternoon of absolutely nothing to do. Unfortunately, he turned down my interview request, having been advised to lay low and save his voice which, again, was plagued by a cold. I moved into Edge's room, collecting Adam along the way.

"What's it like in Dublin now? Are you treated much differently?" I began.

"I don't know, really, because we haven't been home," Edge replied. "Except for Bono, who would be hard-pressed to walk in the center of Dublin and not get torn to shreds, the rest of us can get on with a normal life. In Ireland, I think people are proud of what we're doing, but there's no feeling of awe because they've known us for so long." He laughed, "They realize we're the same old assholes we always were!"

"Adam, when you get back to Dublin, what do you do to relax?"

"Basically nothing. By that I mean, I'll sleep very late and stay in the first two weeks. After that you calm down, because you find you get that adrenalin buzz for the first two weeks at approximately 8:00 P.M., which is approaching stage time. That's what I do, watch a lot of television. It's, you know, very boring. Then, I'm sort of cleansed and I go out and find friends."

"Edge?"

"I have a terrible habit of finding really unimportant, trivial, manual things to do. I'll go mow the lawn, or find some piece of furniture that needs varnishing, or . . . paint the cat. Something like that. It requires very little mental effort—you concentrate on things and your brain sort of unwinds slowly. When I go on holiday, the last thing I want to do is just lie on a beach. I far prefer to go skiing or do something that gets me involved. If I just lie on a beach, I just get totally freaked out because my mind goes into gear five and I can't relax."

I observed that it seemed U2 possessed some magical recipe for success—as its phenomenal rise to fame suggested. Edge offered this in response: "I think there's a sense of unity that I don't see in many other groups. I think we take responsibility for each other in a way that most groups don't. We, as a group collectively, probably are not incredibly talented musically, but what we do is cover for one another, in a way. Ultimately it's sorted out; no one is left with egg on their faces because there's three other guys in the band who are willing to make sure that that's not gonna happen. There is a true dependence in the group on the other members." His serious tone fell apart, however, once he looked over at Adam and started to laugh. "Which is one of the reasons why we have to keep friendly with one another!"

U2's three-night stand at the Centrum was another high point of its tour, especially the second concert. That show began with "Gloria," a song usually reserved for encore time. Bono announced that they wanted to do something special, then led the band into a set of "oldies" that U2 hadn't performed in years. Larry responded with the thudding introduction to "I Threw a Brick Through a Window." With the last note of that song the band neatly dovetailed into "A Day Without Me," Bono throwing in a perfectly tailored verse of "Dear Prudence" to lift the melody to even greater heights. However, his unexpected insertion of the Beatles verse changed the song's timing just enough to confuse his mates' transition into the brief drum roll that usually announces the final part of "A Day Without Me." While Larry had no way of knowing for sure when it was time to kick off the roll, Edge had already flown into his closing notes. Looking back in surprise at the even more surprised drummer, Edge snapped back to the former melody with Adam's bass sticking to his guitar chords like glue. The guitarist laughed and nodded to his rhythm section to try it again; this time the elements clicked together smoothly. It was improvised so well that most of the audience didn't even notice the mistake, but Bono playfully acknowledged the band's fumble. "Well, sometimes you just forget, you know?!" U2 then rewarded the crowd with a rare performance of "I Fall Down."

"Bad" provided some of the concert's best moments, as Bono added a part from "Norwegian Wood" by the Beatles, a sing-along of "Ruby Tuesday," and verses from "Sympathy for the Devil." The band was so comfortable on the big stage that an encore of "Party Girl" lasted a full nine minutes. Bono brought an entire family onstage and rewarded the son, who was having a birthday, with a red balloon — which popped immediately. "You've got to watch these red balloons," Bono said as he quickly arranged for other gifts to be brought out: his black rounded top hat for the boy and a bottle of champagne for the parents. Looking at the hat, Bono said, "There's only one of these in the world, but you're very welcome to it." He uncorked the champagne and toasted the Centrum crowd, "Hey! Let's party!" Then, throwing a barb at the critics who branded U2 for its somber image, he added, "Remember, we're a real serious political group."

11
CAUSES AND EFFECT

U2'S SUCCESS with the American rock and roll audience was undisputed as the summer of 1985 arrived, the band's last three albums having gone solidly platinum and a coast-to-coast arena tour under its belt. But the group had not yet attained the loftier level of success that marked true superstar status. This could be achieved if and when U2 managed to break out of an exclusive rock and roll appeal into mainstream acceptance, joining a circle of select artists whose efforts transcended radio formats and musical styles. Superstars like Bruce Springsteen, Michael Jackson, Phil Collins, and Madonna were all artists who had broken out of their own particular musical genres, crossing over to a much larger mainstream level. Although U2's songs had been played heavily on rock radio and MTV, they were still widely ignored by the bastions of mainstream music in America: CHR radio stations. For example, "Pride (In the Name of Love)" blasted quickly up the *Radio and Records* AOR airplay chart to lodge at number one, but there was no such luck when the single was released to CHR stations. Even though Island Records launched an all-out promotional campaign to alert Top 40 radio programmers about the single's existence and then to feature it on the air, not enough stations became involved to create a national hit. The single stalled at number thirty-three in *Billboard* and then plunged out of sight.

Even though the band members didn't consider themselves a "singles band," everyone was disappointed that "Pride" hadn't done better on the charts. Ellen mentioned later, "I thought, this is it, they've done it, they've actually recorded a Top 40 hit—which seemed pretty amazing after going through the [long and difficult] recording of their album. It wasn't the end-all, although we certainly knew that's the way you sold lots of records; it was another plateau."

Edge reflected about the single during my 1987 interview for Island Records. "As a band we've always been much more concerned with our albums. I would say that singles are like a bonus — if we get a hit single, I'll certainly be delighted. [But] I was a little disappointed 'Pride' didn't do well, it seemed like it could have gone all the way."

Without a hit single and the accompanying crossover to mainstream listeners, U2 still played to its comparatively smaller audience of rock and roll fans — although their numbers were great enough now to fill arenas like Madison Square Garden. It was not typical for an act to grow this popular without the help of a Top 40 smash, but some groups like the Who or the Grateful Dead — both of which could easily sell out any arena or stadium in the land — had proved that it could be done. Bob Catania, who was now Island's director of album promotion, recalled that U2's booming concert business was not going unnoticed, however. Three months after "Pride" had peaked on the singles chart around Christmas, he began to get calls from curious radio programmers. "Suddenly, the big Top 40 stations were calling up, [asking] 'who is this that is selling out Madison Square Garden?'" Catania concluded that "Pride" might have been released too early, preventing the full weight of CHR airplay to be coordinated at one point. Instead, some stations were finished with the track by the time that others were just becoming interested. The effect was that the total airplay of "Pride" was diluted across a period of several months and not in the concentrated burst necessary to send it to the top of the charts.

Island was unsure what to do next. Catania felt thwarted by the murky, experimental nature of the remainder of *The Unforgettable Fire*. He told me: "*War* was a very Top 40-oriented record — you had 'Two Hearts' and 'New Year's Day.' When I got *The Unforgettable Fire*, I was expecting a continuation of that. It seemed to me that the band was making a conscious decision to step back. As U2 went into that arena phase [of its American tour], had there been a follow-up single, we might have been able to break them on that album." "Break" referred, in record industry jargon, to the process of turning U2 into a superstar act — converting a band that might sell 500,000 or a million copies of each album into one that regularly moved ten times that number.

Island didn't feel confident that there was another potential single on the album and scrapped plans to release one, although the title track would come out as a single in Europe. Instead, the label recommended tracks on *The Unforgettable Fire* to American AOR stations since, as Catania mentioned, "there were still many people at album radio to convince." "Wire" was released on a twelve-inch promotional record and lit up the AOR charts for only six weeks (hits often last three times that long). The same strategy on "A Sort of Homecoming" met with even leaner results. Although U2 had not delivered the blockbuster album that Island would have loved, the label was still impressed with its healthy sales that built on the success of the group's previous releases. Greater success was soon to come, but in the meantime U2's members could be proud of executing an artistic shift in their career that was not only satisfying for them, but reasonably lucrative as well.

As soon as the 1985 American tour concluded in early May, U2 released a four-song EP (an extended-play disc with three or more tracks) entitled *Wide Awake in America*, its name inspired by a line in "Bad." The title was somewhat misleading, though, since the live material on the disc was recorded in England and the studio tracks were outtakes lifted from the *Unforgettable Fire* sessions in Ireland. However, it was produced for the American market, and also for Japan, and it became a highly demanded import in the U.K. and Europe. The two live tracks, "Bad" and "A Sort of Homecoming," were recorded in November 1984 and demonstrated the evolution in U2's material that tended to occur during a series of performances. Steadily honed from night to night during the band's rainy tour of Europe, these live versions were quite different from their studio predecessors and were ripe to capture on record.

Kevin Killen returned as the engineer responsible for tying together the loose ends of the concert recording. In an interview for this book, he told me: "Tony Visconti was going to produce a live version of 'A Sort of Homecoming' [to complement Devlin's video], so we were basically trying to get a good live version of that one song. I organized a mobile [studio] and we recorded a couple shows in Manchester [England], a show in Birmingham, two shows at Wembley [Stadium, in London], and Brussels." U2's live version of the song was more direct and focused, without the cloud of Eno-induced effects that had colored the studio original. Bono's vocals kicked with authority in front of an audience that added its own bite by rhythmically chanting throughout the song. Ironically, as Killen revealed, the version U2 eventually used wasn't actually recorded in front of the concert audience, but at a Wembley Stadium soundcheck. "Every night, they knew that they were recording that song and it didn't come together right. We did a version at soundcheck that ended up being the basis for the track, [then] we lifted the applause from one of the live versions because it was played at roughly the same tempo and just fed it in. It had the sound of the arena because it was recorded there, but there was only about fifty people [present]."

In the process of recording the live sets for a good version of "A Sort of Homecoming," Kevin Killen taped a stunning performance of "Bad" as a bonus. Remembering its legal problems with "Send in the Clowns," U2 played a version of "Bad" that omitted Bono's usual embellishments from other songwriters' work. Even so, the *Wide Awake in America* version, recorded at the arena show in Birmingham, stretched to nearly eight minutes. Killen revealed another engineering secret about the EP: "The last note [of "Bad"] was screwed up, so we took the last note from the show two nights previously in Manchester. We just did a multitrack edit of the one note and kept the audience from the Birmingham show."

The pair of unreleased studio tracks completing the EP had not been deemed appropriate by the band for inclusion on *The Unforgettable Fire*, but stood strongly enough when isolated on this release. "Three Sunrises" featured a beautiful melody and choral vocals sliced by angry guitar bursts throughout and "Love Comes Tumbling" was a relatively innocuous companion which strayed little from a simple melody with restrained guitar work. In a *Rolling Stone* review in July, James Henke concluded that *Wide Awake* was merely "a curio that will be of interest primarily to die-hard fans." But for those ever eager to hear more music from U2, this domestic package was an unexpected summer gift.

Wide Awake in America was the American companion to a European release of "The Unforgettable Fire" single that appeared in three forms: a seven-inch disc, a two-record seven-inch EP, and twelve-inch EP, all decorated with gold-tinted photographs taken from a video portrait filmed by Brian Eno. The regular single featured the newly recorded live version of "A Sort of Homecoming" on the B-side. The seven-inch EP added a bonus record with the already mentioned outtakes from *The Unforgettable Fire* plus another entitled "Sixty Seconds in Kingdom Come." The instrumental was an exercise for Edge, who played lightly over a rumbling bass and drum shuffle. Confusing things a bit, the twelve-inch eliminated "Sixty Seconds in Kingdom Come" and substituted a drumless instrumental entitled "Bass Trap." Ambient waves of bass and guitar echoed slowly over and over, serving as a dreamy backdrop for Edge's gentle strumming. This approach would be explored more fully on Edge's forthcoming solo soundtrack record.

While Stateside diehards searched out and snapped up the various forms of U2's latest import single, the easily available domestic *Wide Awake in America* was selling more briskly than anyone at Island had anticipated. Bob Catania maintained that the release of the EP was directed toward U2 fans and not designed to be "worked" by the label to radio stations. "That live version of 'Bad,' though, was just unbelievable — it captivated everyone who heard it." Catania went to his boss, saying that he wanted to promote the track to AOR, but was told that no station would want to play an eight-minute live song because it was too long and had no hook (no catchy chorus). He persisted, though, and finally won permission to "indulge" himself.

Once Catania had instructed his department to begin promoting the song to album radio, he told me, "It went crazy. At WMMR [the most popular AOR station in Philadelphia] they said they couldn't get rid of it." In Boston, "Bad" became one of the most requested songs of the early summer on WBCN. Eventually, after U2 featured the track in the Live-Aid worldwide telecast on July 13, requests for the song increased tenfold, making it WBCN's most demanded and played song from May through the end of August 1985. Catania explained: "U2 had no concept that 'Bad' would ever get on the radio. Every week Paul was on the phone, as we were getting stations to add the track, saying 'Amazing! Amazing! You're kidding!' [Then] they did that song at Live Aid and I'm convinced that it was the song that broke them — it made U2 happen."

U2's involvement with Live Aid was born when Bono and Adam participated in the recording of the Band Aid charity single, "Do They Know It's Christmas?" After the event's founder Bob Geldof raised millions with that record to benefit famine-ravaged Ethiopia, he was inspired to organize a concert that could raise even more. The project grew into a mammoth one-day event at two sites, Wembley Stadium in London and J.F.K. Stadium in Philadelphia, which would be linked by worldwide video and radio communications. By the time Geldof's dream unfolded on the world stage, he had gathered the most impressive array of musical talent and technical support ever assembled for a single event. It would not be a wasted effort: Live Aid was watched across the globe by nearly two billion people, who donated generously to the cause.

U2 was in the midst of performing English and European tour dates when the band first heard about Live Aid. According to Ellen: "We were in Manchester and I got this message that Bob Geldof was looking for Bono and wanted to talk to him about doing this gig. They had been on the road for a year and wanted to go home, but [Bono] looked at all of us and said, 'I just couldn't say no. There was no way I could say no to him because of what we have to do [feed the hungry].' " All of U2's own concert commitments would be completed by July 13, making Live Aid the band's final performance of the *Unforgettable Fire* tour.

The obligation U2 felt to Geldof was typical for a group which had worn the "band with a conscience" emblem for years. Gaining full flower on *War*, U2's cry for political and social change to promote peace marched in step with the growing sentiment of popular music in the early eighties. Not since the reformist spirit of the sixties and early seventies had popular music taken on such a flavor of commentary. After dozens of artists — from John Lennon, Crosby, Stills, Nash, and Young, and Bob Dylan to Creedence Clearwater Revival and Chicago — were galvanized into action by the Vietnam War, the mid- and late-seventies aftermath was characterized by a flight from reality, with popular music refocusing on escapist lyrics and sentiments. The 1976–79 punk movement helped change that, as groups like the Clash, Stiff Little Fingers, the Jam, and the Sex Pistols brought social and political commentary back to rock and roll. After a brief period of flowery, dance-oriented new wave followed, by 1983 bands like U2, Gang of Four, the English Beat, and the Dead Kennedys returned pop music to a more serious agenda. As "New Year's Day," "Sunday Bloody Sunday," and "Pride (In the Name of Love)" were bigger hits than any of these other groups' singles, U2 became a major standard-bearer for the entire movement. Bob Geldof, tapping directly into this revived activist spirit, invited U2 and as many other concerned groups as possible for his 1984–85 Band Aid/Live Aid benefits, which became major symbols of the latest socially and politically conscious wave in popular music.

Geldof's stage managers had assembled a tight schedule at both venues, with acts locked into rigid load-in and setup slots, brief performances, and swift equipment breakdown and load-out periods. From opening up the back of the equipment truck to putting the band onstage, U2's crew had only forty minutes. Because of the continuous television broadcast there could be no interruption in the presentation of the concert, so the acts alternated between London and Philadelphia. The two stadium audiences would be linked via satellite and fed the same TV broadcast on giant video screens so they wouldn't miss any of the action. U2 was scheduled for a 5:00 P.M. (London time) performance at Wembley that was not to exceed twenty minutes in length. The band members planned to begin with "Sunday Bloody Sunday," use "Bad" to fill out the middle of the set, and then build to a climax with "Pride." Perfect on paper, the plan changed drastically once the band members walked onstage for what would arguably become the most important twenty minutes of their career.

U2 began playing after a video-linked introduction by Jack Nicholson from Philadelphia and a technical glitch that briefly delayed the start of the set. Blasting into "Sunday Bloody Sunday," the band's impassioned performance held together a wobbly television sound mix while Bono's constant stage-roving made the cameramen dizzy. Under the gray skies in front of 72,000 people, with unseen billions linked electronically as well, Edge triggered the sequencer to begin "Bad." As Bono breathed his emotional tale and roamed the huge stage, he hopped over the threshold onto a lower platform where groups of cameramen clutched their photo passes and equipment. Here, Bono could be closer to the audience, which strained up against a chain-link fence in front of him. While he sang, Bono noticed someone he suddenly wanted to invite onstage to embrace — not an unusual occurrence at a U2 concert, but much more than he bargained for in this situation.

Bono began motioning for a woman to come to him, but she couldn't squeeze through the densely packed bodies, much less over the chain-link barrier blocking the crowd from the stage compound. A phalanx of security personnel stood above and behind the fence facing outward, unaware of what Bono was attempting. After a couple of minutes, with the singer unwilling to give up on his selected audience representative, he jumped into the no-man's-land between the security team and the fence. There, he tried a direct approach, focusing the guards' efforts on helping what turned out to be a pair of women to climb over the braided cable barrier. Edge's equipment technician, Steve Rainford, laughed at the memory of the moment. "It seemed kind of weird from my point of view [alongside the amplifiers onstage]; the sequencer kept going on and on and on. Paul [McGuinness] was freaking. [He] was yelling to me, 'Get him off! Get him off!' " Finally, Bono was united with the women and escorted them onstage as the massive audience thundered its applause. The three embraced, slow dancing for a few moments before the women were escorted back down to the photo area and Bono finally closed the song.

By the time Bono finished, "Bad" had stretched to almost a quarter hour in length and U2 had used up all of its stage time. The band waved good-bye to the Wembley crowd and television audience. "We came offstage after Live Aid and we thought we had really blown it," Edge revealed during a 1987 interview for Island. "We thought that the idea of doing 'Bad' really hadn't worked, because Bono went into the audience. That was fine, but as everyone saw who was watching the TV coverage, it was like nothing he wanted to do seemed to happen for him: he couldn't get into the audience, he couldn't get the person he wanted out of the audience onto the stage, it was turning into a real embarrassment — a real disaster."

"Did you know that 'Bad' went on for fourteen minutes?" I asked.

The guitarist laughed loudly before replying. "Well, it's quite remarkable that something so extended could become so influential, so remembered. What I think really communicated was [Bono's] persistence and just the fact that he was determined. When it finally happened [getting the women onstage] after minutes of being on pause, it was such a relief and release of positive energy. People were just, kinda, 'YAAAHHH! He did it!' It made up for all the untogetherness of the previous few minutes. But it did mean that we only played two songs, which wasn't our plan."

Bono's episode at Live Aid existed well within the limits each member of the band permitted the others onstage. As an essential part of the magic U2 could weave in concert, this freedom always allowed the possibility that anything might happen. With the exception of Bono's truss-climbing stunts, which U2 had determined to have an overall negative effect, each member was free to improvise. Successful attempts, like Edge's guitar solo in "The Electric Co." or bringing a member of the audience onstage to perform "Knockin' on Heaven's Door," would be tried again. Because of this spirit among the band members, Bono was never personally blamed for his action at Live Aid, as clumsy as it first appeared to the group backstage. As it turned out, the media would exonerate the singer anyway, lauding U2 for an especially emotional moment in a day rife with passionate high points. That was no small compliment with the immense wealth of talent that took the stage during the concert — from steamy sets by Mick Jagger and Tina Turner, Queen, and David Bowie, to such events as Paul McCartney's return to the stage singing "Let It Be" and the reuniting of the Who and Led Zeppelin.

In just a few moments U2 had introduced itself to a vast new audience, leaving in its wake a distinct and powerful impression. Ellen admitted, "Live Aid did have a big impact on their careers, but it was never done with any kind of career motive in mind." The same could be said about the group's next public appearance ten months later in Dublin at a concert to benefit the Irish unemployed, as well as a 1986 charity tour for Amnesty International. U2 demonstrated again and again that it was a group willing to share its talent, as well as its deepest feelings, for important social causes. For the moment, though, with the *Unforgettable Fire* tour officially over, there was time for a welcome return across the Irish Sea and a much needed rest.

During the break after Live Aid, Bono and his wife journeyed to Africa. In the 1987 interview for Island, Bono revealed: "The *Unforgettable Fire* tour really took it out of me, I wasn't sleeping very well . . . only getting about two hours of sleep a night. I suppose I had just lost contact with who I was: the 'me' that writes songs, not the 'me' that performs them. I was very taken up with the Band Aid and Live Aid thing, and I felt that U2 was part of the change in temperature that allowed Live Aid to take place. So, I wanted to see it through, in a way, and I went there with Ali. I got a lot more from Ethiopia than I gave to it . . . I just worked there for five weeks. I didn't bring a guitar because they hadn't even heard of the Beatles over there, let alone U2." The pair involved themselves in very nonmusical pursuits, educating children and their parents about health, hygiene, and some farming methods. Bono continued: "I didn't want to come back, [but] I did because [of] one thing I know now in a way that I never knew before: what I do best is writing songs and singing them. You know, not everyone can go off and be Batman and Robin, and right the wrongs."

Bono had been back in Ireland for only a day when he heard about the Artists United Against Apartheid project. "Little Steven [Van Zandt] had been trying to get in contact with me, [but] there's not many phones where I was." In New York City, Bono's friend was hard at work on a Band Aid–styled album uniting many prominent musicians to protest against South Africa's apartheid policy. Van Zandt, the former guitarist of Bruce Springsteen's E Street Band, had taken a distinct political tack on two solo records, but the *Sun City* collaboration would be his most ambitious and pointed work yet. Working closely with New York producer and dance mixmaster Arthur Baker, Steven's Artists United Against Apartheid stable grew to include Peter Gabriel (whose classic "Biko" from 1980 first inspired Steven to protest against racism), Bob Dylan, Miles Davis, Pete Townshend, Daryl Hall and John Oates, Jackson Browne, Kurtis Blow, Clarence Clemons, Ringo Starr and son

Zack, Gil Scott-Heron, Bruce Springsteen, Herbie Hancock, Bob Geldof, Jimmy Cliff, Peter Garrett of Midnight Oil, Lou Reed, Pat Bena-
tar, Nona Hendryx, Peter Wolf, and many more. The artists were
featured in various combinations on six anthems composed by Little
Steven and they all agreed to donate their performance royalties from
sales of the album to the Africa Fund, a charity developed to provide
feed money for various anti-apartheid causes.

Bono threw himself heartily into the project when Little Steven
asked him if he would add vocals and a spoken message to the album.
He elaborated in the 1987 Island interview: "They sent me the tapes in
Dublin and I [recorded] sixteen-year-old shop assistants who were striking in Dublin city because their chain store owner was selling South
African produce. They refused to handle it and he sacked like twelve or
thirteen young girls. They're singing on 'Sun City.' " Bono also decided
to fly to New York for further recording sessions and a video shoot. "I
didn't know which end was up! One moment [it was] Addis Ababa
[Ethiopia], three days later [I was] in New York. I didn't sleep for a
week, but I was very refreshed and reenergized after spending time
away from rock and roll music."

Peter Wolf picked up the story in my interview with him. "I was
in New York and hadn't seen Bono since we toured together in 1982.
I was in this room with Little Steven, Springsteen, and Lou Reed . . .
Bono comes in — he just got in from Africa, with no sleep. I leaned over
to Lou and said, 'This guy is really into you,' because I wasn't sure if
Lou knew. He [had] quoted one of Lou's things at Live Aid [a bit of
'Walk on the Wild Side' during 'Bad']. So here comes Bono into this
room, with all the greats, near-greats, and ingrates. I see him 'working'
the table and sitting very close to Lou. Then we go down to Washington
Square [to shoot the video] and there's Springsteen, the Temptations,
Hall and Oates, the Fat Boys, Run DMC . . . What's Bono doing?
He runs out from behind the [security] line and starts shaking hands
with the kids!"

Having once lived in Greenwich Village, Wolf decided to visit
a favorite bar to see if he could run into some old friends. Bono asked
if he could tag along, as Wolf related: " 'Aren't you gonna rest?' I asked
him. He said, 'No, man.' 'You want to hang out?' He said, 'Yeah, I'd
love to go with you.' The next scene we're sitting in the bar and somewhere during the conversation, Bono asks me about the Stones — how
he'd love to meet Keith Richards. Well, the Stones were in town recording *Dirty Work*, so I call up the studio and we go up. I forgot that Steve

Lillywhite was doing the album, and Lillywhite and Bono obviously had a connection. To make a long story short, it ended up . . . Bono with Keith on the piano and Mick Jagger singing. Mick and Keith were going through the entire Everly Brothers catalogue, Little Richard, and the blues — that went on for hours."

Meeting the two members of the Rolling Stones was an important event for Bono, as he related in our 1987 interview. "When I saw Keith Richards, he was an inspiration to me. I didn't think he would be such an inspiration, but he really was. Mick Jagger has an amazing voice, and seeing them playing the piano together and just singing these old fifties pop songs and country songs was just amazing to me. Keith's an incredible guy, he puts on the guitar and the lines just disappear from his face. He's in love — that's the way I like to put it — and music is still his first love . . . still a sparkle in his eye. That opened up a world!"

The meeting with Jagger and Richards, as well as Wolf (who was quite a rhythm and blues fan himself), inspired Bono to write a song called "Silver and Gold." Despite the days without sleep, he composed the piece in less than two hours immediately following his overnight encounter while the sun rose on the city. Wolf told me that Bono excitedly called him in the early morning. "He said he had just written this song and was it possible to get ahold of Keith to do it? I thought it would be good for Keith to be part of the *Sun City* thing and I called him. Then, later, I got a call back from Bono — he was in the studio at the Stones' session, and he said Keith was gonna do it . . . with Ronnie Wood too."

"I brought it ['Silver and Gold'] to Keith Richards because I knew he would understand it — and he did," Bono mentioned to me during a 1987 radio interview. The song featured as sparse an arrangement as possible, with stomping foot and acoustic guitar setting the rhythm, and a lone electric guitar soloing economically behind Bono's breathy whispers and bluesy hollering. New York City music critic Robert Palmer was also present, adding some tasteful clarinet notes to the session.

A stab at authentic folk blues, "Silver and Gold" stung as much musically as it did lyrically. "It's set in a prison in South Africa," Bono continued. "A guy is just at the point of violence. My heart breaks when I think of the situation in South Africa. The idea that you are less because of the color of your skin sickens me. It's an angry song written as a result of that." He elaborated further in the 1986 edition of *Propaganda* (the official U2 fan magazine): "The most important verse is: 'These chains no longer bind me, nor the shackles at my feet. Outside are the prisoners, inside the free.' I've always been fascinated by borders, by conflict — and I write about it all the time, because out of it comes real human values. In the book *Night of the New Moon*, by Laurens van der Post, he describes being imprisoned in a concentration camp during the war. The only way he survived was by seeing the insanity of his captors, and seeing the sanity of love. He saw them as being captive, captive to that insanity, captive to that oppression — [the] possession of hatred. He saw himself, the prisoner, as a free man of love."

Little Steven liked "Silver and Gold," which was finished just in time to be added to the *Sun City* master tapes being shipped off to the pressing plant. The cover art for the record, however, had already been finished, so Little Steven and Arthur Baker arranged to have every copy stickered with a notice about the additional song. Although Manhattan Records released the album with much critical success, it sold only modestly. AOR avoided the disc mainly because of its dance-oriented feel, although Bono's gritty blues tune did garner some airplay at these rock stations. College and alternative music radio outlets favored the entire album and the title track appealed to dance stations, but the greatest exposure came from the video of "Sun City," which received regular airplay on MTV. The collage of superstar images from Artists United Against Apartheid's ranks, prominently displayed throughout the clip, made the video a hot request item throughout the fall of 1985.

Meanwhile, Edge had been hard at work on his own full-fledged solo debut, telling *Guitar Player* magazine in June 1985 that he was challenging himself by "tearing up the rule book and saying, 'Okay, given that this is my instrument, what can I do with it that no one else has done before?' " I asked him about the project during an interview for Island two years later. "In 1985 I started writing a few things [which] got me over some of my interests in ambient music, something I enjoy a lot, but stuff that I figured was probably not going to be on a U2 record. So I figured it was probably best to find another use for it and a film was the obvious one. I approached some movie people and eventually hitched up with Don Boyd, who's the producer of what was then called *Heroine*, but since then became known as *Captive*. I met the director and liked the movie, saw the rushes and decided to do it."

"Seeing the rushes" meant that Edge never screened a finished movie, just bits and pieces of the original shoots. The story pitted a wealthy young woman against three abductors in a Patty Hearst scenario that eventually ended with the captive joining her former enemies. Edge found the story intriguing, telling *New Musical Express* in October 1986, "I love the cinematography, it's stunningly beautiful, really incredibly well-shot. The acting's good, especially Oliver Reed as the girl's father. The plot is so . . . so strange at times." The offbeat nature of *Captive* freed Edge from adhering to a rigid musical mold and allowed him to roam the breadth of his imagination. He called his friend Michael Brook, who had developed "The Infinite," an effects device for the guitar, to secure the inventor's help in producing and performing on the album. Largely an electronic effort, *Captive* added many acoustic instruments in places, as on the opening "Rowena's Theme," with its slowly strummed guitar under a floating synthesizer melody. The piece was completed by bells, piano, choral vocals, and a French horn layered throughout.

Edge continued talking, during our 1987 interview, about movie politics and how it affected the recording of the music for *Captive*. "I think the director was delighted with what we did, but it was kinda scary as well because if he had hated what we had done it was too late to change it. The whole way the politics of doing music for films goes [is that] there's no direct chain of authority. You might have the director's creative directive for music, but he's also going to be pressured by his producer and the financiers. So it's kind of hard sometimes to find one guy who can tell you, 'this is right, this is wrong.' I'm kinda glad we were left alone, in a way, because had he been looking over our shoulder the whole time, it may have created a problem."

Edge and Brook were allowed to pursue their musical whims, producing a range of lush instrumental landscapes. "It's definitely for a certain mood," Edge told *Hot Press* in October 1986. "The thing about soundtrack albums is that they fulfill your wish and provide what you're looking for only at certain times. Eno's ambient music is like that, but this has more of a range than that. My ear as a musician has never found a great deal of solace in the blues scale. Instead I've been drawn to sparse, melancholy feels that tend to be European. It doesn't mean I don't like the blues, but there's a difference between loving and appreciating something and then bringing it into your own work."

By far the album's most conventional track, "Heroine" was still far from Edge's usual turf, even though Larry dropped by to add some drums. Sinéad O'Connor, then a budding young singer who had been an early writing partner in In Tua Nua, provided enchanting vocals echoed by a lovely three-note guitar chime from Edge. Not surprisingly, the song was issued as a single in England and Europe after being remixed by Steve Lillywhite. The song failed to chart appreciably, but did spread word about Edge's European soundtrack album in 1986. Virgin Records eventually released the record in the American market the following April.

With the experimental quality and, as Edge described it, the "European" essence of *The Unforgettable Fire* well-documented, it seemed as if U2 might continue on the ambient trail blazed by Eno. Was the band destined to venture even further in that direction on its next album, possibly inspired by the mysterious instrumental passages Edge had forged on *Captive*? He dispelled that conjecture in his *New Musical Express* interview. "I think this has catered for a certain side of my musical taste. Now I feel refreshed and that's all been dealt with, so I think what I'm gonna do with U2 will probably be the opposite to this, whereas previous U2 albums have been more moody." As every U2 album was a result of each of the four musicians' influences and experiences, it was exciting to speculate about what the band would come up with next. How much would Bono's recent blues education affect matters? Edge could only offer this clue in the *New Musical Express* article: "The next album's gonna be a lot more up front. It'll be our best album to date — really."

12

DEEPER INTO BLACK . . . AND BLUES

THE MEMBERS of U2 had relaxed during six months of free time and decided to come together in early 1986 to begin work on the follow-up to *The Unforgettable Fire*. Although many bands entered the studio with their songs already written, arrangements worked out, and lyrics finished, U2 would start the process completely fresh, with only a few snatches of melodies and rhythms in the members' minds. Steve Rainford, who had graduated from guitar technician to U2's ranking overall technical expert, talked about the group's recording process in an interview for this book. "At the beginning of the whole [new album] session [there] was a band rehearsal. It's really the essence of how they do it — they bang around till they make it the way they like and then they record it." Although the band members had enjoyed the expansive recording format used at Slane Castle, they weren't inclined to return to that location, as Steve mentioned: "We were in Adam's place at Danesmoate, all set up. The next logical idea was, 'Well, we should record here.' "

Edge found the idea a natural one, as he mentioned in the 1987 interview for Island. "There's great benefits to taking apart the formalization of recording and doing it in a very spontaneous way. You get back to the original pulse of what the music is all about — it is a simple feeling. [There] shouldn't be a technically complex method of recording, it shouldn't be sterile in any sense, it should be alive and in flux."

Bono added during the same interview that U2's concept while recording the newest album was all about "capturing the moment."

The band members felt that Brian Eno and Danny Lanois made

a well-balanced team that would easily accommodate any musical shifts they found themselves leaning toward, so it was decided early that they would produce the next album. When U2 contacted the pair, Eno and Lanois were delighted at the prospect of working with the Irish band again. Rainford ordered equipment to the production team's specifications. "I contacted Amek for the desk [recording console] and they literally sent us a desk in a humongous crate. It was enormous and it was in several parts, not at all portable. It took seven of us to unload the thing out of a truck when it first came. We put it in Adam's dining room, which it basically filled. We made a Plexiglas door to fit in the doorway between the dining room and the ballroom, and there was a little ancillary room to the right that was perfect for the tape machine." Rainford and his assistants worked around the clock, completing the installation within nine days. The technicians also wired other rooms in the house just as the various chambers at Slane had been utilized almost two years before. "By the time we installed everything, Danesmoate was like a huge cobweb," Rainford added. "Everywhere you went there were cables, and if it wasn't cables then it was flight cases, and if it wasn't flight cases then it was guitars."

Kevin Killen visited briefly to help engineer some recordings, but a previous commitment to work on the new Howard Jones album soon called him away. Killen was disappointed that he couldn't be involved with the sessions, even though "they were still in the embryonic stage," as he recalled. "The week that I worked with them they weren't really trying to record a new album [yet], but they had the tapes rolling just in case they came up with some good stuff. I recorded that song ['Heartland'] that eventually ended up on *Rattle and Hum*. It was a carrying over from *The Unforgettable Fire* period; since the band hadn't really written any new material, what they had was basically evolving from before."

"With the rehearsal routine," Rainford added, "we basically had a policy of 'record everything,' so there was a running record of everything. Things began to evolve and we were trying out methods and ideas . . . then bang! Slap in the middle of recording we had to pack it up."

U2 was committed to participate in a June 1986 benefit tour that would cross America as a celebration of Amnesty International's twenty-fifth birthday. The members had pledged their support after Jack Healey, the U.S. executive director of the worldwide human rights organization, made a personal appeal to them in Dublin. U2 was drawn to the ideals of the movement, which called for the elimination of the death penalty, torture, and degrading treatment of prisoners around the world. Amnesty International sought the release of "prisoners of conscience" jailed for their religious or political beliefs as well as color, sex, ethnic origin, or language — if they hadn't used or preached violence. The organization also advocated the need for fair and speedy trials and worked on behalf of those who were denied justice. U2 soon made this noble cause a priority over all other charities the band could potentially lend its support to. Bono told the official U2 fan magazine *Propaganda* in spring 1986: "On our last tour we toyed with idea of doing a concert in every capital city for Amnesty International. In the end we just did [a benefit at] Radio City Music Hall in New York, which left us wanting to do more in the future."

U2 would be performing on the Conspiracy of Hope tour alongside Sting, Peter Gabriel, Lou Reed, Bryan Adams, Joan Baez, Jackson Browne, and others. During the concerts, Amnesty International USA would attempt to raise awareness of human rights issues around the globe and register new members at well-positioned booths in each venue. Legendary concert promoter Bill Graham agreed to handle the logistics of the tour, slated to begin in San Francisco on June 4. The caravan of musicians and equipment would then stop in Los Angeles, Denver, Chicago, and Atlanta, with a massive finale at Giants Stadium just outside New York City on June 15. The many extra guests added to the last show's roster would stretch a normal evening concert into an all-day marathon. MTV planned to broadcast live from Giants Stadium while Westwood One provided a syndicated coast-to-coast audio linkup for participating radio stations. The widespread excitement generated by the announcement of the tour inspired Amnesty International to set itself an ambitious goal of raising three to five million dollars during the half-dozen concert dates.

Bono told *Propaganda*: "Back in September [1985] we agreed to give them one week, but in effect it will take us much longer than that. Performing is such a different frame of mind from writing and recording, it makes completely different demands on you."

Those demands were stressful, as Ellen Darst confirmed. "This group has a hard time getting started to do an album — the whole process of making records [for them] is not easy. To break rank and go out on that tour was a big strain and sacrifice for them, and it was really hard on everybody [in U2's organization]."

Edge remembered in the 1987 Island interview: "Just before the Amnesty shows we were going, 'No, this is going on at the wrong time! We're in the middle of doing this record and it's gonna take us a month once we get home to get in the swing of things — writing and recording.' "

But despite the poor timing, the band members threw themselves into preparations for the tour. Their attitude was summed up by Bono in the *Propaganda* interview: "The Amnesty International shows will certainly put us back in our plans to release the LP, but I can't think of a better reason to be put back."

Two weeks prior to departing for America, U2 tried out some of its new material and arrangements onstage in Dublin's Croake Park stadium during the Self-Aid concert to benefit the Irish unemployed. After that, the band members hammered out a concise and powerful set to fill its allotted space during each Amnesty show, then flew to San Francisco. This was the first time America would hear from U2 since the Live Aid concert nearly a year before, not counting Bono's solo participation in the *Sun City* project, and the audiences were incredibly enthusiastic. But U2 was only part of a tour that united all the participants with a meaningful common purpose. That bond was evident at Giants Stadium when U2 invited Little Steven, Nona Hendryx, Reuben Blades, and Lou Reed into the spotlights to help on a rousing version of "Sun City," and again when Bono walked onstage to join the three reunited members of the Police for "Invisible Sun."

In the bright sunny bowl of Giants Stadium, the crowd sat back to take in the afternoon performances, many early birds reclining on blankets or towels spread out over the hot plastic sheet protecting the field. Backstage it might have been cooler than under the sun's glare, but the scene was ablaze with sound and motion. Chaos always seemed perilously close, even to the practiced organization that Bill Graham brought to the entire event. Stage crews labored to set up and tear down each band's gear while performers and guest emcees — including the already mentioned regulars plus Joni Mitchell, Miles Davis, Carlos Santana, the Hooters, Joan Armatrading, Peter, Paul and Mary, Muhammad Ali, and Robert DeNiro — were shuttled to and from various dressing room areas. The sheer number of backstage guests made movement difficult and the ever-changing roster of onstage personalities rendered precise planning impossible. Radio, television, and print reporters spilled out of their press area and moved through the various rooms and concrete tunnels, searching for stories. Some penetrated the artists' dining room and lounge which was filled all day with a cavalcade of stars.

Into this swirl of color and ego the members of U2, looking much older and wiser than they had just a year ago at Wembley Stadium, emerged from their dressing room. Bono's hair tumbled past his shoulders over a western-style suede fringe jacket. Edge hadn't touched a razor to his face for some time and had hair as long as Bono's tucked under a black fedora. With an old pair of jeans and a vest he was now U2's hillbilly guitarist. Larry cut the same James Dean figure as before, but Adam had lost a great deal of weight and had worked the remainder into well-defined muscles. His hair was cut very short and he now wore delicate-looking wire rim glasses. With eyes locked forward in concentration, the band members moved through the mass of famous guests, who parted at U2's approach and fell silent until the members passed by on their way to the stage. Suddenly there was a rush as nearly everyone followed the band out of the lounge to secure a position to watch on the huge stage. By now it was dark, with U2 scheduled to appear just before the much-anticipated reunion of the Police. If there was any trepidation in U2's members about playing before the Police, it should have been washed away immediately by the tumultuous roar that greeted them.

Bono struck a typically serious pose for the opening "M.L.K." before following Edge's chunky guitar rhythm into the bouncy and exuberant "Pride." Even as Bono was singing the song's last triumphant note, the sequencer was already introducing "Bad." If Live Aid had featured U2's longest-ever performance of the song, then the Amnesty concert version was certainly the shortest, lasting only five minutes. The band presented "Sunday Bloody Sunday" with a reworked arrangement in which Bono softly sang the first two verses with Edge playing gently behind, before Adam and Larry kicked in their usual militant rhythm. Then U2 took an abrupt departure from what had been a greatest hits show when Bono introduced the next selection as "a twisted Bob Dylan song." Darkly ominous bass notes and a rumbling tom-tom shuffle on the drums set the mood for wildly caustic guitar screeches and moans, then the stinging lyrical protestations of "Maggie's Farm." Without skipping a beat, U2 moved into a verse and chorus from "Cold Turkey," mirroring the raw arrangement and naked lyrics of John Lennon's original before slipping back into "Maggie's Farm. The brooding and metallic interpretation of "Maggie's Farm" had less in common with Dylan's original than "The End" by the Doors — its dark power leaving many in the audience numb and tentatively clapping once it was finished.

Bono later admitted to me in a radio interview the following September that U2 had performed "a pretty twisted version" of "Maggie's Farm." He continued: "It's a kind of classic case of how you can reinterpret a song to your own point of view. We originally performed it at a concert [Self-Aid] for the unemployed people back home in Dublin city. There's a lot of emigration out of Ireland, whether it be to America or, in this case, to the U.K. People have to go there to find jobs and they resent that fact. They don't want to go—they want to stay home, but they've got to go away to work. They have to go away and be under Margaret Thatcher ['Maggie'], if you like. There's a lot of anger in it. I juxtaposed it with 'Cold Turkey' because we've got a real bad heroin problem in Dublin. When people feel that they've got no way out, sometimes they get into finding more dangerous ways out of their situation—like heroin, for instance. There's a lot of pain, and music should be able to be interpretive. If you listen to a jazzman play, he hits those notes, bends the strings, because he's trying to paint a picture. That's all Edge was trying to do, I think it's fair to say. Maybe it seemed self-indulgent to some, but that's the way we viewed it." A recording of "Maggie's Farm" from Self-Aid exists on the *Live for Ireland* album released on MCA Records.

Onstage at Giants Stadium, Bono lightened the mood somewhat by easing the band into a version of "Help!" vastly rearranging the original into a slow lament that clocked in at just over two minutes. Bono didn't need to sing the choruses—the enthusiastic crowd did it all for him. The energy from the audience flowed into U2's closing number, the cover of "Sun City." An apt selection, since South Africa's apartheid policy fell under the umbrella of Amnesty International's many human rights concerns, "Sun City" hit a dizzying peak that brought the entire audience of 53,000 dancing to its feet. The group filed off the stage to rapturous applause, leaving the job of closing the show to the Police. It's not correct to say that U2 outclassed the talents of Sting, Stewart Copeland, and Andy Summers, but it is perhaps fair to conclude that the Irish band represented the present and the future while the Police's reunion, after two years of inactivity as a band, commemorated the past. Bob Catania watched the concert with particular interest, as he was already thinking of the release of U2's next album, almost a year away. He admitted, "To me, it was the changing of the guard from the Police as the megaband to U2. We were watching the moment that it changed."

The members of U2 were more concerned with the help they

had been able to give Amnesty International, as Edge related in the 1987 interview for Island Records. "That was amazing — to be able to help an organization as great as Amnesty International, [which] doubled their total membership after that tour, and have a great time in the bargain. Helping to put Amnesty back on the map was a real thrill." The guitarist had originally feared that the interruption in U2's recording schedule would seriously hamper the creation of its new album. As it turned out, what the members had gained in personal satisfaction and professional stature far outweighed what might have been lost.

Ellen related: "[The tour] certainly didn't hurt U2, although at the time it seemed it might. The two things [Live Aid and the Conspiracy of Hope tour] combined made Middle America aware [of U2] where it hadn't been before."

U2's set during the tour opened wide speculation among fans and the media about the musical direction the group might be heading in. The band was obviously not afraid to embrace other styles, as evidenced by the inclusion of cover tunes in its repertoire which displayed soul, blues, and folk influences. Then there was "Maggie's Farm," a gloomy metallic mystery quite unlike anything the group had previously offered. If anything, these elements indicated a significant change in U2's heading, but the eventual destination was anybody's guess.

Back in Dublin, the band was again experimenting with different recording situations and studio techniques. The Amek desk went in and out of Adam's house at Danesmoate a few times and was used for a while at Edge's place. U2 also used Windmill Lane for some sessions, which included setting up in an old warehouse next door to take advantage of its peculiar echo qualities. Steve Rainford recalled that U2 also accepted an invitation from Windmill to try a new option. "They went ahead, at great expense, and built a new 'live' room which they were very impressed with. We were all hibernating at Danesmoate and got down there to check the place out. Edge showed up with a guitar and Adam set up in an area . . . but Edge didn't like it [the sound], so he said 'bring some stone in.' " It was hoped that playing from behind a stone wall in the studio would improve the sound to his liking. "Within an hour, we had masons in and they laid plastic on the floor, a nice wood floor, and they paved a nice brick wall with stones! No cement, just stacked brick in the corner . . . but that didn't work either."

In the end, U2 did tape pieces of what would become its next album, *The Joshua Tree*, at Windmill Lane, but the more comfortable sessions in Adam and Edge's homes remained the preferred method of recording. As the band members settled down from their trip to America and gradually slipped into a creative studio groove, tragedy suddenly struck. While Greg Carroll (G-Dub) was running an errand for the band, the ebullient roadie's motorcycle was struck by a car in Dublin. He died soon afterward, leaving everyone in the U2 camp shocked and sorrowful. Bono responded by writing a beautiful set of lyrics that eulogized his friend and then delivered them with passionate anguish after he traveled with Larry to New Zealand for Greg's funeral. The song's title, "One Tree Hill," was inspired by the name of the largest mountain overlooking the harbor at Auckland. Later a selection on *The Joshua Tree*, "One Tree Hill" was also released in tribute as a single in Australia and New Zealand.

Deeply shaken, the group forged on with its recording and, by January 1987, under the guidance of Lanois and Eno, had completed the basic tracks and overdubbing. Thirty other cuts were available in various states of completion; U2 would raid this cache for assorted B-sides to its singles during the coming year. Kevin Killen recalled that the band contacted him again to see if he was interested in mixing some of the tracks into final form. "Adam told me that Danny was just exhausted from doing the album and [asked] would I come and help them do it. I really wanted to, but I was committed [to Bryan Ferry and Mr. Mister]. In the end, Steve Lillywhite offered his services and mixed four of the tracks—Danny, Brian, and Edge mixed the rest."

Adam told *New Musical Express* in March 1987: "We'd given ourselves a deadline because we wanted to release the LP as early in the year as was possible. [Steve Lillywhite] was really a fresh pair of ears coming in and adding the finishing touches—they were basically small changes."

Experience had taught the promotion and marketing staff at Island to synchronize the American appearance of *The Joshua Tree* and its first single, "With or Without You," with the release dates in other countries. In 1984, when the "Pride" single had reached British stores weeks earlier than in the States, U2 had become such a desirable airplay commodity to some American radio stations that they searched intensively to locate import copies to feature "exclusively." These stations enjoyed an advance on the normal American release, angering radio competitors who inevitably vented their frustrations on the record company. "I remember getting called out of a business lunch in L.A.," Bob Catania said. "WNEW [in New York City] was going crazy because WLIR [on Long Island] was playing 'Pride.' The song had come [into America] on the 'Rock Over London' show [a weekly syndicated program featuring new U.K. releases]. We then had to rush-release 'Pride' in the States."

Despite the extra care taken to coordinate the release dates and prevent leaks of *The Joshua Tree* to the media and public, Catania's nightmare came true once again. "We had one leak," he recalled. "It was a college station in Scranton [Pennsylvania]." The promotion boss had received an angry call from a major AOR station complaining that the forthcoming U2 album was being illegally featured elsewhere on the air. "I said, 'You're out of your mind — you probably heard a U2 cut you're unfamiliar with.' He starts reading me titles and I go, 'You're right!' So I called up the college station and got the administrator on the phone, told them to cease and desist, and they sent me a reel-to-reel of *The Joshua Tree*." Catania was shocked that the station had gotten hold of the entire album even as it was being pressed. "It turned out that WEA manufacturing [Warner-Elektra-Atlantic Records, which pressed Island products] is in Oliphant, right outside of Scranton. One of the jocks at the station had a relative that worked in the plant; [he] had stolen a tape or a test CD and gave it to this station. They were also trying to peddle really bad cassette copies around."

Island shipped copies of "With or Without You" accompanied by a terse announcement telling stations to adhere to a "no-play" policy until 11:30 A.M. on Wednesday, March 4. It was expected that AOR would rally around U2's single, but Catania also believed that this would be the song to finally crack the stubborn CHR format. "The most asked question was if I expected it to happen on the Top 40 end," he related. "Of course I did! It didn't take a genius to hear 'With or Without You' and realize you had a mass-appeal record." Catania was dead right. With all the CHR airplay and promotional help from an instantly successful MTV video clip, the single debuted on the *Billboard* Hot 100 chart at number 64 and blasted all the way to the top by the first week of May.

A perfect vehicle for Bono's breathy and pensive vocals, "With or Without You" held power at bay, instead wrapping his words gently in musical velvet. The delicate opening was urged along by bass while Edge added sustained notes high above on his "Infinite" guitar, designed by Michael Brooke. The device allowed him to modify typical guitar sounds to resemble other instruments — in this case, the timbre of a violin.

"It's very different," Edge told me during the Island Records interview in Texas one month after the single appeared. "I think 'With' became the obvious choice for the single, not because it's probably the most commercial song on the record, but because it's the one that seems to smooth the transition from the last things to this record. It's nothing like *The Unforgettable Fire* and yet it showcases everything that U2 has been about up to now: Bono's singing, my guitar playing, Adam, and Larry."

The *Joshua Tree* album package was predominantly black, accented by eye-catching gold lettering and borders, framing a picture of the solemn band members in front of an arid mountain landscape. U2 journeyed to Death Valley for the photo session with Anton Corbijn, and while there noticed the lonely Joshua trees which grew stubbornly in the sun-baked dirt. Often standing thirty-five feet high, the plants were named after the Old Testament warrior and prophet Joshua, their branches symbolizing his arms outstretched to heaven as he courageously led his people to the promised land. Edge elaborated in the Island interview: "The image of the Joshua tree seemed to speak for what the album was about and our aspirations for the album, because it wasn't finished at that stage. Just to see it there, so stark in the desert landscape . . . I suppose it just summed up a lot of ideas without being one single thing, it seemed appropriate on many levels." On the back cover, U2's members stood next to the branches of a Joshua tree. A similar pose appeared inside the gatefold sleeve. Once again, Anton Corbijn had captured the essential mood of a new U2 album — that of yet another courageous change to a simpler beauty.

"Very different," Edge replied when I asked him during the Island interview to compare U2's new release to *The Unforgettable Fire*. "It's more finished, more in focus. We attempted from the onset to work within the idiom of the song, which is something we never really thought too much about in the past. If *The Unforgettable Fire* was an album of experimentation and innovation, this was a record that accepted the idea that a song was [a] straightforward arrangement quite stripped down."

"Was it difficult for the producers to adjust to this new approach?"

"Although Danny and Brian worked on *The Unforgettable Fire*, they were very much in favor of this new sort of idea. We never had any fears of them not being able to understand what we were trying to do. Brian is a really naive kind of enthusiast as far as music goes, he's not an intellectual listener at all. He listens to something and he either loves it or he hates it, and his reasons are often very instinctive and not intellectual. He's a huge fan of people like Hank Williams and—"

"Brian Eno is a fan of Hank Williams?" I asked incredulously.

"Absolutely. [Also], before [Lanois] used to be an engineer and producer, he played in a bunch of country bands. So again, his understanding of the song is quite good."

"Does this mean that U2 may come out with a country-western album?" I jested.

Edge laughed. "I don't think we're capable of a pure country record. I think we'll always end up sounding like U2 simply because we have such a strong style—Bono vocally and me guitar-wise. I suppose this record scratches the surface of the blues and I could quite see the same thing happening with country, but no one song represents the record."

The opening track on *The Joshua Tree* featured the familiar sonic touch of previous U2 efforts. "Where the Streets Have No Name" entered with a massive organ introduction before Edge's chiming guitar pattern linked up with Adam and Larry's locomotive rhythm. The lyrics revealed Bono on a quest to break down restraining mental and spiritual barriers, a sentiment echoed in the following "I Still Haven't Found What I'm Looking For," which clearly reflected U2's new stripped-down recording approach and folkier style. Edge picked his way tentatively into the song and a tambourine lazily counted out the time until Larry fell into a four-beat pattern accentuating each final pulse with a drum crash. The next two songs represented opposite musical extremes— from the softly turbulent "With or Without You" to the full-blown metallic angst of "Bullet the Blue Sky." Edge mentioned in the Island interview that the latter was "total guitar anarchy . . . 'putting the war through the amplifiers,' as Bono used to say." The vitriolic lyrics matched Edge's power, and the images of warfare, terror, and death in Central America made "Bullet the Blue Sky" a potent successor to "Sunday Bloody Sunday."

"Running to Stand Still" was a deceptively pretty ballad introduced by acoustic slide guitar and carried with gentle piano accompaniment. Bono's reverie soon revealed itself to be a tragic tale of heroin addiction, with the afflicted refusing to halt an inevitable slide into self-destruction. Haunting in its acoustic simplicity, the song closed with a lonely harmonica's plaintive cry. Propelled by an odd beat, "Red Hill Mining Town" was given added depth by layers of backing vocals and orchestral-size keyboards, making it one of the most technically busy tracks on a relatively unadorned album. Bono's vivid images were disquieting, as he explained in the Island Records interview. " 'Red Hill Mining Town' is about the British coal miners' strike, but it's [also] about the breakdown of a relationship under the pressure of being out of work. That's what you don't read about in the papers or see in the news reports. Guys picking up social security, they've got to go home to families and bring up their kids. The pressure of the miners' strike was breaking up families and I was more interested in that element than the politics of it."

The brightly colored guitar chords of "In God's Country" flew past, with Edge's playing recalling sounds as far back as "I Will Follow." Bono suggested scenic vistas and vast open areas, perhaps Death Valley, with his natural images of desert and fire. Those images continued in "Trip Through Your Wires," introduced by a folky harmonica and decidedly country-western harmonies. Bono yelped and hee-hawed his way into the guitar notes to kick the song into high gear. "It was a hootenanny — a big yahoo!" he continued in the Island interview. "We kind of made it up at the moment and I just blew into the harp."

The light-hearted moment gave way to the somber dedication of "One Tree Hill" for Greg Carroll. Bono's soft-spoken lyrics entered as if he was standing at the funeral and turned away to eulogize his friend. Near the end of the song, his voice suddenly leapt into a mournful wail. The agonizing shouts might have been rerecorded in another studio take, but U2 chose to leave this recording as it was. Bono explained: "If you write a song about a person who's close to you and dies in a car accident while doing a favor for you, you're not going to [be able to] take someone in the control room pressing a button and telling you to 'try it again, please' or 'can you drop it in from the second verse.' I'd just say 'drop dead.' So, as soon as I wrote the words, I cut myself off, I performed it once." U2 added a gospel coda to the song — the band members' final salute to their friend.

Bono admitted that the next track on *The Joshua Tree*, "Exit," was the darkest song U2 ever wrote. Creeping in on low guitar rumblings, throbbing bass, and the shimmering night sounds of insects, the song soon built in intensity with a whirling crescendo of guitar explosions, cymbal crashes, and drum detonations. Threatening danger at every moment, "Exit" retreated slowly after a second screaming crescendo. The final track, "Mothers of the Disappeared," was U2's recognition of the thousands of people who vanished every year in Latin America, murdered by death squads. Along with "Bullet the Blue Sky," the song pointed an accusing finger at America's foreign policy, which supported some of the violently repressive governments responsible for the killings.

Bono's lyrics reminded the listener of the world's detestable human rights record and acknowledged the efforts of Amnesty International.

The press reacted swiftly and favorably: John McCready wrote in the March 14 *New Musical Express*, "*The Joshua Tree* will prove a better and braver record than anything else that's likely to appear in 1987." U2's hometown music paper, *Hot Press*, ran an article by Bill Graham and Naill Stokes who enthused, "It stands out like a beacon against the backdrop of musical murk which characterizes rock and roll in the late eighties." In America, *Boston Globe* music critic Steve Morse concluded in his review, "It is easily the most rewarding rock record of the new year. And to call it the best of U2's career would not overstate the case."

The public responded with similar enthusiasm. In London, Tower Records put *The Joshua Tree* on sale at midnight and over a thousand people, including Elvis Costello, waited in line to grab the first copies. Island Records, noticing the American public's preference changing toward compact discs, ordered CDs to be pressed in abundant quantities. Andy Allen, who served as the label's national director of album promotion, revealed in an interview for this book, "It was the first release to ship record, cassette, and CD simultaneously. [Up to that time] you released the record and cassette, then caught up with your compact discs a month later. We actually held back the release to allow the [CD] manufacturer to catch up. It was the largest shipment of CDs in the industry."

Bob Catania, by then vice president of promotion at Island, added, "When all was said and done, *The Joshua Tree* was the first platinum CD—it sold a million copies of the disc alone."

Rehearsals for a mammoth world tour that would visit America for two months began in Dublin as the album was released. U2's last full-scale tour of the States had ended two years before, and anticipation for the forthcoming visit was huge—multiplying many times the fervor that accompanied the announcement of U2's 1985 concerts. Interest in the band had intensified after the Live Aid appearance raised U2's stature, and the Amnesty tour solidified its reputation not only as a first-class musical unit but also as a socially and politically concerned group. Now, with *The Joshua Tree* widely praised as brilliant in its conception and execution, the band was poised to ascend to yet another level of fame, the rarified heights seen by only a handful of groups.

13

IN GOD'S COUNTRY

THE ACTIVITY CENTER at Arizona State University was a full-fledged arena that could hold 13,500 persons. U2 planned to open its tour at the hall, located in Tempe only a few miles down the road from Phoenix, on April 2 and 3. Then, after swinging through the Southwest for a few dates, the group would head to southern California for seven sold-out arena concerts in Los Angeles and San Diego. When U2 arrived in Tempe one week early to rehearse for the shows, midday spring temperatures soared above ninety degrees. The heat soon rose even higher for the band members, however, who were embroiled in controversy from the moment they stepped off the plane.

Arriving in Arizona, U2 unwittingly entered a statewide political fray that had begun in January 1987 when Governor Evan Mecham repealed the previous administration's act creating a state holiday on Martin Luther King, Jr.'s birthday. Mecham maintained that the holiday had been illegally decreed and not brought into law through proper legislative procedure. Many citizens were outraged that Mecham had used a legal technicality to eliminate what they considered an honorable manner of recognizing a great American; others regarded the move as a slap in the face to Arizona's entire black population. Some citizens organized themselves into a Governor Mecham Watchdog Committee, attempting to heighten public awareness of the situation. It wasn't long before a powerful grass-roots movement to recall the governor from his position began to grow.

At least two acts, the Doobie Brothers and Stevie Wonder, had canceled plans to perform in Arizona as a way of protesting Mecham's action—and now U2 was making a well-publicized splash in the state as it opened its tour there. What made that action shocking to outside observers was that U2's respect for King and stance on human rights had been stated clearly on many occasions. Bono clarified the confusing situation when I caught up with the band a few days later to record an extensive interview for Island Records. "We weren't aware of the exact situation until we got there, and had we known a few months in advance, I don't think we would have played Arizona." Instead of canceling the concerts, however, U2 decided to perform as planned to publicize the movement opposing the governor's action. Bono continued: "We were asked to play by the Mecham Watchdog Committee and we pledged our support to them. Martin Luther King is a great American and ought to be remembered, and human rights in the United States is an area that again people are going to have to rethink. The U.S., of all countries, has opened its arms to so many races, colors, creeds—it's the very essence of what the U.S. stands for. If [the U.S.] ceases to care, then it's really going to be very sad. I think Martin Luther King is a symbol of sorts, he stands for something, for human rights and equality among races. That is a symbol worth lauding—worth lifting up."

As U2 entered the fracas, the governor's supporters were not idle. The *Arizona Republic* daily newspaper reported a comment from Mecham's press secretary Ron Bellus: "Apparently they don't know what's going on, period. Who are they to tell Arizona what to do?" The band, meanwhile, received unquestioning support from its longtime friend Barry Fey, who expressed his outrage in the same article. Fey, who was promoting the two ASU shows, also pledged his aid in raising money for the Watchdog Committee by staging further benefit concerts. U2 backed up its convictions with a sizable and undisclosed cash donation to the organization, then went ahead with rehearsals for the tour. It wasn't long before word about the band's involvement in the state controversy became national news.

Fans were already anxious to see U2 after a two-year absence, but the quarrel with Governor Mecham lent an even greater anticipation to the tour's opening shows. Most of the arena was already packed as Lone Justice finished its opening set and crew members swarmed onto the stage. Barry Fey walked up to a microphone at stage center to read a statement from U2 explaining the group's outrage over the rescinding of the state holiday. Loud cheers erupted when he exhorted, "Mecham is an embarrassment to the people of Arizona!" He looked up after finishing the text and added, "On my own behalf, let us turn to the sixties and let the music lead the way to justice."

The members of U2 strode onstage in semidarkness as the taped introduction to "Where the Streets Have No Name" rolled out of the speakers. Larry added a beat on cymbals while Edge began his chiming pattern of notes, growing slowly louder and more aggressive until Adam's bass and the full drum kit united in an explosion of sound matched by the sudden white brilliance flashing from banks of stagelights. Sporting a multicolored Indian vest with his much longer hair pulled back in a ponytail, Bono was greeted with a rush of applause as he dove into the opening words. But almost immediately, he grimaced in pain and grabbed his throat. Bono had lost his voice on previous opening tour dates, his vocal chords unused to the effort of performing for ninety minutes — but never on the very first song. He bravely attempted to hit even the highest notes, but finally, after five more selections, he had to accept that outside of a small range his voice had been reduced to little more than a ragged whisper.

Bono admitted his difficulty to the audience and asked everyone to help sing for him. He turned the microphone around and pointed it toward the cheering crowd. Even though *The Joshua Tree* had been in stores for only three weeks, the Arizona audience called out the latest material with impressive familiarity and responded thunderously to U2's classics. "Sunday Bloody Sunday" featured only fragments of lyrics from Bono; the rest of the time he used his arms to conduct the thousands of voices as one resounding choir. Untroubled by Bono's vocal difficulties, the exhilarated audience also ignored U2's rather obvious pacing problems: Edge finished playing "October" and stepped away from his piano, guitar in hand, to immediately begin "With or Without You," just as Bono decided that his voice was too far gone to attempt the song. An awkward huddle temporarily killed the show's momentum; Edge emerged to patiently pace back to his amps and select another guitar that he needed for "New Year's Day." Bono shortened the band's set by a few songs and U2 left the stage early, but no trace of disappointment was apparent in the wildy applauding Tempe audience.

Backstage after the show, Paul McGuinness forbade the singer from talking to anyone. The other three members, however, were chumming it up with everybody present, including ex-Go-Go Jane Weidlin. Edge had heard some voice problems from Bono before, but never as bad as that night, he remarked to me. "I didn't know, at any point, if he'd be able to go on, he was in pain all the time." Larry admitted that the band had pursued a strenuous rehearsal schedule that was perhaps too much for Bono. Rather than being upset, though, the drummer was noticeably upbeat, still awed by the Arizona audience's huge outpouring of warmth and energy.

While U2 postponed the next evening's concert for a day to let Bono's throat repair itself, reviews that were as glowing as the audience's reaction came pouring in. The *Arizona Republic* gave a generous stamp of approval and Robert Hilburn of the *Los Angeles Times*, in town to cover the opening concerts as a preview to U2's upcoming California appearances, aptly entitled his review "Grace Under Pressure." He praised U2 for the courage of its commitment in standing up to Mecham and the band's honesty in dealing with Bono's ragged voice. *Newsweek* noted in a full-page article three weeks later that "Bono stormed onstage with his voice so hoarse he could barely croak out the first song. No smoke machines. No revolving platforms or elaborate gimmicks. The Irish rock quartet scored with passionate lyrics, honest guitar-driven sound and Bono's Pied Piper charisma."

"It was one of the most important nights for U2," Bono dejectedly mentioned during our Island Records interview a few days later. When I showed him a copy of Hilburn's article, he added, "I heard it was the same with the *New York Times*; I'm so surprised they gave us the benefit of the doubt." At least Bono could be consoled somewhat by U2's highly publicized political statement. The movement to recall the governor would continue to grow as acts of financial impropriety and obstruction of justice were uncovered in the following months. Mecham was impeached barely a year after U2's Tempe concerts. It would be a hollow victory, though, since the reason for the band's involvement in the first place — reestablishment of the Martin Luther King, Jr., holiday — would become a state referendum defeated by Arizona voters in 1990.

The *Joshua Tree* tour continued through the Southwest in early April 1987. Houston was home for three days while the group relaxed, rehearsed, and took on the 19,000-seat Summit for a pair of concerts. Still not satisfied that they'd achieved their usual standards for a performance on this tour, the band members were determined to finally shake off the cobwebs in Texas. If the timing worked out, I would also be conducting the interview for Island Records between rehearsal sessions. I caught up with Ellen and Keryn for a status report at their base of operations in a suite at the Four Seasons hotel downtown. "Everyone's excited about tonight's show, I think this will be the one," Ellen managed to say before the ringing phone demanded her attention. The remains of breakfast filled some trays scattered on a table and the sunbaked city stretched out below the floor-length windows. Ellen said into the telephone, "What do you mean they can't find the tickets?"

Keryn turned to me and smiled, "By the way—" before her phone also sounded off.

Ellen hung up and said to me, "We'll do the interview tomorrow. Is noon all right? Edge can start and then I'll send along Bono." I tried to answer, but the telephone rang again and Ellen's hand shot toward it, ending our brief exchange.

Bono regained his full voice at the Summit, uniting with a stellar band performance that officially ended the tour's shaky start. "Where the Streets Have No Name" and "Still Haven't Found" opened the show, followed by the veteran rockers "Gloria" and "I Will Follow." Bono's self-confidence and improvisational skills returned once he was assured his voice would last. On "Bullet the Blue Sky," as the stage was dipped in red light, he dedicated the tale of greed and violence to Oral Roberts and Jimmy Swaggart, then assumed the character of a pretentious Southern preacher. "He keeps peelin' off them dollar bills . . . slappin' 'em down . . . one hundred! . . . two hundred!"

Larry's drums crashed mightily after each "hundred" and Edge powered into his hardest-hitting guitar solo of the night. Bono picked up a spotlight and slowly circled the guitarist, drenching him in blinding white light. Edge ended the tirade of notes by facing his amps and creating a wave of feedback that slowly ran down the scale like a doomed airplane spinning to earth. This was U2's brand of heavy metal—a jolt to ram home its furious antiwar protest.

In contrast, when Bono picked up an acoustic guitar and harmonica for the following "Running to Stand Still," his words and the band's quiet accompaniment held the audience spellbound. On "Exit," the moodiness of Bono's vocals exploded into instrumental "choruses" highlighted on the stage and halfway back in the arena by a sequence of white lights flashing in time to the music. Bono began to close the song and then returned from its inevitable fade by chanting "G-L-O-R-I-A, Gloria!" from the Van Morrison classic. The ominous turn in mood was countered by a bright and breezy "In God's Country," which flowed past in just over two minutes.

U2 unveiled a gentle first encore, beginning with a cover of "People Get Ready." Originally recorded by the Impressions with Curtis Mayfield in 1965, the song was a hymn of faith and redemption that

Bono soon had the entire arena chanting along with. Next, "The Unforgettable Fire" provided a haunting, low-key tone rather than U2's typical high-energy ending. "40" was the second encore and the final song of the evening, as it had been for years, and the Texas audience sang the chorus long after the band members had walked offstage and the houselights blazed on. Minutes later, though, as the crowd filed out of the huge arena, those lights abruptly died again and the members of U2 rushed back onstage unexpectedly. While fans dashed for seats, the overjoyed Bono launched the group into "Trip Through Your Wires," his blaring harmonica leading the way. Punctuated with hoots and hollers, the new song became an onstage celebration as the band, now a full nineteen songs into its show, spun out a joyous, country-flavored rave-up. The members left the stage with broad smiles, but not before rattling off a blistering version of Neil Young's "Southern Man" that proved the *Joshua Tree* tour was finally in full swing.

Later, U2's entourage drove back to the Four Seasons and gathered in the hotel bar. Ellen was excited because her premonitions about the night's success had turned out to be correct. Adam only admitted in return, "It *was* good, wasn't it?" Then, when Edge appeared, the bassist asked, "Do you want to go to a bar? We should see some of Houston." This was viewed as an excellent suggestion, so everyone got back in the limos and rendezvoused at a loud and brassy disco. Paul McGuinness and Larry joined Adam and Edge, Bono being the only no-show. Once word spread in the busy nightclub that U2 was holding down one corner of the balcony, there was a nonstop shuffle of fans toward the spot. Once the club closed, the laughing and jabbering crowd tumbled into the parking lot, with U2's members and staff happily mixed throughout. The limos were reboarded and soon sped away, but as the parking lot emptied, Edge discovered that he'd been adandoned on the curb. He accepted a ride back to the hotel in a battered Volkswagen, thankfully arranging to leave tickets to the second Summit show for the friendly pair of fans who'd given him a lift.

The traces of champagne in our systems made the next day's noontime interview a little slow at first, but Edge warmed quickly while sipping tea and talking about U2's latest album. "I'm getting into rock and roll again. I mean, obviously, our style — but with the basic ingredients of rock and roll: guitar, backbeat, bass, drums, vocal. No messing about. That's where I'm sort of leaning now — the direction of the band."

"I think we got a hint of that on the Amnesty tour when you did 'Maggie's Farm.'"

"Yeah, the interest in American music was there. *The Joshua Tree*, for all intents and purposes, is a record based thematically on America. There are some songs that could be from anywhere: 'Where the Streets Have No Name' could be a European situation as well as an American one. But a lot of the songs like 'God's Country,' 'Exit,' 'Bullet,' 'Running to Stand Still' are based on America. They are a result of touring here, meeting musicians who are really tuned into American folk and R & B music — the original roots music of this country — and just becoming fascinated with the culture, the very paradoxes of this place. It led us to start investigating the original music, the seminal influences of music here. Hence, the blues kind of thing on the record."

When Bono joined the interview, he looked even more sluggish than Edge had been, but quickly snapped to alertness while offering an overview about U2's recording of *The Joshua Tree*. "The whole business of recording has to be rethought. I think the idea of our recording session is a good thing as well, and there's not enough of it nowadays. They used to put a band in the studio, they'd just play, and you just put down what the band has played on tape with live vocals and no overdubs. I think that's great! You know, a lot of those Bob Dylan records . . . one of the reasons they sound so fresh is because of the way they were recorded — they really captured the moment. It was with this approach in mind that we went into the recording of *The Joshua Tree*. That approach did not succeed on all tracks, but a lot of the backing tracks were just done live in a studio, in Edge's place, or in Adam's living room. We'd just plug in an outside twenty-four track and start playing in a room."

I said, "This is what the Beatles went through, with their records becoming more and more complex, finally getting to *Let It Be* and saying, 'Let's just put the band in this rehearsal studio and play,' " I offered.

"The Beatles' records were complex records," Bono concurred. "On the white album, you might have 'Helter Skelter,' which is full frontal assault, [but] at the same time you'd have . . . uh, let me think of a good example . . . "

" 'Rocky Raccoon,' " I supplied.

Bono laughed. "I wouldn't go that far! 'Dear Prudence' would be a good example. I think *The Joshua Tree* is almost old-fashioned in that it's like an old Beatles album: a collection of songs — some are experimental and almost orchestrated, like 'One Tree Hill,' others are clear-cut little gems like 'God's Country.' "

Bono headed back into his explanation about the recording of the latest album. "The thing about Dan Lanois and Brian Eno in the studio is that they are very [supportive of] the idea of a session. Dan will be in there with his tambourine standing beside Larry looking him in the eye and whacking the cymbal here and there. They get really carried away with [it], and we get carried away with them getting carried away with it. It's just a vicious cycle in the right sense of the word. Yeah . . . 'Trip Through Your Wires' was fun, 'God's Country' . . . actually, 'God's Country' sounds more fun than it was now that I think!" he laughed.

"This 'back to the roots' approach in your recording, is it a reaction to your own music? Did you feel that you were going too far in one direction?"

Edge chimed in: "I suppose to an extent each record is a reaction to the last one, [but] it's not a conscious reaction necessarily. U2 is changing all the time and our own interests and tastes are changing all the time. [It's] almost [that] we need to requalify what the last record was by some new statement. Inevitably, the pendulum seems to swing."

Bono looked at me and asked: "Records haven't gotten any better, have they? They're supposed to sound better with this CD thing now and digital recording . . . but the records themselves haven't gotten any better. There's no point in hearing a bad record clearly; I'd rather hear a good record through crackles and scratches. A big reason why we have so many bad records in the eighties is that people are being cut off from the music they are making. [Recording] is an assembly line with a singer and guitar player just part of the process."

"Yeah," Edge agreed, "production has become the important thing now. Production was originally just the means at arriving at a recording, simply trying to capture what was already present between the band members, now it's become 'where it's at maaannn!' What we are really saying with this record, and to a certain extent *The Unforgettable Fire*, is that music should have that spontaneous live aspect. Modern production is all about control . . . our sessions, when they're the most successful, are totally out of control."

Bono jumped in, adding: "You get a lot more self-confidence as you make a few records, [but] when you start out you're intimidated by the process of recording. I remember when we started making *Boy*, I was nineteen or twenty and I was still living at home with my father, just the two of us. I would come home, maybe three or four o'clock in the morning. I'd be sneaking up the stairs 'cause I didn't want to wake him up — he'd be in a bad mood. [But] he'd wake up and say, 'What time is it?'

IN GOD'S COUNTRY   161

I'd say, 'It's, uh, one [o'clock].' He'd say, 'How long have ya been working on that record?' and I'd say, 'A week.' He'd say, 'How long is the record?' I said, 'Forty minutes.' He'd say, 'Jeez, have ya not got it right
yet?' " Edge and I laughed while Bono continued. "I used to laugh at
that, you know—'the old man doesn't understand what it's like in the
recording studio'—but now I think he's right."

"He has a point," agreed Edge.

"He has a point!" Bono emphasized. "So, as we've grown older,
we've learned not to be intimidated by the process of recording . . . and we've seen through it as well. A lot of it is just bullshit.
You know, you walk into a recording studio and it's all this plate glass
and red lights and technology. It's all there to dazzle you so you don't
see what it's really about. It's about the moment when Edge hits a chord
that way or Larry backs up on a beat. That's what it's about. Think back
to your great records, probably a lot of them were recorded in the sixties
on four-track."

If U2 had gained fresh inspiration from a less-is-more approach
in recording the music, what about the songwriting? If anything, Bono's
words were even more complex than before. I commented to him, "You
can strip the music away from *The Joshua Tree* and read these lyrics as
poetry."

"It's not poetry," he replied, "it's words . . . but it's written
from the point of view of a person who believes in the power of words.
If that means a poet, sure. It's the first time I really wanted to write
words for songs; I used to make it up as I went along and just occasionally write down some words. 'Sunday Bloody Sunday' . . . we wrote
words to that. Actually, it was Edge's idea to approach that issue [of violence on 'Sunday Bloody Sunday'], [but] everybody thinks it's me because I'm the guy with the flag," he chuckled.

Edge, who had been gazing out the window, remarked, "So I
get the blame now."

Bono smiled and continued. "So, occasionally I used to write
down words on a piece of paper or tear my hair out while I was trying
to write words into the music, but now it's different. I think the success
of *The Joshua Tree* is that despite the bleak landscape of some of the songs,
somehow or another it's an uplifting record. You see, we got this thing
we got to carry around with us about U2—we're uplifting, we're supposed to write these anthems—"

"Well, you've built the house," I retorted.

The two exploded in laughter before Bono conceded, "Okay!

Got to live in it! The way to be optimistic is not to shut your eyes and close your ears. As a word writer I had to write things with a lot more detail on this record than I ever did before. That meant lifting the stones and writing about what was underneath the stones—the underbelly of the landscapes . . . what was under the skin of it."

"U2's sense of humor doesn't really show through this album," I commented.

Edge laughed and replied, "That's . . . very true!"

"Does it show through any album?"

"I don't know if it ever does," answered Bono. "It's probably on stage more than it is on record. I think 'Trip Through Your Wires' is a laugh a minute myself 'cuz it's an antagonistic song with a wink."

Edge added, "Ask Leonard Cohen what he feels like—poor guy probably gets this all the time." Then, turning serious, he added: "[But] I don't know if I'd want Leonard Cohen to laugh in his records . . . you know what I'm saying? Some people can express certain emotions powerfully and others not so well. We've never tried to have a laugh on record, maybe we instinctively know that it's not going to be for us."

Bono continued, "It's just like a filmmaker who's attracted to making a certain kind of film, like Martin Scorsese or even Alan Parker. These are men that make movies about the 'other side,' and we're interested in the 'other side.' By that I mean I'm interested in violence . . . I despise violence, but I'm interested in it. I'm interested in the spiritual side of the human being, but I'm also interested in the sexuality of people. There's nothing I don't want to write about, but as a word writer and as a band, we don't get into this sort of 'hey-ho, let's go' kind of thing. We just haven't worked that out—"

"We're all closet Beastie Boys fans, really!" shouted Edge as he got up to leave for soundcheck.

"I'm into Megadeth!" Bono shouted after him.

After Edge left, I asked Bono about the American folk, blues, and country music influence on U2 that Edge had been talking about earlier. "You're joining a grand tradition of musicians coming over [from Europe] and discovering the 'roots.' "

"When we started off as a group, the last thing we wanted was to sound like anyone else. In fact, we rejected rock and roll in the old sense, you know . . . the twelve-bar blues format. We really rejected it because so many bands back there on Baggot Street in the strip in Dublin were playing this music into the ground. With U2 we wanted to develop an original sound and bring a new point of view to rock and roll, and I think we've done that. So now we are in a position where we can open ourselves up to outside influences in a way that wouldn't have been so good for us early on. But, I don't think we want to be overcome by these influences; we want to learn from the spirit of it rather than the form of it."

He continued excitedly: "There's a great spirit in those bluesmen — as a writer [I find] there's a poetic spirit at the heart of Robert Johnson to see. 'Blues coming down like a hail, blues coming down like a hail' — these are words that I would write. I much prefer the American writing — like Irish writing, there's a more generous spirit at the heart of it . . . it's a lot more folk-oriented."

"You're in love with our heritage."

"Yeah. I read of Woody Guthrie, you know . . . 'This Land Is Your Land' . . . and these are good songs. That's why we're playing 'People Get Ready' in the set — because it's a great American song and it's so simple. That line: 'Faith is the key to open the doors and the borders,' says it all to me as an Irishman."

"It's like 'Knockin' on Heaven's Door.' "

"Yeah, a gospel song. I learned the chords [to 'Knockin' on Heaven's Door'] from the Alarm, from Mike [Peters]. I'm a real shit guitar player; if I ever sit down with somebody who's got a guitar, I'll see if I can steal some chords."

"I think a lot of people have this impression of Bono being a very together person who knows exactly where he's going and exactly what he wants."

"I'm not at all like that," he laughed. "I find it amusing that people think I'm together [because] I'm the most untogether person I know. In the band, they just say, 'here comes chaos.' Oh, I want to be together — it's my ambition to one day get my own life in order and tie it up with string and be as organized as somebody like Adam."

"Adam's organized?"

"Clayton's unbelievable. Field Marshal Clayton! For a guy who can stay out all night, if he needs to be up at eight o'clock, he'll be there at eight o'clock on the button." Bono turned more serious, adding: "Music is the one thing I really look after . . . I don't look after myself as much as the songs I write. As a result, personal relationships suffer . . . your friendships . . . your family. I might be untogether as a person, but not as far as U2 is concerned. I'm very grateful to be in U2 and I care about it, so I look after it. Without it, I wouldn't know where I'd be as a person — I think I'd make a pretty shit bank manager! You know,

I worked as a petrol pump attendant once. Can you imagine me as a pet-rol pump attendant? It was pretty bad. I took the job 'cause I could write words while the cars weren't coming in. Then they had this oil strike and there were queues of cars, and I had to stand there at the pumps. I had to give it up."

"Despite success, you haven't compromised your music at all to cope with a larger audience," I observed.

"You see, rock and roll music — if it's to be inspirational, it's got to be challenging. You've got to find new sounds on the guitar, you've got to find new ways of approaching a four-four beat. Rock and roll still needs innovation and there's a lot out there. It might mean that you sell less records because you're not doing what people want you to do, but what difference does it really make to us? We've been blessed with suc-cess, no worries about where the next dollar is going to come from. We're well looked after and therefore we can do what we want to do. What a great position to be in! I think the only commitment we must make is to continue to do that."

That night, U2 tore into its second Summit show, all traces of onstage rustiness gone. Spirits were running high afterward, the hum of backstage conversation positive and excited as I ran into Bono. "You coming?" he asked.

"Huh?"

"Ask Ellen, she'll take care of you!" he shouted, disappearing down the hallway. Apparently, Paul McGuinness and the band mem-bers had decided that it was a good time to throw a party for its hard-working staff, so Ellen directed me to a waiting limo with Edge and two of his cousins who lived in Texas. Out of the arena and into the warm Houston night, the caravan motored through the city streets on its way to a secret destination. As midnight closed in, the cars pulled up to a bar called the L.A. Club. Far from the world of neon lights, pulsing sounds, and crowds suggested by its name, the nightclub seemed sleepy, with scarcely more than a dozen patrons hanging around to watch a talented country-rock band perform. Paul arranged a deal with the manager to close the doors to the public, offering to cover the bill for the U2 en-tourage plus anyone who was in the club when we arrived.

Video producer Barry Devlin had brought a film crew from Dublin to film the band from its opening rehearsals through the South-west leg of the tour. Accompanied by Anne-Louise Kelly, who had been freed from her desk duties in U2's Dublin management office to organize the project, Barry's team would turn out a minidocumentary for Irish television and also MTV in the States. The video crew had been every-where: in the hotel for interviews, onstage during U2's thunderous shows, and in the dressing room when the sweaty band members were tossed towels after their concert. Not about to miss this action, Devlin's team arrived at the club in time for the first round of drinks. While beer was the item on most everyone's mind, Bono suggested that in the spirit of the great Southwest, as many as were able should drink tequila shots. Devlin's team walked around the room, hanging a microphone on a long boom over everyone's heads while the camera caught all the gaiety. But the video crew soon recorded something much more substantial when Bono, Edge, Adam, and Larry decided that they wanted to play some music.

Borrowing instruments from the country-rock group and ac-cepting accompaniment from a couple of its members, the Irish band-mates shuffled somewhat unsteadily across the dance floor to the stage. Surprised, everyone in the party crowded around in a semicircle as Bono led the group into Johnny Cash's "I Walk the Line," liberally changing the verses to make jokes about Edge, Larry, and Adam. Edge fondled an acoustic guitar and his voice took on a lazy drawl to sing the thirties country standard "Lost Highway." Bono accompanied on gui-tar, Larry lightly slapped the snare, and Adam curled up to the side with a bass. It was easy to imagine the four of them sporting straw hats and homemade instruments on the dusty porch of some rural, weatherbeat-en shack. The lucky gathering of forty or fifty people slipped into true hootenanny spirit, dancing and shouting encouragement along with the music. Anne-Louise, Barry, and the television crew were mesmerized, and even Paul McGuinness and his staff stood captivated.

Although it was easy to imagine the members of U2 sitting to-gether in rehearsals working out new songs in this way since the time they had come together as a band, to actually see them onstage strum-ming through an acoustic rave-up of American country standards was quite revealing. The impromptu club session underscored everything that Bono and Edge had been speaking about that afternoon — U2 was getting back to the roots, obviously enjoying every moment of their mu-sical journey. The band stripped "I Still Haven't Found What I'm Look-ing For" to the bare bones, and the acoustic treatment sounded as noble and powerful as it had during the Summit concert. Then they slipped comfortably back into the country groove, finishing up with another Johnny Cash standard, "Folsom Prison Blues." The small crowd burst into applause as the band stood up and thanked their accompanying musicians. They downed a few last-call drinks before heading back to the hotel. Barry Devlin smiled while his crew packed up their equipment; clearly he'd been in the right place at the right time. If one tried to capture U2 in a single picture frame, one might choose a shot of the band raging onstage or intimately creating together in the recording studio. But what Devlin had on tape was the best of both: U2 as a musical unit in its most candid state.

The view from behind stage—April, 1985.   (DEBORAH PADOVA)

Sharing at the Worcester Centrum—April 1985.
(HEIDI LA SHAY)

"The audience is our backdrop"—Edge, Adam, and Larry playing "360" in April 1985.   (DEBORAH PADOVA)

U2 returns to the Paradise Theater—Edge and Adam at a Boston press conference at the club on September 21, 1987.   (LORRAINE M.)

U2's ace in the hole—Boston press conference September 21, 1987.   (LORRAINE M.)

"All I got is a red guitar, three chords, and the truth"—Bono at the free San Francisco concert November 8, 1987.   (ROBERT SOMOHANO)

Filming *Rattle and Hum*—onstage in San Francisco.   (ROBERT SOMOHANO)

U2's front line—Hampton Coliseum, Virginia, December 1987.   (SUSAN AND
VALERIE SASSAMAN)

Bono as the Fly—Boston Garden, March 17, 1992. (TED GARTLAND, copyright
© 1992 *The Boston Herald*)

14

FUSS AN' HOLLER

ESS THAN a week after U2 hit its stride onstage in Houston, the band arrived on the West Coast. After a pair of shows in San Diego, the group settled in Los Angeles for a five-night stand at the Sports Arena, taking a one-day break in the middle for Easter Sunday. When Bob Dylan surprised everyone by showing up at one L.A. show, the band invited him onstage for an obligatory rendition of "Knockin' on Heaven's Door." While U2 huddled with the legendary artist, an incredible din of anticipation filled the arena as the capacity crowd waited impatiently for the song to begin. This was not the first time Bono and Dylan had performed together—Bono had jumped onstage at Dylan's Slane Castle performance in 1984—but once again the occasion was completely unrehearsed, as Edge mentioned during a live interview program I cohosted for the D.I.R. Radio Network in September 1987. "We were [onstage] trying to work out the chords of 'Knockin' on Heaven's Door' and Bob didn't remember them! It made me feel a bit better." They proudly picked their way through the song, then tackled "I Shall Be Released," to the delight of the screaming audience.

"As we were leaving stage," Bono related in the interview, "I said, 'Those songs are gonna last forever, Bob.' And he said, 'Your songs are gonna last forever too—the only thing is, no one's gonna be able to play them.' They're hard to figure out, you know?"

If the series of 15,000-seat-arena sellouts wasn't evidence enough of U2's popularity, *The Joshua Tree*'s ascent to number one on that week's *Billboard* album chart certainly was. Instead of spending months building steadily in sales to climb the chart, the new release had blasted to the top in only four weeks. Backstage, Adam remarked that U2's number one amazed him. "I never thought we'd be in a battle with Madonna for the top of the charts!" Todd Everett, writing for the *Los Angeles Herald* on April 20, confirmed that U2 "draws the kind of audience response which has come to be associated with only a small number of pop icons. What had been, only a few years ago, a small, fanatic following has become a large fanatic following, comparable to Springsteen disciples and (Grateful) Deadheads."

Chris Willman, reviewing the concerts for the *Los Angeles Times*, noted that the group exuded a new maturity onstage. "[Bono's] stage antics have sometimes bordered on theatricality disguised as spontaneity. This time, though, there was little of the overt crowd manipulation that he has indulged in so heavily before, and more sense of genuine humility. Of course, being less manipulative, [Bono] runs the risk of being less charismatic. But for those to whom the music means more than charisma, it's worth losing a little of that old electricity for the sake of seeing U2 mature musically — and the group will need that maturity to make the transition from 'Band of the Eighties' to band of the nineties."

Not only did U2 receive acclaim from the Los Angeles press and a glowing album review from *Rolling Stone*, but in April the band also advanced into the pages of both *Time* and *Newsweek*. These bastions of mainstream American culture were not often penetrated by rock and roll, but U2 crashed through the barrier with articles only one week apart. The *Newsweek* feature, entitled "An Irish Pied Piper of Rock," reported: "In concert, the grandeur of their music fills an arena like a pipe organ in a cathedral. U2 is tapping a big audience tired of the empty glitz of oversynthesized pop." The group secured the even greater honor of nabbing *Time's* cover story, "Rock's Hottest Ticket," a feat that even the most ardent U2 supporter probably couldn't have predicted. The band members stood under the familiar magazine logo while a tiny photo of Mikhail Gorbachev peered from the upper right as if in reproach to the four young Irish lads who had stolen his international spotlight.

Bob Catania's premonition about the Top 40 potential of "With or Without You" was confirmed as the single soared into the upper reaches of the *Billboard* chart. By the members' own admission, U2 had not attempted to design a song for success on the singles charts, but they were astounded by the ease with which "With or Without You" flew past the band's previous highwater mark of number thirty-three (reached eventually by "Pride" in 1984). In retrospect, it's clear that Island

Records and U2 had all the necessary elements for the chart assault perfectly in place. First, without catering directly to the pop format, the band had penned a remarkably versatile single; soft and lilting in mood to please conservative mainstream tastes, yet visceral enough to satisfy most rock and roll fans. Urged along by its lovely, indelible melody, Bono's description of a painful, frustrating relationship that was impossible to disengage from touched a common sentiment in listeners. Next, U2 had achieved a significant level of national fame without the benefit of a hit single. The band's further success was almost assured as it sold out arena after arena and the members' faces appeared in America's most widely read magazines and newspapers. Situations were now reversed: Top 40 radio scrambled to become involved with a phenomenon that many of its listeners were already clamoring about. Finally, Island Records unloaded the largest promotional budget in its history to ensure that the single and album would not be lost in the flood of new releases each week. The label backed up its promotions with a massive merchandising effort to guarantee visibility of U2's product once it was in stores.

When "With or Without You" hit number one in *Billboard* on May 8, the band members shared the rare distinction of not only possessing their first top-ranked single and album, but having them both in that position at the same time. The event occurred during U2's three-day stint at the Civic Center in Hartford, Connecticut. Onstage, Bono didn't make a big deal about the achievement — he just mentioned the fact near the end of the show and thanked the audience for its support. The main celebration was found backstage among fifteen Irish journalists who had flown in to review the concert and follow U2 through a series of tour dates in the New York City area. That the group had captured the number-one-selling album *and* single slots in America's most widely accepted record sales chart left no small impression on the Irish writers, who labeled the event proof that U2 had conquered the United States. *Hot Press* writer Liam Mackey noted that the chart positions, wildfire media coverage, and skyrocketing demand for U2 concert tickets had turned the *Joshua Tree* tour into *the* tour of 1987. But he also reminded his readers that in the midst of all the hoopla, "the four people who make up U2 have still to do what they've been doing an awful lot for the last ten years, albeit now against a backdrop of staggering dimensions — they've got to walk onstage, pick up their instruments, and for around one hundred minutes, show committed fans and first-timers — and perhaps even remind each other — just what it is they've got that's raising all this fuss an' holler."

Immediately before its march into Hartford, U2 had completed a three-night stand in Massachusetts at the Centrum, where the band uncovered some new surprises in concert. Paying homage to the seminal American rock and roll that had grown from country-western and rhythm and blues roots, the band churned out a gritty and suitably sloppy version of Eddie Cochran's 1959 classic, "C'mon Everybody." On another night, they strolled onstage while the arena's houselights were still brilliantly lit, joining in with John Lennon's version of the 1961 Ben E. King hit, "Stand By Me," which had been playing over the P.A. system as warm-up music. Most people in the crowd were still talking with friends or finding their seats when they realized that Bono was singing duet with Lennon's vocals and Larry was echoing the drumbeat. The lights were killed, the tape faded, and U2 continued on with the song, receiving a tumultuous greeting. Bono mentioned backstage afterward that the group had also performed the unexpected opening during its final concert in Los Angeles. "I enjoy seeing the surprise on everybody's face when we walk on the stage with the lights on."

A glance into that vast sea of faces would confirm the constantly changing makeup of U2's audience. The group's longtime supporters were now being joined by a new breed of fan spawned by the popular success of "With or Without You" at Top 40 radio. Many of these people were younger listeners for whom CHR and MTV provided the greatest exposure to pop music. Some hadn't even reached junior high school when *Boy* was released in the States, but were now discovering U2 through its new hit single. With the band's exploding success, these mainstream-oriented fans turned out in ever increasing droves, soon outnumbering the veteran U2 fans they were joining. Although it's fair to assume that many of these recent converts were inspired by U2's social messages, a great portion of them were clearly far more interested in the band's popular appeal and star status. In the competitive battle to obtain tickets to any U2 concert, these new supporters began to gobble up more and more of the available seats. At the Centrum, U2's members became exasperated with some of these fans while performing a version of Peggy Seeger's sobering ballad "Springhill Mining Disaster," which described the poor working conditions and frightful sufferings of coal miners. Frequent interruptions by screaming fans threatened to destroy the delicate power of the piece, prompting Bono at one point to halt the song and yell in frustration, "This is not the Beatles! This is U2!"

Since its Stateside debut in 1980, U2's popularity had grown at a fairly even pace, allowing the band to adjust gradually to the mounting demands of fame. But now, with success accelerating at a frantic rate, the band members were finding it difficult to cope with the rush of attention. The *Boston Herald* reprinted quotes from a pair of U2 interviews, with Irish deejay Dave Fanning and Dublin's *Sunday Tribune* conducted in the summer after the band returned home from its U.S. tour, indicating that the members were displeased with the compromises they had been forced to make. Larry observed: " 'The more press we get, the more difficult it becomes to be a human being in [America]. It's the price you pay, unfortunately.'

" 'We try to find manageable numbers of people to talk to, outside of record shops or a few hours after a gig,' said bassist Adam Clayton. 'It's just if you've got like 5,000 people outside a venue, you can't go out and talk to them. It's a pointless thing.'

" 'We *are* cut off and we *are* separated from our fans. I don't like it but we've got to live with it,' said Bono. 'I miss being able to meet someone after a concert and go back to their place and have coffee, or sleep on their floor.' "

During the spring tour of America, U2 maintained an aftershow hospitality suite which various members of the band visited. Although Edge and Adam were the usual envoys to this backstage area, Larry and Bono often walked down to the room as well. Their guests most often included radio and music retail personnel, contest winners, or longtime friends. The band members, however, were more interested in meeting other fans — the loyal ones who had waited in line for hours or days to buy tickets, the people who were forced to purchase seats far back in the arenas' rearmost areas, and those for whom U2 had become an important inspiration and comfort in their lives. Bono, in particular, was determined to make sure that he could still step from behind the protective screen that Paul McGuinness had assembled around the band and meet these "authentic" members of his audience. After one Centrum concert, he vanished for over an hour, finding a safe spot at the backstage door to sign autographs and chat with an eager group of fans clustered tightly around him. Bono's disappearance caused no small stir in U2's security ranks before he was finally located. On another night, Bono stood in the sunroof of his limo as it pulled away from the Centrum, shaking hands with an overjoyed crowd until he was submerged in outstretched hands and had to be dragged down through the hatch into the car.

U2 completed its tour with six nights in New Jersey's Meadowlands Arena, then left for Europe and a pair of hometown concerts at

Croke Park, where the Irish media examined the Dublin heroes in further detail. As the country's most successful music group ever and a major export from the Emerald Isle, U2 commanded the highest level of attention from the rock press and the country's mainstream newspapers. Much of this scrutiny was particularly intense because the band members had become multimillionaires in a country where unemployment and poverty were typical for much of the population. Some press members called into question U2's ability to be a champion of spiritual and humanitarian causes when it had achieved vast financial success in America. "I'm often asked how I can write a song about being unemployed when I'm very much employed," Bono told Dublin's *Sunday Tribune.* "The answer is I can't—but I do and will continue to do. The question of course is why the system hands out prizes to its greatest critics . . . I feel we *must* bite the hand that feeds us, even if it's making us fat."

B. P. Fallon, on the air at R.T.E. radio in Dublin, pressured Edge (who still drove around the city in a beat up Volkswagen beetle): "When you're touring, and traveling around, you do it on quite an expensive level, don't you? I mean, your own plane and stuff like that."

"We do it now 'cause we can afford to do it, and to be honest, whatever we can do to make touring that little bit easier, we will do. Because, what tends to happen is the shows start to suffer if you're wiped out by traveling forty-eight hours in a bus, when you could be actually on a plane doing the journey in three. As far as backstage, it's like we just look after people as we hope we'd be looked after at other shows. But I don't think it's ever wasteful or inappropriate for the situation."

U2's position in the face of such criticism was easily defensible, but the members were now answering many more questions about the pressures, and their accountability and responsibilities with regard to success than about the particulars of their art. This trend continued, with U2's name even reaching the international gossip columns. With much of the media focused on U2's stardom and away from the band's substance, there was a constant need for the members to reaffirm that they played in a rock and roll group that existed for the primary purpose of satisfying their creative needs. Success had certainly arrived for the four young lads from Dublin, and artistic advancement had been the aim and driving force that got them there. But, in a rush for headlines, the press often ended up ignoring U2's greatest asset: the enduring power and beauty of its music. Irish writer John Waters commented in a June 1987 piece for *In Dublin* magazine, "U2 are important not because they drive around in stretch limos, or get on the cover of *Time*, or get to play with Bob Dylan, but because of their music. That seems axiomatic, but sometimes you get to wondering if it needs to be said. The media in recent months has been focusing on the shadow of U2's achievement and not enough on the substance."

Bono added in the same article: "Some of the recent pieces on us have concentrated perhaps too much on the U2 *phenomenon* and my comments, and forgotten above all we're a rock band. The music is articulate in a way that I'm not. I'm almost a liability to the group because I'm so open — I haven't yet learnt how to hold the cards close to my chest. But we really don't take ourselves too seriously, *really*. The music's serious."

The single package for "With or Without You" was a good example of U2's seriousness. The stark black-and-white cover photo, taken by Anton Corbijn with a Death Valley backdrop, pictured Edge staring wearily from a crouch — as if he'd just dragged his fingers through the expired topsoil or was waiting for a passerby's sympathetic handout. On the back cover, the band members loitered in front of an abandoned, dilapidated building, with bleak expressions on their faces. The entire photo design, projecting an atmosphere of desperation, perhaps out of the Great Depression era, would be repeated for each successive single from *The Joshua Tree*. The seven-inch and twelve-inch versions of "With or Without You" both featured two extra songs not available on the album. "Luminous Times (Hold on to Love)" slowly built a dense web of instruments around a simple echoed piano, while "Walk to the Water" began in a shimmering glissando of piano notes that gave way to guitar and a slapping tom-tom beat.

Taking its cue from the enormous positive reaction to "I Still Haven't Found What I'm Looking For" on album radio, Island released the track to CHR stations in June as U2's second single from *The Joshua Tree*. The artwork for the release used the same colors and format as the first single, incorporating another photo from the desert shoot. This time Larry was pictured, leaning against a wooden wall with his eyes squeezed shut and his face a mask of pained resignation. Two more nonalbum songs were utilized on the B-side, including the stunning rocker "Spanish Eyes," a fully produced gem that nabbed its own significant share of AOR airplay and showed up in some live sets that fall. The track was one of Edge's favorites from the *Joshua Tree* sessions, as he revealed during the Island interview in Houston: "I think it's one of the best things we've done for a while—from the sort of 'three-minute magic' standpoint. It just comes in and WHAM!—it's rock and roll." In contrast, the other extra track, "Deep in the Heart," was a spacey concoction of echoed guitar squawks and psychedelic feedback.

CHR responded enthusiastically to "I Still Haven't Found What I'm Looking For," turning the song into one of the biggest hits of the summer of 1987. Once again, in its new direction toward a leaner, more roots-oriented folk sound, U2 had unconsciously produced a single with massive popular appeal. The title, conceived by Edge, was developed by Bono into a set of lyrics about spiritual yearning that easily evoked a universal image of searching for the perfect love(r). Radio airplay was heavily reinforced by an eye-catching video that had been filmed when the band played Las Vegas in April. Capturing the members strolling through the sights and sounds of the city's neon-lit strip, the colorful video became an MTV staple. The appealing musical attributes of the single plus its unprecedented exposure catapulted it into the number one slot in *Billboard* by early August, making U2 a two-time visitor to the pinnacle of the chart in only four months. Throughout the summer, the band's circle of popularity widened exponentially to include both young and old converts who didn't even count themselves as fans of rock and roll. It was no wonder that tickets for U2's fall visit to America vanished instantly, even when massive stadium concerts were added to the schedule.

For the album's third single, Island once again followed the precedent set by album radio, releasing a song to CHR that had been highly successful on rock stations. "Where the Streets Have No Name," the fiery opening track from *The Joshua Tree*, hit record stores as U2 reached America in September for its latest tour. As with the two previous singles, the cover featured a solitary member of U2 in a striking black-and-white Corbijn photograph. This time, Adam was tapped for the honor, his body nearly lost in the shadow of a rusted tin wall as he gazed over the lonely ruins of a ghost town. "Where the Streets Have No Name" took U2 to the now familiar upper reaches of the *Billboard* singles chart, hitting number thirteen by November. The video for the song was filmed during a surprise rooftop performance in Los Angeles which had lured hundreds of bystanders and snarled traffic before it was shut down by police. Inspired by the Beatles' legendary 1969 set from atop its own Apple headquarters in London (partially preserved in the *Let It Be* movie), U2's filmed performance did much to bolster the success of the single it accompanied. Bono commented during the D.I.R. Radio

Network interview: "It's just that a lot of bad things often hold up a city. That day it was some good things — rock and roll music held up the city, stopped the traffic. I'd like to see a bit more of that, wouldn't you?"

The twelve-inch single package added some exciting extra tracks, including U2's version of "Silver and Gold," previously written by Bono and performed with Keith Richards and Ron Wood for the *Sun City* album two years before. The song had been re-recorded during U2's summer break, updated from its smoldering folk-blues treatment into a full-fledged rocker. During the D.I.R. interview, when I asked Bono about the reworked track, he responded: "I've listened to Jerry Lee Lewis's 'Whole Lot of Shakin' Going On' a hundred times today. That's sort of what we're interested in at the moment. 'Silver and Gold' is rock and roll — U2 style." The band included another B-side track called "The Sweetest Thing," a bouncy love song in frolicking reggae style which contrasted with the more melancholy tone found in much of U2's recent music. A disarming piano figure introduced the melody before whip-cracking drums snapped the beat to attention. Bono's occasional falsetto made him sound like a schoolboy high on his first love, and the infectious chorus begged the listener to sing along. The twelve-inch version of "Where the Streets Have No Name" also featured one additional cut entitled "Race Against Time," a diversion with snatches of vocals and heavily distorted guitar that would have sounded comfortable as a chase sequence on some sci-fi movie soundtrack.

It seemed inevitable that Island would release another single — if only to complete Corbijn's set of four black-and-white sleeves. In November, "In God's Country" appeared, with a photo of Bono crouched on a rocky field glancing bitterly at the camera in front of an abandoned factory and water tower. U2 had depleted its store of extra material, so the B-side featured two tracks from the album: "Bullet the Blue Sky" and "Running to Stand Still." As album radio rushed to embrace the single, CHR showed only a cursory interest and it floundered on the charts, failing to hit even the Top 40 in *Billboard*. A rippling, fast-moving rocker, "In God's Country" was a bit raucous for most mainstream radio stations. Matters certainly weren't helped by Island, which didn't heavily promote the song or even create a video to accompany it. The record company's absence of support was purely a commercial concern, since by that point the phenomenon of *The Joshua Tree* was largely over. However, U2's desire to release the last in a series of four artistically consistent singles won out, and "In God's Country" was released in the States anyway. (In Australia and New Zealand, the same picture sleeve was used for the single of "One Tree Hill," released to honor the memory of Greg Carroll in his native land.)

Since the latter part of the *Unforgettable Fire* tour in 1985, U2 had maintained a policy of not visiting local radio stations while on the road in America. Political infighting between radio programmers, Island Records, and U2's management was inevitable if the band members visited a station and then failed to drop in on the competition. In August 1987, Ellen invited me to participate in a plan to help U2 circumvent this political problem while simultaneously reaching out to its fans. A special live interview program in which listeners could phone the band members on the air was set for September 8, just two days prior to U2's first fall tour date. The D.I.R. Radio Network, source of the "King Biscuit Flower Hour," would provide its satellite link from a tiny studio in New York City to subscriber stations all across North America. The show, entitled "Trip Through Your Wires," was structured to combine questions from three cohosts and live phone calls from fans, interrupted occasionally by some unreleased live versions of U2 songs.

Norm Winer, program director at WXRT-FM in Chicago, would anchor the broadcast along with Linda Ryan from KUSF-FM in San Francisco and myself. Ellen had expressed U2's continuing concern that America's noncommercial college radio stations be represented, and had invited Ryan, the enthusiastic music director at the University of San Francisco's campus station, to participate. When we arrived more than two hours before the broadcast, the incoming phone lines were already jammed with callers waiting on hold to speak with the band members. Surrounding the circular conference table covered with microphones, headphones, and notepads was a ring of ungainly-looking professional movie cameras. Their presence was quite unexpected — despite extensive preparations and an elaborate briefing, no one on U2's staff or from D.I.R. had informed the hosts that a documentary on the band was being filmed during the fall visit. The youthful movie director, Phil Joanou, was quick to apologize, and expressed confidence that the filming procedure wouldn't affect the interview program in the least.

When the band members arrived, their relaxed and jovial mood actually loosened the tension in the studio as airtime approached and D.I.R. staffers rushed about. Caterers brought in platters of food and drinks — Bono and Edge chose mineral water, Adam and Larry reached for beers. When Joanou mentioned it would be best for everyone just to act naturally and forget about his battery of movie cameras and operators, Bono thanked him facetiously for reminding us that they were there, earning a big grin from the director and laughs from all present. Hot, bright camera lights were switched on as the final moments counted down and the seven of us took our seats. Mitch Maketansky, D.I.R.'s broadcast coordinator, regularly called out the remaining minutes and yelled for everyone to put on their headphones as volume levels were set. In the final confusing moment, a caller who had resolutely waited on hold for over two hours to speak with the band was accidently disconnected. No one had time to worry about that, though, because Norm Winer's taped introduction to the show was already being broadcast to stations throughout the United States and Canada. The last technicians hurriedly exited the studio and ran into the adjoining control room to plaster themselves to the glass, wary for signs of trouble. "Good evening and welcome to 'Trip Through Your Wires' with U2 . . . . "

In contrast to the overriding image of seriousness associated with *The Joshua Tree* and its creators, the tone of the interview was light and often humorous. It began with the band members roasting their own drummer. Edge turned to Larry and asked, "Any jokes, Lawrence?"

"No, Edge."

"You've got a drummer joke," Bono reminded Edge.

"Okay. What do you call a guy who hangs around with a pile of musicians? The answer is . . . a drummer!"

As everyone laughed, Bono urged, "Hey Lawrence, tell them your drummer joke."

"That's a bit mean, asking a drummer to tell a drummer joke," Larry replied, but he told the joke anyway. "Three guys are sittin' down having a rap and the first guy says, 'I'm a nuclear scientist and I have an IQ of 170.' The next guy says, 'I have an IQ of 140 — I'm a neurosurgeon.' The next guy says, 'I have an IQ of seventy.' The other two guys say . . . ['You're a drummer!']."

Larry supplied the punch line when U2's first caller got on the line. The fan asked if the band members had any interests other than music. Bono began, "I'm particularly interested in petrol pumps at the moment, Edge grows flowers, Larry's very interested in Harley-Davidsons — the list goes on. I don't think the program's long enough for the list. What are you interested in?"

"Music!" the caller instantly replied.

Larry jumped in, "We've got very little interest in that. We're into lots of other things."

The next caller succeeded in introducing a more technical level to the program by asking Edge, "Which guitar neck feels most comfortable? I'm a guitarist and I study Edge very much, [but] I can't seem to get it professional sounding."

"I'm not a man who feels comfortable discussing such technical details as guitar necks," Edge began. "Generally I'm not particularly interested in the nuts and bolts so much—"

Bono interjected, "I heard somebody ask Edge the other day [while] showing him a pile of guitars which was his favorite, and he just said, 'The black one.' If you're a musician you should try to work it out for yourself. I think Edge would be the first to say don't copy him, don't copy anyone. Everybody's got something interesting to say, whether it's writing words or making music—just do it your own way. Trying to work out what Edge does, I've even tried to do that. I've picked up the same guitar, I've had it exactly on the same settings that the Edge puts it, put my fingers where he puts them, and just this godawful noise comes out!"

I ventured, "I heard you started doing your own music because you couldn't do other people's tunes when you first started."

"We were probably the worst cover group ever," Bono conceded. "We started out with a few Rolling Stones songs, even the Beach Boys. Can you imagine U2 playing the Beach Boys? We just started playing our own songs for that reason."

"Isn't it funny, here we are [almost] in 1988 and can't play any of our own songs—we're doing all these cover versions!" Larry added, cracking up everyone at the table.

U2 had discussed the fascination traditional American musical styles held for them in earlier interviews. Now, the band members illustrated their love of one of those styles in particular when Edge replied, purely tongue-in-cheek, to a question about possible U2 side projects. "We plan to form a country-western group called the Dalton Brothers and we're going to give up the rock and roll. See, I was told by a very wise old man that there was no money in rock and that country was where the real money was to be made." At that point, an acoustic guitar was produced and the Dalton Brothers (Bono and Edge) performed a maudlin country-western tearjerker called "Lucille." At the end of the program, they also took a stab at "Lost Highway."

"My hero at the moment is Willie Nelson, as you just heard," Bono admitted. "I think he's the coolest cat and I like the way he sings."

Perhaps a more obvious inspiration to U2 was the music and

lyrics of John Lennon. Certainly the words of "Sunday Bloody Sunday" and "Bullet the Blue Sky" echoed Lennon's stance on behalf of the peace movement. It was also no accident that his version of "Stand by Me" was the last song played from the speakers before U2 walked onstage each night. A caller asked Bono, "What are your thoughts about John Lennon and what he had to say?"

"I like the way he wrapped up the truth in a simple phrase or two, like 'all you need is love.' I like the way he could write a soul song like 'Crippled Inside.' It's just so simple — 'one thing you can't hide, is when you're crippled inside.' He spoke the truth about himself." Revealing a sore spot that would result in next year's "God Part II," Bono continued by venting his rage at author Albert Goldman. "Some guy is writing a book about him [John Lennon], the same guy that wrote the book about Elvis Presley and attempted to portray Elvis as a rock and roll idiot. This same asshole is going to try to really do John Lennon over and portray him as a rock and roll fool, probably. Well, the difference is this: John Lennon already told us he was an asshole, so we don't need to hear it from somebody else. That's the difference between John Lennon and a lot of other performers: he put his life on the line for all it was — good and bad. I respect him for that."

Winer asked Bono, "There have been certain performers over the years who have committed themselves to social and political concerns. What do you feel your role is in terms of making people aware of reality?"

"I wouldn't take on the job of making people aware of reality, I'd take on the job of making *myself* aware of reality," he answered. "Being in a rock and roll band certainly removes you from reality, so it's a full-time job." (Bono clarified his answer to me after the broadcast. "We can't tell people what to do, they'll just continue to come back and never think for themselves. We sing about issues that have an effect on us and hopefully that causes some in our audience to think about them too.")

As "Trip Through Your Wires" entered its second hour, Bono responded to my question concerning U2's rise to fame. Was he afraid of being placed on a pedestal by fans and worshiped as a rock and roll icon? "I'm not afraid of them, but I don't like it, none of us like it," he replied curtly. Then in a reassuring tone he added: "It's a good thing to be into music, it's a good thing to be into a rock and roll band. I'm into rock and roll bands! It's a good thing to respect somebody . . . I respect a lot of people and I like to be respected. But when it goes further than that — when people want to find out the meaning of life just because you can sing in tune, because you can write some songs . . . you've got the wrong guy. I heard that John Lennon, when he used to be sitting in bars, before people would even get up to him he'd say, 'Look, I don't know the truth! You probably know more than I know!' I feel a bit like that . . . especially because I've got a faith, because I believe in God. People think I've got all the answers when in fact I've just got a whole list of questions."

I had another question. "There are a lot of bands who go out on the road with huge corporate sponsors to pick up the tab on their tours. As of yet U2 has not resorted to that, do you think there'd ever be a plan to?" I asked.

Bono practically dove on that one. He answered sharply, "You might as well put on a suit and tie and go work for them! There are rare exceptions when it's okay to stand beside something: Larry stood beside Harley-Davidson and put his name to that because it's an American company making something special — the Harley-Davidson motorbike. But the idea of getting involved in the whole big business thing is just not interesting. It's not the right thing for a rock and roll band to do, I feel."

"The problem is that we've never found a beer that we liked enough to be sponsored with," Edge joked. "Guinness, we might consider."

Bono and Edge closed the live interview by slipping into their Dalton Brothers routine once again, harmonizing on "The Lost Highway." Joanou's cameras had whirred quietly for the entire ninety minutes, but the footage would never be used in the movie, *Rattle and Hum*. The film crew began to dismantle their equipment for the next shoot as the taped closing credits rolled past on the radio and the door to the studio burst open to admit a dozen D.I.R. managers and technicians who offered their congratulations. The celebration spread as photos were snapped and the band members signed autographs. Following the interview, how did the members of one of the world's most popular bands on the eve of a mammoth U.S. tour spend the remainder of their evening? They returned to one of their favorite haunts — a dusty pool hall down the street in Manhattan where no one recognized U2, and wouldn't really care if they did.

15

THE DALTON BROTHERS RIDE AGAIN

THE ITINERARY for U2's 1987 fall tour of the United States was announced in a nationally syndicated broadcast from New York City on August 14. Ticket sales information for individual concerts was released soon afterward by each city's local media, sending fans across the country into a flurry of preparation. The rush for seats intensified when rumors began to circulate that this would be U2's last tour for a few years. On September 10, after only one day's rehearsal, U2 opened the tour by tearing up Long Island's Nassau Coliseum in a two-hour extravaganza. At one point, Jimi Hendrix's Woodstock festival version of "The Star Spangled Banner" screamed from the P.A. speakers. As much as any song, Hendrix's incendiary flailing of the national anthem vividly recalled America's turmoil during the Vietnam War years. As Edge launched out of the recorded wall of Hendrix feedback with his own shrieking intro to "Bullet the Blue Sky" and Bono hurled himself into the song's stinging lyrics, U2 provided a subtle but sobering reminder that not much had changed in eighteen years — only the dates, locations, and body counts. From the metallic glory of "Bullet the Blue Sky" and throughout the remainder of the two shows in Nassau Coliseum, U2 exhibited a seasoned control of its enormous energy.

For the first time in America, U2 would include many stadium concerts in its tour schedule. The band was no stranger to these massive shows, having pulled off the 1983 US Festival, concerts in Dublin's 50,000-person-capacity Croke Park, the 1985 Live Aid appearance in London's Wembley Stadium, the Amnesty International tour finale at

Giants Stadium, and various European festivals over the years. Following the same logic that had brought them from clubs to theaters and then into arenas, the move into stadiums was necessary to satisfy America's demand for tickets. But the decision to perform in venues originally designed for sporting events — huge and impersonal surroundings for any concert — immediately drew fire from critics. Edge explained to James Henke in *Rolling Stone*: "It was a difficult decision for us, because we've always tried to create a feeling of intimacy in any show. People said we couldn't do it in arenas, and I really believe we did. When it came to stadiums, we really had to make the move, because if we didn't, it meant playing twenty nights in an arena, which we just couldn't face. Bruce Springsteen seems able to do that and retain his sanity, but any more than about six shows in one town and we start going totally wacky. It becomes like a job."

"A lot of times people talk about the good old days back when we used to play clubs," Bono mentioned in the "Trip Through Your Wires" interview. "I actually prefer being onstage in the open air or in a big place, because I think U2 make big music and we weren't really that good of a club band. We're all a little bit nervous playing these big stadiums, but we think that our music's going to work in that way."

Edge also responded in the March 1988 *Rolling Stone* interview to those who suggested that U2 had added the stadium shows to its itinerary purely for the sake of raking in more money. "There's no doubt that if you do exclusive stadium shows, you make a lot of money if they sell out. But what we did was a mixture of stadium shows and arena shows, which is the most uneconomical thing you can do. We didn't feel confident enough to play only stadiums, but we also didn't feel like we wanted to spend six or seven months just touring the United States [in arenas]."

Leapfrogging from arena concert to stadium show, U2 left the opening dates on Long Island for appearances in Philadelphia and New Jersey before reaching New England for a pair of concerts at the Boston Garden. Even though the legendary arena hosted two of the most successful sports teams in America, it was actually a decaying structure built over seventy years earlier with layers of fresh paint and two rows of modern skyboxes failing to obscure its creaking obsolescence. Joe O'Herlihy's usually superb sound mix was doomed in the sea of roof girders that crisscrossed high overhead. But from that same daunting mass of rafters hung a battalion of hockey and basketball championship flags, a rallying point for Boston's enormous pride in the Garden. It would be worth the extra trouble for U2 to perform here. In the spring, the Boston Garden's manager, Larry Moulter, had arranged for the band members to shoot baskets on the fabled Celtics parquet; now they were returning to do what they did best — play rock and roll.

Balconies brimming with fans hung down close to the stage and nearly every one of the Boston Garden's 15,500 seats was occupied by the time U2's crew declared itself ready to bring the band on. Little Steven and the Disciples of Soul had finished up a rhythmic set highlighted by a blistering version of "Sun City" and selections from Steven's latest album. The brightly dressed guitarist swirled onstage in his silks and scarves, a modern-day gypsy singing danceable yet strongly barbed protest anthems. U2 began with a leaden pulse, the taped Hendrix wail and angry thump of "Bullet the Blue Sky" ominously accompanied by stagelights drenching the band members in red and spotlights raking the audience with searching white fingers. Muscling its way into "Where the Streets Have No Name," U2 opened this show with a powerful one-two punch from *The Joshua Tree*.

Bono and Edge sported trophies from their southwestern visit — the former with a cowboy hat and the latter in his multi-colored Indian vest. But Edge's bright garment, as well as most of the stage, was suddenly plunged into darkness when nearly all of U2's spotlights and overhead stage lamps abruptly winked out. Since it was difficult for the band members to find their way around onstage, even for Bono to locate his microphone to make an announcement, the show ground to an immediate halt. With each passing minute it became more apparent that this problem wouldn't be remedied quickly, so rather than delay the performance any further, Bono called for the houselights to be turned on. "Our lighting rig has broken down," he explained. "[But] rock and roll doesn't need all these expensive lights and smoke bombs, [because] we have the spirit of Larry Bird with us tonight!" A tremendous shout went up at the mention of the Celtics' basketball star. U2 began "I Will Follow" and continued playing for another hour in the naked glare usually reserved for sporting events. Bono spent a lot of time chatting with the crowd, which he could now see clearly, and succeeded admirably in converting the hollow arena atmosphere into a warm nightclub glow. When Bono's vocal monitor broke down after "I Will Follow," preventing him from hearing himself through the band's sound mix, he sat down on the broken speaker cabinet, smiled resignedly, and said, "It looks like it's going to be like the old days — nothing works around here." Then he whipped out a harmonica and shouted, "I bet Larry Bird can play a better harmonica than I can!" With that, the band rolled into "Trip Through Your Wires" and Bono had no trouble matching Edge's rave-up guitar solo with a fine harmonica blow of his own.

"One Tree Hill" was a surprise addition because Bono had adamantly stated that his emotional studio performance of the eulogy could not be repeated. But now, with over a year between the band and Carroll's death, U2's members had decided to bring the song to life on-stage as a nightly tribute to their friend. The effort required much advance planning, however, since a synthesized background had to be created to handle the multilayered string and keyboard parts. U2 also added "Silver and Gold" to its set, though the scattered applause at Bono's announcement of the song indicated that only the most ardent fans recognized it. His long explanation about the anti-apartheid message and *Sun City* inspiration seemed to educate the remainder, though, and a strong reaction rewarded him by song's end. Some familiar cover choices, including the gospel-tinged "People Get Ready" and the slow arrangement of the Beatles' "Help!" rounded out U2's selection of twenty songs.

After scrambling about for an hour, the stage crew finally restored the stagelights. Someone killed the houselights and the crowd cheered, but it was actually disappointing to lose sight of the entire Boston Garden audience joyously dancing at its seats. The frenzied crowd eagerly recalled the four band members back onstage, Bono now clad in a Celtics jersey, to perform two encores, including the traditional concert-closing "40." Afterward in the dressing room, Bono was jubilant about the crowd's reaction, "especially with all of that . . . chaos." He felt invigorated enough to spend most of his after-show time checking out a Harley-Davidson that had been driven into the Garden's backstage tunnel, then disappeared on the borrowed bike with Ali, his wife, to show up later at a local rock club.

The following day, word spread about U2's memorable performance in the face of its technical obstacles. Local critics responded with barely controlled enthusiasm. The *Boston Globe* stated: "The poor spotlight operators might as well have gone back to their hotel. U2 carried on like troopers, forging an even closer bond with the audience." The mayor of Boston capped the celebratory spirit by bestowing honorary citizenships on the band members before they returned to the Garden for their second concert. During this show, U2 rearranged its set list — introducing more of the latest material, digging deep into its song catalog, and blasting out a potent metallic version of the Beatles' "Helter

Skelter." Once Bono began "I Still Haven't Found What I'm Looking For," the rapturous audience took over and sang two full verses a cappella before Larry even touched a drum. This inspired the group to attempt a version of "Spanish Eyes," which Bono declared as U2's first live performance of the song. Facing each other and counting out the start, the band members pounded into the beefy rhythm while Edge tossed out the jangling chords. Within seconds U2 had slipped into an assured control, but after Bono finished his lyrics it became apparent that the players still hadn't worked out a way to end the song in concert. The rhythm churned along while Bono glanced at his comrades in amusement and asked, "How do we end this?" Edge shrugged his shoulders, so Bono turned to Larry. "Try the drum break again." A spot to wind the song down was found there and U2 finished in laughter.

Curious about what the band members would do before and after their gigs, the Boston media trailed U2 like a pack of bloodhounds. Hordes of fans staked out the band's headquarters at the Four Seasons hotel across the street from the Boston Common. Rumors raced through the city: "The band is shooting a video on the North Shore!" and "They're playing a surprise gig at the Paradise tonight!" Although difficult to separate from the rest of the wild conjectures, those two speculations were actually based in truth, since Phil Joanou was still busy filming all aspects of the band's Boston visit, including an afternoon press conference held at the Paradise, the club where U2 had first played in Boston. But how different this visit to the Paradise was. In 1980, when an unknown Irish band finally landed in America with another equally anonymous headlining group, the media had barely blinked. Now television and newspaper reporters scrutinized U2's every move while local radio stations whipped their listeners into a frenzy by giving concert tickets away and fighting for exclusive interviews. Still, with the media storm churning all around it, the U2 camp remained calm. Edge slipped out to browse at some record stores while Bono hung out at a local rib grill, unperturbed by the patrons who walked over to converse and get autographs.

Joanou's movie project was not simply a television documentary or video clip, but a multi-million-dollar film feature backed by Paramount. U2's members had been impressed with the director despite his youth and relatively thin resume — twenty-seven with a U.S.C. film school diploma, two episodes of Steven Spielberg's *Amazing Stories*, and a feature film debut called *Three O'Clock High*. Joanou unexpectedly edged out competition from other directors including Jonathan

Demme, whose *Stop Making Sense* concert movie with Talking Heads had been widely hailed as one of the best in the genre. U2's members wanted something more personal than *Stop Making Sense*, so Joanou's enthusiasm and open-mindedness tipped the scales in his favor. In May 1987 he met the members of U2 on the road for the first time; quickly confirmed as their choice, he began sketching cinematic plans during the summer.

By August, U2 and Joanou had finalized their idea to film the group on the road during the fall leg of its American tour. With the band's music being the focus of the movie, Joanou would concentrate his efforts onstage at rehearsals and concerts, conducting interviews with the members and covering any relevant side projects such as hit-and-run studio recording. He occasionally veered a bit off course in his efforts to chronicle U2's tour, as *Rolling Stone* reported in February 1988. After Bono fell on a rain-soaked stadium stage in Washington, D.C., dislocating his shoulder, he was surprised by Joanou, whom he had lovingly dubbed "E.T." "They put me in an ambulance . . . I look up, and there's E.T. standing over me with this camera and his lights. I said, 'E.T., what the fuck are you doing in my ambulance?' And he said, 'Hey, you wanted me to make a documentary!' " That sequence would eventually be chopped from the final version of the movie, but Joanou still had plenty of footage to choose from. During three and a half months of following U2 around America, the crew would shoot 350,000 feet of sixteen-millimeter documentary film, 450,000 feet of thirty-five-millimeter concert footage, and a further 100,000 feet of interview segments. Joanou eventually edited this massive amount of film into a ninety-six-minute movie with about 9,000 feet of tape.

Two days after Bono's shoulder mishap, U2 returned to the Boston area for a concert at Sullivan Stadium, the outdoor home of the New England Patriots located thirty miles south of the city. The band had easily sold all of the football stadium's 60,000 tickets, even with its recent Boston Garden sellouts. Tucked behind the massive complex of steel girders towering over the stage, Joanou held a late afternoon strategy meeting in the film team's command center. As frequent outbreaks of rain pelted the protective tent cover, a bank of monitor screens gazed blankly at the assembled technicians. Voicing instructions through a microphone headset, the director would coordinate his operators' efforts by observing their camera work on this control board. When U2 arrived, Joanou quickly wrapped up the meeting and grabbed a hand-held camera to personally film the band's soundcheck. Bono appeared with his arm in a sling and gazed across the empty stadium at the low rain clouds with much more than his usual level of concern.

A few hours later, showtime at Sullivan Stadium approached as the final bank of showers rolled through the area and soaked the early arrivals in their seats. Specially added to this concert, the Pogues brought the damp audience to life with an opening set of its own bawdy mix of Irish traditional sounds and rock and roll, followed by a spirited set from Little Steven. For most of the assembled throng, the members of U2 would be little more than dots moving about on the huge stage. Curiously, though, the usual provisions to beam live video of the concert onto huge screens for the benefit of those sitting a football field away had not been made. Edge told *Rolling Stone* in March 1988 that U2 preferred a more spartan approach to stadium concerts than most bands. "It's the music that makes the atmosphere. There's no laser show, no special effects. If we succeed or fail, it's definitely down to our own ability to communicate the music." Once again, U2 pulled off its unexpected entrance while the lights were still on during "Stand by Me." As usual, the band members surprised most people, who did not notice them climbing onstage in the distance. Bono could easily be identified, though, by the triangle of white cloth supporting his injured shoulder and arm. Despite the discouraging prospects of playing Sullivan Stadium with its appalling sound qualities and a cold, damp wind blowing through the huge bowl, the group's sheer exuberance, along with Joe O'Herlihy's ability on the sound board, enchanted the crowd during the entire ninety-minute show.

Jimmy Iovine, the effusive and tireless producer who had worked on *Under a Blood Red Sky*, wandered the backstage area, his trademark baseball cap perched atop his head. "We've got a [recording] truck back here," he mentioned to me. "We're recording ten shows, [but] I'm not sure what it's going to be used for. They just want to have it — we'll listen to it when the tour's over." As it turned out, he taped twenty concerts, with selected cuts from those shows appearing in the movie soundtrack, which Iovine was officially hired to produce only a few weeks later.

As U2 took its latest material on the road, with recording truck and film crew in tow, the basic theme and framework of the movie assembled itself. While *The Joshua Tree* had been a demonstration of the members' fascination with American song forms, *Rattle and Hum* would document U2's continued search as it toured through the birthplace of blues, gospel, soul, country-western, and rock and roll. Not only would the band members open themselves to the influences close at hand, but they planned to accelerate the process by seeking out certain people and places which could help further their education. This thematic focus to the film explains why certain high-profile events during the tour, such as Bruce Springsteen joining U2 onstage at Philadelphia's 100,000-person-capacity J.F.K. Stadium, were omitted from the final version.

The first stop on U2's American music journey was a small church in Harlem, home of a gospel choir named the New Voices of Freedom. The band members were fascinated by the choir's soulful interpretation of "I Still Haven't Found What I'm Looking For," which had been released as a single by the small New Jersey label Doc Records. The idea for a collaboration soon emerged and the members of New Voices of Freedom were invited to augment U2 onstage during the band's September 28 Madison Square Garden appearance. Bono, Edge, Adam, and Larry journeyed to the church for a hastily arranged rehearsal session; Joanou was on hand to capture the moment when the choir filled U2's song with a deeply moving passion, giving its writers an authentic, spine-tingling gospel lesson. At Madison Square Garden, under the tutelage of musical director Dennis Bell, the choir and its soloists George Pendergrass and Dorothy Terrell lifted U2's performance of "I Still Haven't Found What I'm Looking For" to a majestic new height. This version was recorded and used for the soundtrack album, while the rehearsal filmed at the church appeared in *Rattle and Hum*. In keeping with U2's desired theme, the Harlem sequence pictured the band members as admitted novices in search of, and embracing, their musical lessons.

The tour moved south to Memphis, Joanou following the band members as they playfully explored Graceland and visited Sun Studios. There, in the legendary studio where Carl Perkins, Jerry Lee Lewis, and Elvis Presley had recorded some of their most memorable rock and roll, U2 booked some time between tour dates. The recording session would result in three songs for the *Rattle and Hum* soundtrack album, including "Angel of Harlem," a tribute to American rhythm and blues that U2 dedicated to Billie Holiday. The song featured the Memphis Horns section, which had added its trademark sound to many of the original soul hits on the Stax and Volt record labels in the sixties and seventies. Bob Dylan visited the session for "Love Rescue Me," lending his distinctive voice to back up Bono on the slow blues number. A rave-up collaboration with legendary guitarist and singer B. B. King resulted in the soulful holler "When Love Comes to Town"; King's guitar leads were layered over Edge's rhythm and his vocals joyfully powered each chorus. A rehearsal of the song was filmed and eventually represented one of the best moments in the movie.

With the chronicling of U2's seminal American music discoveries as the primary focus of *Rattle and Hum*, the movie's concept was enlarged to include the band's interest in classic sixties rock as well. By incorporating selections from three of the genre's greatest contributors — Bob Dylan, the Beatles, and Jimi Hendrix — U2 acknowledged the wealth of music which had influenced popular culture years before the Irish band ever set foot in America. Longtime fans of Bob Dylan's writing, the members decided to present one of his songs in the movie. Rather than record one of their frequent performances of "Knockin' on Heaven's Door," which would have been easy, U2 tackled another Dylan track, "All Along the Watchtower." What made this particular selection so interesting was that the band members learned it only moments before stepping onto the stage at a free outdoor concert in downtown San Francisco; Joanou's cameras were present as the band huddled in their trailer and worked out the chords and lyrics to Dylan's 1967 masterpiece. A few days later, during two Denver concerts in McNichols Arena, U2 tipped its hat to the Beatles by recording a blistering interpretation of "Helter Skelter." Finally, cameras and tape machines caught the crowd's excitement as the shattering Hendrix version of America's national anthem introduced "Bullet the Blue Sky" in front of 60,000 fans at Arizona's Sun Devil Stadium.

Joanou filmed the bulk of the concert sequences in black and white at the McNichols gigs and in color during the tour's closing pair of shows at Sun Devil. Returning to the city where the tour had begun nearly nine months earlier, U2 added the two final shows for the specific purpose of capturing essential footage for *Rattle and Hum*. This was Joanou's last chance to acquire the dramatic shots he needed, so he pulled out all the stops, ordering additional stagelights, a giant camera crane, and a helicopter for airborne glimpses of the massive crowd. Ellen mentioned to me that the band had charged a special low price for admission to the shows because Joanou's twelve cameras and crew of 120 would no doubt be far more aggressive during this particular shoot and disrupt the performance somewhat.

Bad luck dogged the film crew's efforts during a rehearsal the night before the first concert. Heavy thunderstorms interrupted the production as Joanou struggled with the show's opening sequence of "Where the Streets Have No Name." With the exception of this staged portion, the members of U2 were adamant that there be no simulations in the movie. Nerves became frayed during the rehearsal's long hours of takes, interruptions, and retakes. Bono found his own performance hollow and bloodless without an audience from which to draw energy and inspiration. *Rolling Stone* writer Steve Pond reported that at one point the singer stopped the action, wondering aloud into his microphone, "Listen . . . Phillip . . . I mean, what's my motivation?" The uneasy feeling didn't end after rehearsal, either. Alienated and distracted by the close presence of Joanou's equipment, which frequently blocked the band members' view of the crowd, and vice versa, U2 turned in an average performance during the first Sun Devil concert. Bono mentioned to Pond: "I felt torn when I was out there. On one hand, I really want to reach out to the people who've come to the show. But that part of me is directly conflicting with the side of me that knows that on film it'll look completely over the top if I do that."

Now there was only one chance left to capture the onstage essence of what U2 audiences had been raving about for years. The odds were stacked firmly against the band, its members clearly uncomfortable in front of the glaring eyes of a dozen cameras, their contact with the audience distant as the needs of the movie intruded on the spontaneity of their performance. But, as in their commanding rise to form at Red Rocks more than four years earlier, U2's members managed to focus on their strengths as a performing unit and forget about the film equipment and financial pressure. The concert was a triumphant success, highlighted by the group's impassioned unfolding of "Bullet the Blue Sky" and a stirring version of "Bad." Joanou was ecstatic about the show and his crew's equally successful efforts, which gave the director the color concert footage he required.

Too early the next morning after an all-night celebration, the dead tired band members caught a flight home for the holidays. Joanou headed in the opposite direction, toward Los Angeles to begin editing the concert sequences and 150 hours of documentary footage into an initial rough cut. The *Joshua Tree* chapter of U2's career was now officially over, and the *Rattle and Hum* period that would culminate in the film's premiere in November 1988 was now fully launched. Most of the new year would be taken up by steady work—Joanou editing, then flying to Dublin in May to film more black-and-white documentary footage as the band rehearsed and recorded new studio material for the project, then re-editing. The members of U2 worked virtually nonstop since, as Jimmy Iovine explained in an interview for this book, "the record and

the movie had to come out at the same time and you can't push movie
deadlines back. We had a lot of work to do—we had to mix an album
of studio tracks and live tracks and also mix the movie. I think part of
why I got the job is my temperament; I can do something like that. *Rattle
and Hum* came at a point in my career where I had just finished [produc-
ing albums by] the Simple Minds and the Pretenders and took a year
off to work on my Christmas record. *Rattle and Hum* really gave me a shot
of life," Iovine continued. "It really gave me purpose to make records
again."

U2 and Iovine were reunited before the *Rattle and Hum* project
when the producer asked the band to donate a song to his *A Very Special
Christmas* compilation album which would benefit the Special Olympics.
"I've been wanting to do a Christmas album all my career," he explained
about the collection, which reached stores in October 1987. U2 recorded
a version of Phil Spector's classic "Christmas (Baby Please Come
Home)" which, as Iovine explained, "is a song that Darlene Love [origi-
nally] sang, and she [also] sang background on the U2 version. It's exciting because we did it very quickly at a soundcheck in Glasgow, Scotland
[in July 1987], but it really works." His production of the track closely
resembled the famous sixties wall-of-sound technique that Phil Spector
had pioneered in the studio with Love, Ike and Tina Turner, the Crys-
tals, and the Ronettes. U2's version had all the feel of Spector's famous
touch with its jingling bells, dense and booming instrumental mix, and,
of course, Darlene Love adding a definite feeling of deja vu.

A Very Special Christmas included all-star performances from
Bruce Springsteen, Madonna, Sting, Run D.M.C., Stevie Nicks, and
others. Iovine's efforts to record the impressive array of talent took him
around the world, but he'd be rewarded for his exhausting travels with
a hit album that sold in the millions that holiday season and continued
to move out of stores each successive Christmas. The sales during the
1987 holiday resulted in an eight-million-dollar donation to Special
Olympics International. Iovine later related to me that by the end of
1990, *A Very Special Christmas* had sold over four million copies.

U2's members involved themselves in another side project that
eventually bore fruit in the opening days of September 1988—a tribute
album dedicated to the music of blues legend Leadbelly and folk music
hero Woody Guthrie. The roots of America's great folk and protest
movements in the early sixties could be traced back to the Depression-
era songs of these two performers, who shared a political consciousness

and in human dignity. Bob Dylan, for one, had cut his teeth learning the Woody Guthrie songbook. Both Guthrie and Leadbelly had been visited by representatives of Folkways Records, who roved the country before World War II with their primitive recording equipment, searching out local blues and folk performers to preserve another piece of America's rich musical heritage. To forever protect those precious Folkways recordings and the priceless music catalogs of Leadbelly and Woody Guthrie as national archives, the Smithsonian Institution purchased the lot with private donations and profits collected from the sales of the tribute album, *A Vision Shared*.

The album compiled the efforts of several artists performing a variety of Woody Guthrie and Leadbelly songs, including Arlo Guthrie singing his father's "East Texas Red," Dylan singing "Pretty Boy Floyd," and Bruce Springsteen contributing a pair of Guthrie covers. Little Richard teamed up with the rocking funk masters in Fishbone to blast out Leadbelly's "Rock Island Line," Taj Mahal sang "The Bourgeois Blues," and Brian Wilson performed the bluesman's biggest hit, "Goodnight Irene."

For a band on a voyage of discovery to America's musical roots, the folk blues tradition of Woody Guthrie and Leadbelly was right where U2 wanted to be. The members gladly accepted an invitation to participate by recording Guthrie's "Jesus Christ." That particular track also gave them an opportunity to comment strongly about the religious hypocrisies occupying more and more of the evening news. Bono mentioned in a promotional interview record accompanying the radio release of *A Vision Shared*, " 'Jesus Christ' is a song that has to be sung . . . U2 has to sing it. It's more relevant today than it was even when he wrote it. We decided to do that because of the line, 'the bankers and the preachers they nailed him in the air.' I've said it before, but these people we see on our television sets, TV evangelists, literally are stealing money from the sick and the old." Bono also revealed why U2 felt close to the spirit of Guthrie's music. "I suppose the songs of Woody Guthrie had something to do with the truth, whatever that is. There's a lie that's very popular right now, which is you can't make a difference, you can't change our world. A lot of songs on the radio perpetuate that lie, for me. They have words, but they don't mean anything, they have a melody but the music sounds the same. It's the same song and it puts people in this big sleep. I think Woody Guthrie's music was much more . . . awake than that."

Keryn Kaplan called WBCN in September when U2 was in

town for its Boston Garden dates to request a copy of Woody Guthrie's original "Jesus Christ." Bono "kind of knows the song," she related, "but wants to make sure he gets the words right." A copy was found at the station and delivered to the band at soundcheck. A few weeks later, when U2 reached Memphis and dropped in at Sun Studios to record the three tracks for *Rattle and Hum*, the members also taped a hootenanny-style rave-up of "Jesus Christ." The austere original was energized into a rollicking shout with Bono's chorus of alleluias echoed by a set of soulful female vocals. The drumbeat tumbled underneath in a light shuffle that blended well with Edge's simple electric playing. Larry hollered out a one-two-three-four count after the song's lulling middle break to return the band to its chugging locomotive pace.

Played on many college stations across the country, "Jesus Christ" was mostly avoided by AOR. Some were discouraged by criticism they would likely receive for airing a piece of "religious music," and others simply didn't view *A Vision Shared* as a prominent enough project to promote; instead they devoted airtime to other, "more important" songs. However, the limited airplay of U2's contribution plus other tracks, especially Bruce Springsteen's version of "Vigilante Man," managed to spread word about the album. CBS Records released a seventy-two-minute video with even more songs documenting the artists' tribute to Woody Guthrie and Leadbelly, including a group sing-along of "This Land Is Your Land" which Bono heartily joined.

For the first time in four years, Bruce Springsteen didn't win the Artist of the Year award in the *Rolling Stone* readers poll for 1987. That honor went to U2, which also captured awards for Best Album, Best Single ("With or Without You"), Best Band, Best Live Performance, Best Songwriter (Bono), Best Album cover, and even Sexiest Male (Bono). A second portion of the poll tallied the opinions of *Rolling Stone*'s critics, who likewise dubbed U2 the Artist of the Year and Best Band. An even greater demonstration of U2's year of success occurred at the Grammy Awards ceremony in March 1988 when the Best Rock Performance by a Group and Album of the Year honors were bestowed on the band. Carrying home the former trophy acknowledged U2's effort in rock circles — a great honor indeed — but securing Album of the Year for *The Joshua Tree* meant that the group had won out over a field of artists encompassing the entire range of popular music.

The band members flew to New York City to attend the Grammy Awards show at Radio City Music Hall. Edge injected some humor to the nationally televised moment by thanking a variety of people from Martin Luther King, Jr., and Bob Dylan to James T. Kirk and Pee-wee Herman. *USA Today* commented that, "the win elevated the Irish group to the Grammy elite, a contingent not known for the far-out and the radical. Bono asserted, 'We're slipstream, not mainstream. I have a lot of records that haven't won Grammys. But we are a part of a wave of groups that have gotten through the safety net.' " As U2's members hit the Grammy parties, the legendary Roy Orbison announced he was writing a song with Bono and Edge. U2 was the toast of the town and the country. Published accounts of U2's 1987 world tour put its gross at $35 million and global sales of *The Joshua Tree* at $14 million.

Although the band members enjoyed the rewards for all their hard work, the group's exploding popularity did cause worry, as Edge mentioned to James Henke in *Rolling Stone*. "This year's been a dangerous year for U2 in some ways. We're now a household name, like Skippy Peanut Butter or Baileys Irish Cream, and I suppose that makes us public property in a way we weren't before. We've seen the beginning of the U2 myth, and that can become difficult. Like, for instance, Bono's personality is now so caricatured that I worry whether he'll be allowed to develop as a lyricist the way I know he can." After years of outspoken statements in interviews and conviction in his lyrics, Bono had gone well over the self-righteous line in the eyes of many. Combined with what *Boston Phoenix* writer Owen Gleiberman called the "front and center ego of Bono's stage persona," this created an almost messianic figure that fell easy prey to mimickry and even derision. There were the "Bono thinks he's Jesus" jokes, comedian Bob Goldthwait's hilarious imitation of the singer, and even a U2 parody group called the Joshua Trio. In addition to defacing U2's biggest hits in laid-back lounge style, the Irish band also performed such originals as "Nobody Cares," featuring these telling lyrics: "What about unemployment? What about the ozone layer? Nobody cares. No, wait . . . Bono cares!"

Bono himself was quite aware of the problem, admitting to *Spin* magazine in a January 1989 article entitled "Hating U2," "People think, 'There goes Bono running all over the stage. And unlike Mick Jagger, Bono doesn't do it with a wink. That's the problem. Bono actually believes in the people that come to the concerts and believes in what he's doing.' Everything I say becomes some sort of statement, something of vast importance. I could go on stage, unzip my pants, and hang my dick out and people would think it was some statement about something."

"Being taken too seriously is a problem," Edge emphasized in

Henke's *Rolling Stone* piece. "It seems that no matter what we do, people place this huge weight of importance on it. Importance out of the realm of music, whether it's political importance or something cultural. I think that can be bad." Henke asked how U2 could avoid the trap, if possible. Edge replied, "by being in love with the music."

Amid this fallout of fame, with the American tour finished in early 1988, U2 disappeared into the studio to redouble efforts on the *Rattle and Hum* project. After recording several new tunes with Iovine in Dublin, the group moved to Los Angeles for six months to work in the producer's favorite facility, A & M Recording Studios, which Iovine and Yakus had upgraded into one of America's foremost state-of-the-art recording centers. Here, U2 completed its latest songs for the album while Joanou toiled close by to finish the movie. Filled with a barrage of fresh U2 music, much of it stunning, the *Rattle and Hum* soundtrack album reached radio stations on October 5, 1988, with the film premiering one month later. A single, "Desire," arrived at the beginning of September and was on its way up the charts two weeks later. But despite the appearances of another typical U2 success, the entire project would create an unexpected and unwelcome reaction in the ranks of the American media and public. The backlash would eventually prompt the band members to begin a three-year moratorium of the States, wary of returning until a new studio album was ready in late 1991.

16
RATTLE AND STUMBLE

WHERE'S MY MATE Keith Richards?" shouted Bono from
the stage of London's Dominion Theater. U2's first concert appearance in nearly eleven months had been hastily
arranged to close a special charity show that included sets
from Ziggy Marley, Robert Cray, Womack and Womack, Tom Tom
Club, and others. The October 16, 1988 Smile Jamaica concert, broadcast on British television and American MTV, was organized by Chris
Blackwell to benefit thousands of victims of Hurricane Gilbert. The
highlight of U2's twenty-minute set came when Richards appeared onstage to add guitar and raspy backing vocals to "When Love Comes to
Town," followed by a spirited finale of "Love Rescue Me" on which Ziggy Marley also joined in. Topping a bill that featured reggae, blues,
soul, and dance music, U2's performance at Smile Jamaica was a testament to the members' continuing fascination with black rock and roll
roots. It also served as the perfect, if inadvertent, introduction to the
Rattle and Hum album which appeared three weeks later.

Island had released the single "Desire" in early September, its
thumping bounce inspired by Bo Diddley's famous guitar beat. Culled
from the 1988 Dublin studio sessions, the song leapt onto album radio
and then stormed the singles charts two weeks later as CHR stations welcomed U2 back. Debuting on the *Billboard* chart at number fifty, "Desire" peaked at number three during the week in November that U2's
movie premiered. The single featured an extra track that wouldn't be included on the upcoming album—"Hallelujah Here She Comes," a more
acoustic-based mover recorded in Los Angeles and featuring the backup

vocals and organ of Billy Preston (who, incidently, had been the only outside musician included in the Beatles 1969 rooftop session). A twelve-inch version of the single added an extended "Hollywood Remix" of "Desire," incorporating extra vocals, sound effects, and snippets of southern California news broadcasts. The swirl of local color in the remix complemented a video filmed in Los Angeles by Richard Lowenstein. The video's dizzying parade of images showing U2 and the American city that had been its home for the entire summer was blitzed on MTV. This outstanding fall success of "Desire" was an auspicious beginning to the *Rattle and Hum* project, which reached its next phase on October 5 with the release of the album to radio.

The cover of *Rattle and Hum* used the same black-and-white Anton Corbijn photography and stark brown lettering as the "Desire" single, which had featured a shot of Larry intently snapping out a beat. This time the artwork incorporated a photograph of Bono illuminating Edge onstage with a brilliant spotlight. Available as either a double record or single CD, *Rattle and Hum*'s seventeen tracks combined live performances from the previous tour and studio efforts that complemented the movie. The later sessions from Dublin and Los Angeles produced five selections for the album as well as a mother lode of extra songs which U2 stockpiled for use as upcoming B-sides of singles (and extra tracks on the CD and cassette singles which were quickly replacing vinyl).

"The feelings were really captured on that record," Jimmy Iovine told me. "Usually, what's going on around the studio never makes it on a record because today, albums are recorded under very similar circumstances . . . very calculated . . . very straight. This was like the Stones' *Beggars Banquet*; you get a real feel for what was going on around the group during the sessions. What's on *Rattle and Hum* is what it felt like making that record, and you don't get that a lot anymore." Reflecting the American music lessons learned on the road during 1987 and right up to the recording of each track, U2's studio sessions were exciting explorations for the band members. After studying Bo Diddley in "Desire," Edge sang mournful lyrics on a slow country-western styled "Van Dieman's Land" and Bono hit a steadily building soul groove on the six-and-a-half-minute "Hawkmoon 269," the latter featuring a rich gospel-styled backup by three female singers and Hammond organ from the (now frequent) visitor Bob Dylan.

A more familiar sounding, harder rocking U2 pounded out "God Part II," a stinging rebuke of Albert Goldman's 1988 biography, *The Lives of John Lennon*. U2's song title cleverly reprised Lennon's own

"God" from his *Plastic Ono Band* album of 1971 and, like the original, served as a vehicle for a bitter diatribe. With this song, Bono elaborated on the angry denouncement of Goldman he had made during the "Trip Through Your Wires" broadcast the previous year. Iovine's use of phasing, a sixties production trick that generated rapid tone shifts across the recording, flashed back to the psychedelic climate in which Lennon's beliefs had been born. U2 also offered a beautiful romantic, spiritual (or both) love song, "All I Want Is You," to close the album. Resembling the haunting title track of *The Unforgettable Fire* more than U2's latest rootsier recordings, the melody was inspired by a lengthy coda that Edge had added to the end of "With or Without You" during the 1987 tour and featured an eerie, supernatural sounding string arrangement by Van Dyke Parks. The remainder of the studio material on *Rattle and Hum* included the three tracks recorded in Memphis and the Kevin Killen–Daniel Lanois engineered "Heartland" from 1986.

Dissent came with the first major review of the soundtrack album. Jon Pareles titled his devastating *New York Times* article, "When Self-Importance Interferes with the Music." Beginning by labeling the release, "a mess," he continued: "The plan, clearly, was to retain the moral fervor of *The Joshua Tree*, yet to vary U2's much imitated style, to pay homage to American music, and to regain some of the sponaneity that superstar status can crush. Unfortunately the band's self-importance got in the way. *Rattle and Hum* is plagued by U2's attempts to grab every mantle in the Rock and Roll Hall of Fame." Pareles concluded, "Mass popularity can be hard on performers, particularly a band like U2, which has always tried to make the sincerest statements possible. From the beginning, U2 has had an unguarded quality, a sense of urgency and vulnerability that it maintained even as its audience grew into the millions. But that urgency has curdled on *Rattle and Hum*, where U2 insists that clumsy attempts at interpreting other people's music are as important as the real thing. What comes across is pure egomania." Tom Carson came to a similar conclusion in the *Village Voice*, and other critics were not far behind.

There were many positive press reviews which came out at the same time, however, most finding *Rattle and Hum*'s quilt of songs acceptable enough. Although the *Boston Globe*'s Jim Sullivan agreed somewhat with Pareles, determining, "When approaching covers, U2 too easily crosses the righteous/self-righteous line," he added, "these are minor flaws, there's too much to rave about." Anthony DeCurtis's review in *Rolling Stone* conceded that "*Rattle and Hum* seems a tad calculated in its supposed spontaneity. Rather than a documentary, it's merely a document of events that often were staged and arranged for the express purpose of being filmed and recorded." But he concluded that the album represented "the sound of four men who still haven't found what they're looking for — and whose restlessness assures that they will be looking further still." At the end of November, *Time* reasoned: "some grumpy reviews fretted about a scope that went way too wide and a cohesion that remained elusive. Indeed, *Rattle and Hum* is careeningly ambiguous, but what fixes its focus is the band's passion to rediscover and remake themselves. U2 has never sounded better or bolder."

Despite the generally positive nature of most album reviews, the presence of several particularly critical stalwarts in the music press managed to paint a negative or at least mixed overall image of *Rattle and Hum*. Adam Block interviewed Bono for *Mother Jones* early in 1989, asking him if any of the criticisms had "hit home." He replied, "I must say I was generally very disappointed in the community of critics. It's funny. I would've thought that what people would have expected us to do would've been to put out a double live LP, cash in on *The Joshua Tree*, and make a lot of money for very little work. That is what big rock bands do. When we didn't do that, I expected people to recognize that. When we put the records out at a low price, stripped away the U2 sound, then just went with our instincts as fans, and just lost ourselves in this [American R & B] music, in a very unselfconscious way . . . the spirit of it has been completely and utterly missed. The spirit of it is unlike any record of a major group, for a long time. That spirit is the very essence of why people get into bands and make music. And it's not about being careful. And it's not about watching your ass . . . "

U2 could be consoled by its legions of fans, though, who firmly ignored the mixed impressions given by critics and raced into stores to purchase the album. Within a month, almost three million units (records, cassettes, and CDs) of *Rattle and Hum* had been sold in America, while another two million were sold abroad. After debuting on *Billboard*'s album chart on October 29, 1988, the release shot up to the top slot two weeks later and remained there for an additional five weeks. It was the first double record set to reach the coveted number one position since *The River* by Bruce Springsteen in 1980. As "Desire" blazed a bright path on CHR, album radio had similar success with the song as well as other new tracks: "When Love Comes to Town," "Angel of Harlem," and "All Along the Watchtower." "God Part II" and "All I Want Is You" would receive AOR's attention the following year. With all the hoopla surrounding the album, even a companion book was a resounding success. Paramount couldn't have been more pleased with the visibility of the *Rattle and Hum* project as the release date for the movie closed in.

With the U.S. opening set for November 4, U2 and Paramount collaborated on a few high-profile charity premieres to be held in Dublin, Madrid, New York City, and Los Angeles. The American debut, on November 1 at the Astor Plaza Theater in Times Square, benefiting the youth crisis center Covenant House, promised the attendance of all four members. U2's New York fans responded in earnest, completely filling Forty-fourth Street in front of the theater. Their ranks swelled as rumors of an unannounced U2 acoustic performance around the corner in Times Square ran rampant. That impromptu concert would never happen, though, since steady rains throughout the day and into the night had already scrubbed the band's plans to stage such an event. As the time for U2's arrival approached, police lines bulged under the force and weight of the crowd, but held open a narrow corridor for the lucky few with tickets to the premiere.

Inside, about a thousand people waited anxiously for the band members to appear. Racing through the doors, panic-stricken about being late, I had the peculiar experience of watching all the eyes in the entire theater quickly swivel toward me. Not recognized as a member of the band, I returned to being an anonymous part of the assembly within a moment. The lights were dimmed and the premiere began with a roar from the audience, which soon settled down to all the usual excitement of watching any flick at a local theater . . . until officials ushered the members of U2 inside under the supposed cover of darkness. A frantic room-wide shuffling occured as word shot around and most everyone craned their necks to get a better view (or whatever view was possible in the darkened theater). Many bolder patrons stood up and jockeyed toward the band members' seats, forming a parade of autograph-seekers that soon blotted out the movie for much of the audience. Before the film ended, the four musicians escaped the ever tightening crush of people around their chairs by fleeing to a post-premiere party in Greenwich Village that also received the type of overwhelming audience and media attention usually reserved for Hollywood's most glamorous.

But "Hollywood" was what U2 had deliberately courted when it set about making the *Rattle and Hum* film. Accordingly, the band members now engaged with a critical community with whom they hadn't had much contact before. The experience turned out to be a bloody one, many film reviewers showing little mercy, or at least tempering any praise with demerits for the movie's inconsistencies. *USA Today* called the film "overdirected," pointing out, "[It] distracts by going from black and white to color and back; neither fans nor critics, knowing or unknowing, are given much sense of what the Irish band has meant to the eighties." Michael Wilmington of the *Los Angeles Times* lauded the musical moments of the film but noted that their context was "muffled." Owen Gleiberman, writing in the *Boston Phoenix*, charged that U2's members projected a "superstar aloofness" in a movie that, "offers next to nothing of U2's history, their offstage routines, their spirit away from the camera." He also echoed Jon Pareles's piece on the album by commenting, "Bono and the boys visit Graceland and the original Sun Studio; it's hard to say whether the scenes are there to demonstrate the kinship they feel with Elvis or the desire to usurp his crown," adding that the scene with the New Voices of Freedom was "a transparent attempt to make the band members seem like good liberals."

Phil Joanou's camera work received mostly high marks and his visual interpretations of many U2 concert selections were applauded, but most reviewers seemed to want more out of *Rattle and Hum* — answers, for instance. The movie provided very few of those, steering away from direct interview sessions in favor of presenting U2's music. With the concert segments and documentary episodes left unadorned by explanation, the viewer was left to interpret the intent of each segment. Some concluded that the movie was an entertaining document of the Irish band in concert and on its innocent, fact-finding musical journey across America. But it was easy for others to suppose that the now world-famous U2 had grown arrogant, determined to prove itself master of and as important as its American music lessons. To these reviewers the group that had strived for so long to remain honest and authentic came off as distant and unapproachable, its ego-driven members relinquishing any affinity with their loyal audience.

An inevitable consequence of the band's growing popularity, the possibility of misinterpretation of U2's movie resembled the problem faced during the group's stadium concerts. In the enormous environment of the stadium, distances from the stage for most of the crowd were so great and conditions for enjoyment so limited that U2's power to entertain was highly dependent on each audience member's faith in the musicians. The only thing that could compensate fully for a fan's disappointment at being a football field away from the stage was the excitement of believing that the band actually cared for everyone there, even those in the last row. These same conditions could be applied to *Rattle and Hum*; if there was no faith, then misinterpretation and even disgust might easily follow. In a film that refused to spell itself out, instead rendering its answers through the music, fans that believed in U2 and understood the group's messages could experience an enjoyable near-concert experience. But to those who had no knowledge of or faith in the band's integrity, *Rattle and Hum* remained an enigma easily construed as arrogant. In theory, the danger was that the movie wouldn't make much sense to those outside U2's core of support. In practice, that's exactly what happened, with the negative film reviews being the first glimmer of dissent.

The second indication of trouble occurred after U2 fans marched into movie theaters nationwide, making *Rattle and Hum* the second-highest grossing picture, at $3.8 million, in its first weekend. Once the initial and most fervent battalions of fans had seen the film, though, mainstream moviegoers failed to be lured into the theaters, despite an aggressive advertising campaign by Paramount and Island Records. Ticket sales fell off sharply, and the film was taken out of most theaters before December. Jeffrey Ressner reported in a *Rolling Stone* article entitled "Bono Less Than Boffo at Box Office" that *Rattle and Hum* earned $8.3 million in domestic theaters while it cost $5.6 million to produce, but, "movies must usually gross three times their budget to be profitable — the film still has a long way to go if it is to make money." Earnings from cable rights and a February home video release that would feature extra concert selections were expected to bring the project into the black, but Paramount and U2 had to be disappointed that the movie wasn't received with more enthusiasm.

Support for U2's music began to erode at CHR, many programmers interpreting the lack of interest in the movie to be a sign of popular disenchantment with the band. In January, "Angel of Harlem," accompanied by another fast-paced Lowenstein video, toughed it out to the number fourteen position in *Billboard*, but the following single, "When Love Comes to Town," only reached number sixty-eight. Phil Joanou's video clip incorporating *Rattle and Hum*'s images of U2 and B. B. King performing the song failed to push the radio single to spectacular heights, but was smartly timed, nevertheless, to re-promote the movie to potential videocassette purchasers. In June, U2 would offer a last gasp from *Rattle and Hum*, issuing "All I Want Is You" as a single, with a stunning video filmed by old friend Meiert Avis. The beautiful love theme imagery, revealed through the actions of a small circus troupe, brought new attention and a fresh appreciation of the song from MTV viewers. Although album radio responded fairly well to the single, CHR barely noticed "All I Want Is You," which debuted on *Billboard*'s Hot 100 at number ninety-three and peaked a mere ten positions higher.

As Edge had once affirmed, U2's members never considered themselves to be in a "singles band," but Paramount and Island's great expectations of success with the *Rattle and Hum* project placed a huge weight of importance on the single releases. U2 again demonstrated its customary attention to artistic detail in the packaging of the singles. "Angel of Harlem," with Adam pictured on the cover cradling his bass, featured an extra unreleased studio track, "A Room at the Heartbreak Hotel," driven by three soulful female backup singers. The twelve-inch and CD versions also added the live "Love Rescue Me," recorded with Keith Richards and Ziggy Marley at the Smile Jamaica concert. U2 displayed a rare moment of photographic humor on the cover of the next single, "When Love Comes to Town," which pictured Edge grinning at the camera while riding an imaginary horse across the sand. More previously unissued recordings surfaced here, including a version of Patti Smith's mysterious "Dancing Barefoot," as well as an extended remix of the B. B. King–U2 collaboration. The final single, "All I Want Is You," featured a brooding Bono on the cover and included unreleased performances of the often-covered soul classics "Unchained Melody" and "Everlasting Love."

While the movie struggled in theaters and CHR backed away from the singles, album and alternative radio stations remained a bastion of support for U2 in America. Despite any inconsistencies, *Rattle and Hum* provided a solid source of highly desirable songs to rock and roll stations for nearly a year. The first three singles each climbed into the top echelon of *Radio and Records*' AOR chart: "Desire" and "Angel of Harlem" hitting the number one slot, "When Love Comes to Town" reaching number three, and the fourth, "All I Want Is You," claiming number thirteen. Island released "God Part II" as an album radio emphasis track in February 1989 and it became the most successful non-single selection from *Rattle and Hum*, climbing to number seven in *Radio and Records* by April. "Dancing Barefoot" and "Everlasting Love" made inroads on some AOR stations, but really caught on at alternative radio. This continuing support of U2, even as the band was buffeted by mainstream America, confirmed that most rock stations and a huge audience still believed in the group.

The continuing loyalty from its core of fans was confirmed in March 1989 when U2 swept the 1988 *Rolling Stone* readers poll. Once again nabbing Artist of the Year and Best Band, U2 also won best of the year trophies for album (*Rattle and Hum*), album cover, single ("Desire"), video ("Desire"), producer (Jimmy Iovine), songwriter (Bono), male singer, drummer, and bassist. Edge narrowly lost out in the Best Guitarist honors to Eddie Van Halen. But in the critics poll portion of the music awards, U2's absence was a resounding statement of the disappointment within the writers' camp over the band's 1988 efforts. One year before, the *Rolling Stone* critics had chosen U2 as Artist of the Year and Best Band, also doling out second place honors for *The Joshua Tree* as Best Album right behind Bruce Springsteen's *Tunnel of Love*. This year there were no trophies; U2's name failed to appear in any category, even as a runner-up.

Outside of U2's core following, America's mainstream music consumer had apparently had enough of U2 by the spring of 1989. Since the release of *The Joshua Tree* two years earlier, the band's singles had dominated CHR airwaves while its tours regularly criss-crossed the country. U2's videos were shown on MTV with ever increasing (and eventually annoying) frequency, magazines and tabloids spotlit the band almost daily, and the supposedly calmer rock and roll media had doled out lavish praise portraying U2 as the new savior of rock. Then the multimedia juggernaut of a heavily promoted movie with its attendant soundtrack album, singles, and book arrived. But, as Steve Pond pointed out in the *Rolling Stone* readers and critics poll issue, "U2's problem is more than simple overexposure. After years of favorable fan and press reaction to the band's music; years of dramatic stage performances; years in which underground credibility turned into mass success; years of articles based on intense conversations with a socially minded lead singer and his three more retiring band mates; years of grainy black and white photos of deadly serious, brooding faces, growing from dewy-cheeked youth to bestubbled adulthood; after all that, the U2 backlash has set in." Bob Catania, then vice-president of promotion at Island, told me during an interview in June 1989: "The backlash is that they take themselves too seriously. Now U2 is in a corner, there has been a slide and Island is in a marketing dilemma."

"*Rattle and Hum* is a messy but revealing collection that has some terrific songs," Steve Pond elaborated in his *Rolling Stone* piece. "But it doesn't say anything definitive. 'The statement,' says Bono, 'was that there was no statement.' But when you throw in a $5 million movie and a lavish marketing campaign, you get a project that demands to be taken as a Major Statement. And in the gap between what people thought U2 was promising and what the band actually delivered, you had the beginnings of a backlash, of a potential crisis in the career of a band whose seat atop the rock pile isn't quite so secure these days." In only a few months, the perception of U2 as a white knight fighting the good fight for rock and roll mutated into a "not U2 again!" grumble in the music industry and mainstream audience. Even Edge felt compelled to tell Pond, "I'm sick to death of reading about U2!" With its overpowering image constantly in the media, could a line of U2 dolls, trading cards, and chewing gum be far behind?

The members of U2, weary from working on the movie for a year straight, actually predicted the trouble before *Rattle and Hum* premiered, as was revealed in an earlier *Spin* interview which didn't hit the streets until January 1989. Edge told the magazine: "The only important thing about this film is that we survived it. Of course, whether we survive the bullshit hype with our marbles intact remains to be seen. Having avoided a lot of the bullshit for so long, this film will mean us walking into a mountain of it. We were stupid enough to agree to do the film in the first place. We only had ourselves to blame." But by that point, U2 had invested $5 million of its own money to shoot and edit *Rattle and Hum*, while the band's significant partners, Paramount Pictures and Island Records, were similarly involved to the hilt. With pre-release promotion at a fever pitch, U2 had advanced too far into the *Rattle and Hum* project to ever consider backing out. But, even if that was possible, it is still doubtful that the band members would have abandoned the film. Bono stated in the March 1989 *Rolling Stone* piece: "They say in the eighties that rock and roll is dead. I don't think it's dead, but if it's dying, it's because groups like us aren't taking enough risks. You know, make a movie. Put yourself up there against what's out there, *Robocop* and *Three Men and a Baby*. That's great for rock and roll, not just for U2. I think you've got to dare." One unfortunate result of the eventual backlash would be that many listeners failed to credit the movie and album for some truly rewarding musical moments as U2 sought to take their own dare and move forward.

The band members took the next logical step by hitting the concert trail, spotlighting their latest rhythm and blues lessons in the international Love Town tour. Although the band would visit most of the world in its four-month concert swing, no plans were made to visit America, a complete reversal from U2's usual touring pattern. Paul

McGuinness and the band members were well aware that to further expose U2 during the American backlash was too risky. Following *Rattle and Hum*'s media overload so soon with another highly publicized U2 event would only generate further hype and debate with every stop on the tour. At the very least, attention would be focused firmly on U2's image problems and not its music, an uncomfortable situation for a band that had always held art as its goal. By avoiding the U.S. for a time, the band at least allowed for the possibility that in the future its work would be taken seriously on its own merits, unencumbered by questions of integrity, attitude, or motive. Edge told *Rolling Stone* in March, "The safe thing to do would be to wait three years and then do the next record." Bono added, "There is a sense of 'Up drawbridge,' cut ourselves off."

Meanwhile, there was limited backlash against U2 elsewhere in the world. The overseas press didn't display much of the antagonism of its American counterparts when U2 reinterpreted rhythm and blues roots in *Rattle and Hum*. Plus, the crushing media overdose experienced in the States was significantly diluted or completely absent elsewhere because U2 simply hadn't toured the rest of the world in recent years. Outside the U.S., reaction from critics and fans alike was warm and jubilant. The road trip began in September 1989 with twenty-three concerts in Australia and four more in New Zealand. These countries had last been visited five years earlier on the *Unforgettable Fire* concert swing, and were neglected during U2's 1987 breakthrough tour in support of *The Joshua Tree*. After performing extensively "down under" and then in Japan and the East, U2 moved on to Europe and eventually wound up with four shows in Dublin between Christmas and New Year's Day.

The Love Town project included two months of exhaustive rehearsals, during which U2 revamped its stage set-up and worked out many fresh song arrangements, resulting in one of the group's most musically ambitious and extensive tours to date. The band members indulged themselves in lengthy practice sessions in Dublin and then Sydney, Australia, enjoying the relative wealth of time available after years of jamming crucial stage rehearsals into the brief periods between recording and touring. To provide the proper rhythm and blues kick that fueled the Sun Studio songs from the soundtrack, the band members invited B. B. King and his six-piece "orchestra" to join them onstage nightly. During a central portion of the show, the expanded lineup performed "Angel of Harlem," "Love Rescue Me," and (of course) the signature tune of the tour—"When Love Comes to Town." Bono humbly offered during a network radio interview from Sydney in October that

U2 was actually B. B. King's backup band. "It's a bit embarrassing singing next to him; he is one of the greatest blues singers alive."

It was a great loss to Stateside fans when they missed U2's concert collaboration with B. B. King and the exciting live debuts of *Rattle and Hum* studio songs. The group opened many shows with a dramatically building "Hawkmoon 269" and regularly played "Desire," "Van Diemen's Land," "God Part II," and a riveting "All I Want Is You" (which seamlessly flowed into "Bad"). The group was in joyous form, tighter and more versatile than ever with a wealth of new songs, cover versions, and older material to choose from. Reflecting the quiltlike content of the *Rattle and Hum* collection, U2 presented anything from the metallic angst of "Helter Skelter" to the plaintive strains of "Slow Dancing," a country-western tune that Bono had written and demoed for Willie Nelson (Bono wasn't kidding during the 1987 "Trip Through Your Wires" radio special when he mentioned Nelson as an inspiration). "She's a Mystery to Me," the tune Bono and Edge presented to Roy Orbison, who recorded it before he died, appeared in some set lists, as well as an acoustic "In God's Country" and the revived "Two Hearts Beat as One." While U2's musical choices constantly changed from night to night, Bono's ability to forge a bond with each audience hadn't changed at all from previous years. In city after city, fans felt touched by the band's passion, or even found themselves onstage slow dancing with U2's lead singer or suddenly strapping on an acoustic guitar to play with the musicians.

The Love Town tour's final concerts were held at the Point Depot, a brand-new performance venue in Dublin that had been rebuilt from a decaying structure which had housed some of U2's *Rattle and Hum* rehearsals (and the movie sequence for "Desire"). The group capped its four-night hometown stand, the tour, and the entire *Rattle and Hum* project with a live midnight broadcast of its New Year's show throughout Europe. Ushering in the very start of the nineties, U2's radio concert reached an estimated seven hundred million listeners from Iceland, across Britain, down to Spain, and deep into the Soviet Bloc. The fading recorded notes of "All You Need Is Love" from the Beatles announced the start of U2's set as the band members walked onstage to a tumultuous roar from the Irish audience. "Where the Streets Have No Name" was the first of twenty-two songs, which included old favorites like "I Will Follow," "Gloria," and an optimistic juxtapositioning of Dylan's "The Times They Are A-Changin' " with "New Year's Day." After a rousing encore with B. B. King and his musicians, then an obligatory

"40," U2 left the stage and signed off from its most historic broadcast yet. Later in the year, the band's official fan magazine, *Propaganda*, would print a track-by-track listing of the 100-minute show and provide a free, brightly decorated cassette cover for those who taped it. This was an official blessing from the members of U2, who usually frowned on bootlegging, but encouraged the trading of this very special concert among fans.

U2's New Year's Day performance stood at the brink of a passing era for the band and the new decade to come. At the time, there was a tension among fans and the media, reinforced by Bono's onstage statement during the second night of the Point Depot series. He announced: "We've had a great ten years, but we've got to do something else for awhile . . . just to get away for a little while. These gigs are like a party for us and you, and we can't go on doing this forever." When some interpreted the statement to mean that U2 was breaking up, causing a rush to Paul McGuinness and Ellen Darst for clarification, the band's management only deepened the mystery by making no announcements concerning the group's future. For fans, this led to much heartbreaking speculation about the end of U2.

But there was much less anxiety for those aware of U2's past history of "breaking up" and reinventing itself before each new album. This period of rest and reevaluation that Bono hinted at fell within the band's typical pattern. The possible exception to the rule was U2's frenetic year between *The Joshua Tree* and *Rattle and Hum*, in which there might have been no rest, and certainly some sort of continuing exploration of American music. In the revealing *Mother Jones* interview in April 1989, Bono affirmed the need for the members of U2 to remain engrossed in their music, adapting and not ending their quest. "Ten years ago, when I thought about being in a rock and roll band, I saw so much. I saw everything: being on the radio, television, making movies, records, being on the road. It was huge, like a really wide spectrum of things that were very important. Now that spectrum has shrunk down to nothing. The essence of what it is to be a rock and roll band to me, now, is just that three-and-a-half minutes [of a song]. Not giving interviews, not being on television, not all that goes with it. What has drowned out the sound of the rock and roll circus has been the rock and roll song. Just that one thing. That's the most exciting thing for me." He continued, "I come back to that line in our song 'In God's Country': 'We need new

dreams tonight.' The job is to dream up a world you'd want to live in."
Given these words, it seemed that U2's career was far from complete.
The band members retired to their homes and families, beginning a self-
imposed retreat from the world that would eventually become a full two-
year sabbatical.

17

CHOPPING DOWN
THE JOSHUA TREE

WHEN U2 DISAPPEARED from America in 1989, the group really had no choice. Loyal U.S. fans had exalted the four band members to the status of rock and roll deities while their former champions in the media had crucified *Rattle and Hum* as a deliberate or careless slide into self-indulgence/self-importance. U2's heartfelt anthems, "Sunday Bloody Sunday" and "New Year's Day," had been reduced to mere sing-along opportunities for the audience, diluted of meaning and becoming a sort of "stadium-speak," as John McKenna wrote in the December edition of *In Dublin* magazine. By early 1989, the group that had always thrived on expressing reality through its songs was in danger of being utterly crushed by its own larger-than-life image. Under the weight of their oppressive myth, could the band members ever create effectively again? If and when it arrived, U2's next musical statement would not only have to characteristically rebel against its predecessors, but also deal effectively with the post–*Rattle and Hum* combination of myth and backlash engulfing the band by the end of the eighties.

Clearly, a period of rest and then intensive reevaluation was required. Andy Allen, soon to be promoted to senior vice-president and general manager of Island Records, related, "*The Joshua Tree* and *Rattle and Hum* were almost A and B of the same project: we rolled from one album directly into the other and literally had to stop promoting *The Joshua Tree* to set up the next. Then, *Rattle and Hum* was a beast in itself because it had this tremendous film aspect to it, so it took the marketing and commercialism to another level. When we got to the end of the project, we realized there had been supersaturation. I remember being in an airport gift shop and looking at the magazine rack, U2 was on the cover of three or four magazines simultaneously. It literally looked like a U2 gift shop. Yes . . . they *had* to take a vacation."

During the period that the band was absent from America, Chris Blackwell surrendered Island's independent status by selling it to the international Polygram Label Group (PLG) based in Germany. "U2 profited greatly from the sale of the company because of deals Blackwell had made with the band leading up to the sale," Allen mentioned. To keep the star band on his label and thereby retain vast bargaining power, the owner signed off percentages of Island to U2, netting the band members and McGuinness millions when the sale to PLG was concluded. Soon, Island Records' field promotion staff was eliminated and its management team trimmed. The move allowed the label sovereignty in signing its own acts and recording them, but promotion and distribution of the product would now be Polygram's responsibility. Even though the massive conglomerate already had a worldwide promotion and marketing network in place, the release campaigns of several Island artists were disrupted by the transition. Allen observed that U2 managed to avoid the worst of it, however. "It just so happened that U2 was in between its projects when the sale happened in October 1989, so all the transition confusion didn't hurt them at all as it did some of the other artists. By the time they approached their album release date, the Polygram staff had been together for a year and had ironed out most of the kinks."

There was little fanfare over U2's role in and profit from the Island sale. The same could be said about domestic news coverage of the band's overseas Love Town concert tour. As U2 optimistically crashed out of the old year and into the new with its jubilant Point Depot performances, virtually no word arrived in America concerning the whole cacophonous affair. Even when Bono sparked intense conjecture onstage in Dublin about the band's possible break-up, the few bulletins received in the States were noticeably subdued. McGuinness had encouraged the band members to remain out of the limelight and severely limited media access as their sabbatical lengthened. The blackout continued for over a year and a half in America until October 1990, when U2 finally broke the silence with a new song.

U2 contributed a track and eventually a video to *Red, Hot + Blue*, an international musical project designed to heighten AIDS awareness and raise money for AIDS organizations through sales of an album compiling twenty modern interpretations of classic Cole Porter songs.

The music of this popular American songwriter of the 1930s was target-
ed because of its bold stylistic sophistication and progressive lyrical content promoting the power and surrender of love. Somewhat out of vogue
since the rock and roll era began, the Porter catalogue was a fresh reser-
voir of music that seemed to speak to the coming decade and certainly
the need for love and understanding in the face of the AIDS crisis. Many
of rock and pop's new stable of stars donated their talents, including
Sinead O'Connor, Neneh Cherry, David Byrne, Jody Watley, Debbie
Harry and Iggy Pop, the Fine Young Cannibals, and Annie Lennox
from the Eurythmics. U2 selected "Night and Day" as a suitable cover
choice, turning out a dark jewel that glittered ominously with its thick
wash of synthesizers, chilling melody, and assertive dance beat. Color-
ing the dance music of "Night and Day" with the same energy and feeling
employed on the gloomy, hard rock version of "Maggie's Farm," U2
came up with a moody, yet powerful and ultimately triumphant piece.
Arranged and recorded in Edge's basement in June of 1990, "Night and
Day" was basically a keyboard piece with congas added from Noel Eccles
and an Infinite guitar layered throughout. Bono entered with a low and
foreboding tone, contrasting this threatening approach with friendlier,
normal-voiced choruses. He would use this concept to powerful effect
again on "The Fly," the first single from U2's next album, to be released
the following year.

For fans with memories of U2's hootenanny sessions and rootsy
American music discoveries echoing from the three previous years,
"Night and Day" was a curve ball that had more in common with the
smooth "European" feel of *The Unforgettable Fire*. Dance-oriented as it
was, the track found little favor in album radio circles, but helped drive
the *Red, Hot + Blue* album to the top of the alternative radio charts. A
ninety-minute television special which incorporated videos from several
of the project's artists, including U2, was presented on ABC–TV in December 1990, helping to spread word further about the compilation
album.

Was "Night and Day" an early indication of a new artistic direction for U2 or a mere diversion for the group? There was evidence to
support both interpretations: the band had reinvented itself with each
new album but had also left the recorded artifacts of many experimental
sidesteps in its path. The surprising truth was that the members of U2
were just as mystified about the band's future direction as anyone else.
Eno revealed in a piece he wrote for *Rolling Stone* in November 1991 that
the members spent a great deal of time discussing what to do next and

what kind of direction to take: "U2's records take a long time to make not because the band members are stuck for ideas but because they never stop talking about them. U2's state of mind going into this record was similar to that before *The Unforgettable Fire*: ready for something bigger, rebelling against its own stereotypes."

The band journeyed to Berlin for two lengthy visits in the fall of 1990 and early 1991. After filming the "Night and Day" video with director Wim Wenders and then assembling the familiar team of Daniel Lanois and Brian Eno as album producers, U2 began work in the legendary Hansa by the Wall recording studio, where Eno himself had helped David Bowie craft the *Low* and *"Heroes"* albums in 1976 and 1977. The studio team's usual arrangement with U2 was altered, Eno being expected only for regular consultations and the bulk of the production being accomplished by Lanois with assistance from engineer Flood (Mark Ellis). Edge admitted in a March 1992 *Musician* magazine interview that U2 began the album with a great deal of difficulty. "It really tested everyone very severely. It was just a real testing of the way we write our songs, the creative system within the group. . . . For a week or two at the beginning in Berlin, it was so hard to get things happening and get inspired and get working on the same wavelength. To put it in a word, the magic just wasn't there. Whether it was the playing, the material, the arrangements, the direction, the studio, the flute sound — who knows why? It just wasn't happening."

Not only did the members of U2 have trouble at first, but Lanois was finding it difficult to relate to what was in fact turning out to be a departure for the band. Edge continued: "It didn't help that Danny didn't really get it. He was a little unsure about the direction. But Brian came in, and Danny and Brian work off each other very well. So Danny was kind of tuning in on what Brian was feeling and thinking, based on what we were saying and playing. Danny really started to get it then, and that was good." U2's magic returned with the song "One" as Edge's exploratory chords inspired the other three members to layer their own instruments in. "There was a tangible feeling in the room," Edge commented in *Musician*. "Suddenly it had jelled. It had clicked and everyone knew it."

The members of U2 threw all of their preconceived notions of music, especially their own previous work, out the window and set to work with a completely new palette. Eno wrote: "Buzzwords on this record were trashy, throwaway, dark, sexy, and industrial (all good) and earnest, polite, sweet, righteous, rockist, and linear (all bad). It was good if a song took you on a journey or made you think that your hi-fi was broken, bad if it reminded you of recording studios or U2." The eventual album, *Achtung Baby*, represented a riot of influences, from caustic industrial sounds to rap-inspired electronic hip-hop beats. It was a testament to U2's ability to move with the times, incorporating not only the musical sounds around it but the environment as well in constantly creative ways to remain fresh. Berlin itself became a backdrop for the record, according to Eno. "The Berlin of the thirties — decadent, sensual, and dark — resonating against the Berlin of the nineties — reborn, chaotic, and optimistic — suggesting an image of culture at the crossroads. In the same way, the record would be a place where incongruous strands would be allowed to weave together." Other bands in U2's place might have enclosed themselves in a bubble and churned out a crowd-pleasing remake of *The Joshua Tree*, but the inevitably successful seller would have only represented a holding pattern, effectively dooming the band to its creative death. U2 had always been about change, so another one should have been expected.

After setting the tone for the *Achtung Baby* project in laborious rehearsals and hammering out songs from the musical fragments that emerged, the U2 recording entourage packed up and headed for home. In late March 1991, the band moved into Elsinore, a refurbished house on the Irish coast about ten miles south of Dublin. Virtually repeating the arrangement followed in recording *The Joshua Tree*, the band had a studio desk hauled into the old home and a vast network of electrical cables laid throughout the premises to connect the control room to its studio areas: a ballroom and a large downstairs chamber. With the Irish Sea foaming on the rocks outside, U2 spent several months at Elsinore honing the songs that would become *Achtung Baby*. Steve Lillywhite was brought in to help in the final mixing of the album, which also required booking some time at Windmill Lane Studios. Eno candidly described the team in his *Rolling Stone* essay: "Bono, the Mother Theresa of abandoned songs, compassionately argues for every single idea that has ever experienced even the most transitory existence. Larry and Adam are reliable wide-anglers when things start to lose perspective or become too narrowly focused. They become the voice of musical conscience. Edge, the archeologist of the rough mix, delves back through earlier strata in the song's development, emerging triumphantly with a different version on a battered cassette. Steve Lillywhite, a welcome addition at the mixing stage, comes in fresh and enthusiastic, free of history, and trusts his gifted ears. Dan listens to feel, to the skeleton of the song, and draws at-

tention to things that everyone else has stopped noticing. Flood rea-
wakens sleeping songs with brilliantly original mixes after we've all gone
home. I trust my instincts, wax doubtful or enthusiastic, grumble En-
glishly and contradict myself."

While the band and its recording team labored on at Elsinore,
copies of a bootleg tape of pirated material from U2's Berlin sessions
emerged in Germany, Holland, and England. Since the Hansa sessions
represented the very beginning of the *Achtung Baby* project, the songs and
studio fragments were in very rough form, containing several musical
dead ends that U2 had quickly abandoned. Bono commented to the
Irish press, "I don't know why anyone would be interested in them." His
casual attitude was beefed up by Island Records' threat to prosecute any
record dealers or stores that imported or sold the rough tapes. In an
official band statement Paul McGuinness announced, "There is always
a strong demand for U2 material, but these tapes are very early recordings and I don't like to see people being ripped off." Just how the Berlin
session material had leaked to the public remains a mystery, but the fervor with which McGuinness and Island Records attempted to strangle
the tapes' distribution illustrated that both had assumed a greater
responsibility in further restraining public access to the group. The flow
of information to the media was studiously contained: interviews with
the band members were curtailed and recording sessions closed. Andy
Allen at Island Records revealed, "Paul purposely did not let them talk
to the media, he was like a governor on a motor. He didn't want to see
a *Rattle and Hum*–level splash on U2, choking the media."

As U2 moved closer to the fall 1991 release of *Achtung Baby*, its
continued restrictions on publicity threatened to offend some members
of the press. The policy of limited access was actually quite justified. In
an attempt to refocus the attention of the media and fans onto music and
away from image, the band members needed to stay out of the limelight
and let their music take center stage once again. "Everyone has this sort
of caricature impression of what we are like," Edge told *Musician* in one
of only a handful of interviews. "*Achtung Baby* is definitely a reaction to
the myth of U2. We never really had any control over that myth. You
could say we helped it along a bit, but the actual myth itself is a creation
of the media and people's imagination. There is little resemblance to the
actual personalities of the band or the intentions of the band." During
the summer and fall, U2 released information, decidedly musical in nature, about its sessions (including quotes from the band members) solely
in *Propaganda*, the official U2 fan magazine. Its *Achtung Baby* issue,

provided for sale to newsstands for the first time, was the primary and most objective source of news about the upcoming album. By the time *Achtung Baby* actually arrived in stores in November, the only other available domestic piece with inside information about the new album was Eno's beautifully analytical essay in *Rolling Stone*.

Andy Allen was Island's principal player in the marketing strategy for the forthcoming U2 release. "When we approached *Achtung Baby*, it wasn't with fanfare. There wasn't the idea of coming out out with a huge, blockbuster single. As we discussed the marketing with Paul and the band there was an effort made to reestablish U2 as an alternative group." In the aftermath of its long string of single hits in 1987 and 1988, U2's history as a cutting-edge band had been replaced by its new reputation as a CHR and album radio commodity. "We knew they still had credibility in the alternative area because of *Red, Hot + Blue*, which went immediately to the number one spot on the alternative chart, mostly driven by the U2 track. It was very important to the band to stay there, so that originally launched the idea of coming with 'The Fly' first. They knew it was going to be a difficult track at commercial radio, but it gave us a chance to set the mood for what the *Achtung Baby* album was going to be."

On October 9, 1991, promotional CD singles of "The Fly" arrived at domestic radio stations. At WBCN, a first listen by several deejays and management staffers provoked common looks of surprise and wonder. Larry's deadly drum thump kicked off a brutal guitar riff that snarled throughout the song, matched by Bono's electronically distorted, low and breathy verses. The dark, stampeding mass pulled up at each chorus, lifted by the singer's angelic falsetto. A dark and forboding rock and roll intrusion, "The Fly" would surrender its alien presence after a few listens, but in that time take the listener on a musical journey all the way to the vanguard of nineties rock. Edge commented on the music in *Propaganda*: "All I know is that it feels like what I want right now, it's raw and rough and straightforward and down to the essence of things, quite unpolished in some ways." Bono clarified: " 'The Fly'? Well, to me it's the sound of four men chopping down *The Joshua Tree*."

As expected, alternative radio embraced the single with unrestrained delight, and album radio wasn't put off at all by its raw and challenging metallic nature. Enough stations played "The Fly" in the first week for it to debut at the number three position in the *Radio and Records* album tracks chart. After two more weeks there, it darted into the top position but tumbled suddenly down the song survey the week after. "The Fly" also made significant inroads on many mainstream CHR stations, jumping onto Top 40 playlists briefly before abruptly dropping off near the end of the year. After its surprising initial success, the quick death of the single on radio was ensured by Island's release of *Achtung Baby*'s second single, "Mysterious Ways," only five weeks after the first. Album radio and CHR stations found this new track's soulful, hip-hop dance feel to be much more palatable than the angry snarl of "The Fly," which was rapidly ditched in favor of its successor. "This album was going to originally come out in September, but the finishing touches took a bit longer than expected," Allen elaborated. "We knew that we'd be getting this record out very late in the selling season [before Christmas] and traditional marketing sense says that if that is going to happen, you put your most commercial track out A.S.A.P. to sell the upcoming album. We literally threw that approach out the window when we went with 'The Fly' and then came back very quickly with the more multi-format, more mass-appeal track. 'Mysterious Ways' did go to number one at album radio [remaining on top for seven weeks] and Top 40 could also play it." "Mysterious Ways" peaked at number nine in *Billboard*'s Hot 100 singles chart in January.

Videos for "The Fly" and "Mysterious Ways" appeared in conjunction with their radio counterparts. The former, filmed in Dublin and London, cast Bono as a manic street prophet dressed up in leather and striking black bug-eyed sunglasses. Feeding vicariously off the situations and emotions of others for inspiration in his role as an artist, Bono was ignored or rebuffed by the people filmed around him. In a flashing parade of situations and mostly dark images and shots, "The Fly" video exposed a U2 willing to observe and express the sensual and even, perhaps, the perverse. The video for "Mysterious Ways," filmed during the summer in Morocco, swirled with color and psychedelic special effects. The appropriately sexual feel of the video quickly blasted apart any illusions that the song was aimed at familiar U2 targets: political situations, drug abuse, or social injustice. It was obvious that on at least these two *Achtung Baby* tracks, the band was moving away from the black-and-white issue-oriented stance of *The Joshua Tree* and exploring the chromatic and complex world of emotion. The light smirk of the album's title also hinted at the changes.

Achtung Baby appeared in stores on November 18. Its neatly organized series of sixteen photographs on the front cover and sixteen more on the back showed black-and-white images of the band in Berlin mixed with colorful pictures shot in Morocco and Ireland. Quite a departure for U2, whose previous album covers had each employed a powerful, singular image, the new release presented multiple frames showing the band in various poses along with grotesque silver U2 rings, German Trabant cars, a bull and a snake, Edge's glittering pair of pants, and even a fully naked Adam Clayton. This last photo on the back cover raised a few eyebrows and stirred up some controversy at first, but the publicity soon settled down, and the only enduring effect was that the cover was censored in America. "Yeah, we had to put a black X over Adam's . . . well, U2's fifth member!" Allen laughed. "Apparently America was the only country that had to do that." Island voluntarily adjusted the covers when many stores threatened to not stock the album if it was released with full frontal nudity. Collectors may be interested to know that only the cassette and CD were censored; the few records produced for the dwindling U.S. vinyl market featured the original artwork.

Allen revealed that U2 had had an active role in the CD packaging of *Achtung Baby*. "U2 took the stand that they would not issue their CD in the typical long box, which is only used in America." The cardboard envelope, traditionally used in the U.S. to package compact discs into a larger form more difficult for shoplifters to conceal, was completely discarded after purchase and had been indicted as a major wasteful addition to the country's landfills. Public and industry outcry called for alternatives to the oversized cardboard wrapping. "We released the U2 album in a traditional plastic jewel-case [without the long box] and also in 'digi-pak' form, which is a long package without disposable materials [except for two narrow plastic strips to hold it open] that folds into a small CD unit. Most consumers have told us they like the jewel box better, but some retailers wouldn't take the release unless it was in 'digi-pak' — so we put it out in both forms. This was done in a very quiet manner," he added. "The issue was not to make an issue of it. The band wanted the music of the album to speak."

Achtung Baby's songs revealed some of U2's most exotic musical changes to date, the opening "Zoo Station" immediately staking out the album's ambitious territory in both its sound and Bono's frank lyrics. Carving its rhythm and some melody out of a series of distorted and strikingly non-musical noises at the beginning, the track then added comforting layers of guitars and keyboards to take full flight. Bono's voice, electronically mutated into the weird robotic tongue heard on "The Fly," entered with expressions of his search for a bold, new change: to let go of the steering wheel, inhale the laughing gas, and accept a new shuffle of the deck. The breezy "Even Better Than the Real Thing," driven by Edge's classic guitar chiming, was loaded up with the kind of light sexual innuendo common to much pop music, but nearly absent from any previous U2 song. A sentimental tale of an untouchable partner, "Who's Gonna Ride Your Wild Horses" glided over Edge's murky guitar distortion and was followed by a companion piece, "So Cruel." The use of hip-hop rhythms common to pop, but new to U2, blended smoothly with Bono's emotive singing to produce another bittersweet tale of unrequited passion. The light, danceable flow of "Tryin' to Throw Your Arms Around the World" followed in similar danceable hip-hop fashion as it described a lonely, drunken soul on his pre-dawn path home.

These unusual U2 offerings were combined with more traditional-sounding tracks like "One," which traveled the sentimental road established by "With or Without You," both in its instrumental approach and in the description of a tormenting relationship of embrace and rejection. "Until the End of the World" returned the band to driving, hard rock form; it appeared with a different mix in director Wim Wenders' film of the same name. In this particularly powerful set of lyrics, Bono assumed the character of Judas Iscariot as he confessed his betrayal of Jesus and asked for forgiveness. "Acrobat" built from the same rising and falling dark energy that had powered "Exit" from *The Joshua Tree*. At first listen a song about love and life under attack by pressures on all sides, "Acrobat" really contained Bono's most naked statements about U2's defensive posture in the aftermath of *Rattle and Hum* and recalled that period when the band members didn't know what they should do next or even if there was any inspiration left.

Achtung Baby ended bleakly with "Love Is Blindness," possibly a comment about Edge's marriage, which had broken down the previous year. He told *Musician*: "I think what was going on in my life had an influence on Bono and therefore on the lyrics to some of the songs. I think there's a lot of stories in there and it's not just my story. It's not a very comforting ending, is it? I suppose that's what we've learned. Things aren't all okay out there. But that's the way it is." First stated on organ, the slow and mournful melody accompanied Bono's hushed singing and inspired Edge to release a few wrenching guitar notes that seemed the beginning of a howling blues guitar solo, something that would have been completely out of character for him. Pulling back, though, Edge returned the spotlight to Bono, the ominous power of the haunting piece established without the need for a solo.

The album received high marks from most critics. U2 was lauded for the integrity of its artistic risks, which far outweighed any deficiencies in the actual recording. Elysa Gardner in *Rolling Stone* gave *Achtung Baby* a whopping four and a half stars out of five, commenting that "U2 is once again trying to broaden its musical palette, but this time its ambitions are realized. We're reminded why, before these guys were the butt of cynical jokes, they were rock and roll heroes—as they still are." *People* reported: "Most of this odd, often intoxicating concoction would not be identifiable as U2 were it not for Bono's distinctive voice. From the wah-wahing guitars on 'One' to the trippy vocals of 'The Fly,' the style can only be described as psychedelic. And that turns out to be wunderbar, baby."

Despite the significant changes in U2's style, the band remained as marketable as ever. In its first week in stores, the album sold over 300,000 copies and debuted on the *Billboard* chart at number one. Playing tag with Michael Jackson's *Dangerous* and country superstar Garth Brooks' *Ropin' the Wind*, *Achtung Baby* remained within the top twelve U.S. album slots for over four months, with sales of three and a half million units. By then, "One," the third single from the album, was streaking toward the familiar upper echelons of the *Billboard* singles chart, promising to spur album sales even further.

On February 29, 1992, U2 returned to the American stage for the first time in just over four years with a concert in Lakeland, Florida. The Zoo TV tour, named for a phrase conceived by Bono, moved quickly across the country with one concert in each of thirty-one cities (except two at the Los Angeles Sports Arena) to finish up in Vancouver on April 23. The hit-and-run tour, with shows in arenas much smaller than the sold-out stadiums of U2's fall 1987 visit, couldn't hope to satisfy America's demand for tickets. But, much like the brief *Unforgettable Fire* tour before Christmas 1984, this swing was designed as a quick reminder to fans that U2 was back and had a new album in the stores (the band planned to return in the summer for a stadium tour). Understandably, competition for tickets was as fierce as in any concert tour in history. The warm-up concert for just over 6,000 fans in the relatively small Lakeland Arena sold out in four minutes. In the first hour that tickets were on sale for U2's St. Patrick's Day concert at Boston Garden, with a two-ticket limit per person, a half-million calls were received. After several million calls in four and a half hours, during which New England Telephone's system was hopelessly jammed, the 13,000 available seats were finally sold out. Steve Morse interviewed Joanne Waddell, a

New England Telephone manager, for the *Boston Globe*: "It was complete gridlock," she told him. "I don't know how else to describe it. We expected a lot of calls . . . but this was unbelievable. They bombed us right out of the water."

In a move designed to foil scalping, U2 had required the Boston Garden's tickets to be distributed through the telephone network only. Typically in New England, professional scalpers and legitimate ticket agencies would hire dozens of people to stand in line, sometimes for days, to buy tickets that would eventually be resold with exorbitant markups. U2's system certainly couldn't prevent all of these scams, but it did succeed in disrupting the attempts of many established profiteers. At other arenas, some tickets were sold out of the box office to fans who had obtained a wristband from the arena a few days before. In these cases, the wristband announcement was made on the radio only moments before they were distributed, a move that helped limit the professionals' chances of arranging mass purchases. Moments before the doors opened at most concerts, U2's organization released tickets to the box office, hoping that those about to pay inflated scalpers' prices would purchase good seats at face value instead. U2 operatives even ventured into the streets on occasion, selling correctly priced tickets before fans could spend hundreds on a scalped seat.

U2's musicians demonstrated through these extraordinary measures that they were still concerned about their fans. In Boston, they reinforced that reality by regularly stepping out of their week-long home at the Four Seasons hotel to greet the knots of supporters that waited in constant vigil. These spur-of-the-moment meetings were the only sources of personal information about U2 for fans, as Paul McGuinness's press blackout was still being firmly enforced. Bono did grant a brief interview to MTV, but through his nervous and abrupt manner, he signaled that perhaps he wasn't supposed to be doing so. When asked why U2 was performing so much of its new album in concert and so little of its earliest material, he replied: "We're into it, and I think the real U2 fans that have been around [will] be into it. We might lose some of the pop kids — but we don't need them." The final sentence angered some industry insiders and media pundits, who saw it as an example of U2's continued arrogance. But the statement, however poorly worded, did express the band's need to continue forging ahead artistically whatever the risk; if U2 had wanted to cater to pop superstardom it would have churned out a blatantly commercial follow-up to *Rattle and Hum*. Even if the music industry took some offense at Bono's answer, however, the incident caused no ripples among U2's massive following, which jammed every concert and continued to add to *Achtung Baby*'s impressive sales figures. Perhaps they simply didn't see themselves as the "pop kids" to whom Bono referred.

     The Zoo TV tour carried U2's concept of live performance to a whole new level. Previously committed to playing on an unadorned stage with attention firmly focused on the four band members, U2 added a myriad of stage props to its arsenal for the first time. Largely the result of collaboration between lighting and set designer Peter Williams (Willie) and the band, the elaborate staging was based on video, with a complex network of television monitors pointing in every direction. While U2 played, live camera shots were combined with pre-produced images by Brian Eno and other artists, as well as actual television broadcasts (the band hauled its own satellite dish on the road for this purpose). Most of the twenty-two songs performed on typical nights, including ten of the twelve selections from *Achtung Baby*, were accompanied by a companion video. This new television-conscious stage show was sponsored, appropriately enough, by MTV (despite U2's non-corporate stance in years past).

     The Zoo TV stage featured six Trabant cars hung from the lighting truss, their shells painted with brightly colored words and flowers and their inner workings removed to make way for spotlights. A runway extended from one side of the stage halfway back into each arena, where a much smaller platform waited for U2's mid-set "unplugged" segment. Before each show began, another Trabant with a glittering mirror-ball surface sat on the platform, occupied by Irish deejay B. P. Fallon who played a set of rhythm and blues and rock and roll favorites from a mixing console inside. After Fallon exited, during the band's entrance, the car was lifted up to the rafters to be used as a rotating oversized mirror-ball during Bono and Edge's rendition of Lou Reed's "Satellite of Love." Two other balls glittered brightly during "Ultraviolet (Light My Way)" and a belly-dancer was employed on "Mysterious Ways." Throughout the performance, elaborate lighting effects added a colorful dimension never before seen at a U2 concert.

     A generous liberal breeze, reviving the sixties American "Summer of Love" spirit, had blown through European pop circles over the previous three years, no doubt fanned by the brightening political and social environment in Germany and the Soviet Union. U2 had embraced these feelings, instilling a "love vibe" throughout its concerts — from B. P. Fallon's mostly-sixties music set, to the color-drenched "Mysterious Ways" video, to the flowers painted on the dangling Trabants and the words "I'd rather be tripping" inscribed on one of them. This atmosphere combined with the heavier, industrial textures pioneered by urban alternative bands like Ministry and the Jesus and Mary Chain (which had inspired and powered "Zoo Station" and "The Fly") to come up with a powerful, distinctly nineties concoction that invaded and overpowered each audience's senses in a hundred-minute show.

Bono appeared every night during the spring tour in black leather, hair slicked back, with the dark "Fly" sunglasses hiding his eyes. As the band tore into "Zoo Station" with grinding, metallic swipes from Edge, the stage plunged into near-darkness lit only by sudden murky images flashing from the television monitors. Swirling shapes and indistinct images together with live footage taken by several cameras, including one on the catwalk to the smaller stage, paraded past on the video screens. Bono leapt onto the walkway, playing tag with the camera and even humping it suggestively at one point (parodying a rock star or being a rock star?). Opening with eight songs from *Achtung Baby*, the new U2 took control as it had never done before: Bono as the Fly took the audience through the new album's various shades of emotion. This segment was precisely calibrated to synchronize with the video images and lighting effects from the Zoo TV stage set, U2's performance of the songs nearly identical to the original studio versions on every night.

Ending this *Achtung Baby* portion of the show with "Tryin' to Throw Your Arms Around the World," Bono took off the sunglasses and ditched his Fly persona, coaxing Edge, Adam, and Larry to join him on the small stage for a spirited acoustic rendition of "Angel of Harlem." Surrounded on all sides by a rapturous audience, the U2 of old reemerged and took over. On occasion the band tossed in other songs at this point, including Edge's "Van Diemen's Land" and a rousing version of the Pogues' "Dirty Old Town" that featured a rare appearance by Larry at lead microphone. This heartfelt section of the show continued with the band back on the main stage for "Bad" and a snippet of "All I Want Is You," then flaming crosses filled the video screens as U2 blazed into "Bullet the Blue Sky." Donning a baseball cap and head-mounted wireless microphone, Bono stalked around the stage and out to the smaller platform where he remained for a vastly re-arranged "Running to Stand Still," which ended with the singer enveloped in smoke.

Familiar anthems concluded each show after this point, with videos from U2's Death Valley visit accompanying "Where the Streets Have No Name," and "Pride (In the Name of Love)" accented by a segment of a filmed speech from Martin Luther King, Jr. The latter was the earliest song from its repertoire that U2 would perform. Bono assumed his next character, an overt parody of a pop superstar, by appearing onstage for the encore in a silver lame suit. Grasping a mirror at some shows, he'd kiss his image and yell, "You're fucking bee-yoot-iful!" After a cacophonous rock and roll attack on "Desire," the band settled down through "Ultraviolet (Light My Way)," "With or Without You," and dropped to a passionate crawl on "Love Is Blindness." In Hartford, they skipped the last song but still maintained the subdued, and unusually somber, tone of its farewell.

U2's high-tech, multifaceted show left most fans amazed and inspired. Even though the combination of "new U2" and "old U2" in the tight framework of a designed, non-spontaneous show threatened to offend older fans weaned on the band's passionate past, these changes boded well for a group that had all too recently teetered on the brink of self-parody. The implacable *New York Times* correspondent Jon Pareles nodded approvingly: "Bono was every bit the modern star, enigmatic behind his shades and in his lyrics, yet the master of a multimedia hullabaloo, a rush of noises and images and ideas. U2 wants to have its artifice and its sincerity at the same time — no easy thing — and it hasn't yet made the breakthrough that will unite them. The music can only improve when the band starts to play its new songs with abandon rather than rigor, letting their noise pour out. In the meantime, a U2 that doesn't mind being trendy or funny is a vastly improved band."

The most common complaints about the show concerned the band's decision not to perform pre–*Unforgettable Fire* material (particularly the politically inspired "New Year's Day" and "Sunday Bloody Sunday'), the contrived impression left from the use of some stage props, and a lack of spontaneity in concert. But what outweighed these admittedly valid points was the question of where U2 could have gone in its previous incarnation. Having carried the passion of flag-bearing and fist-raising to the point of being bitterly criticized for its self-righteousness, U2 had most certainly reached a dead end with that stance. Continuing on that path would have been artistically anticlimactic even if possibly lucrative for a time. Breaking up was a viable alternative which the members considered seriously for a while. U2's solution, though, was an abandoned leap toward another style, which fortunately produced the radically different and refreshing *Achtung Baby*. Barely sidestepping the trap of superstardom brought on by the strength of its own original commitment was the greatest challenge of the group's career. Now, U2 seems less preoccupied and serious, even poking fun at itself and its stardom. Enough air has been let out of the U2 myth that the group can once again be appreciated for its music.

Cynics might argue that the members of U2 could just be acting out a new role, traveling even further from their real personalities and feelings; that *Achtung Baby* and Zoo TV are one huge contrivance designed to stun, amaze, and rake in profits. Knowing the members of U2 and witnessing their attention to the fans, as well as the organization's attempts to distribute tickets fairly, I disbelieve this view. U2's album and tour had to be somewhat designed anyway, to react against what the band had created before and to combat an image that threatened to destroy. Within these limits the band has produced an album of seemingly limitless possibilities, vaulting onto an entirely new stage. Its fans once again guessing, U2 has regained the high ground and its role as a true Pied Piper of rock.

THE PEACE
MUSEUM

For anyone whose heart has been stirred by the lyrics of John Lennon's "Imagine," the recording of a fiery Martin Luther King, Jr., speech, or the antiwar plea of U2's "New Year's Day," a visit to the Peace Museum in Chicago could be the next logical step. For over ten years the brick walls of the museum have been filled with the sounds of children playing in its rooms, and then growing silent to listen carefully to the lessons spoken by a museum guide. The galleries have echoed with deeper philosophical discussion from wiser adults while recorded messages crackled from hidden speakers placed regularly through the maze of exhibits.

This may be the only museum in the world where peace is the central theme. If others exist, this is certainly where the idea originated. Co-founded in 1981 by antiwar activist and artist/designer Mark Rogovin (who became the first curator) and Marjorie Craig Benton, a U.S. representative to UNICEF, the museum was envisioned as a center where peace could be taught through the arts. Marianne Philbin, an eventual curator and the director for five years, became involved when the Peace Museum only existed on paper. Interviewed for this book, she stated, "The idea was to reach people in a way that was direct and personal, maybe even a little emotional, that helped them make the connection between what was happening in the world and their own abilities to make a contribution or change." Philbin added that the concept of peace education through the arts was a novel one, but even the idea of teaching peace was itself new. "In school you tend to learn history in terms of war-to-war-to-war instead of what happens in between. You learn about the battles and the generals, but there's less of a tradition in teaching about the peacemakers who have worked in nonviolent ways."

With the help of many dedicated volunteers, the museum opened its original location at 364 Erie Street in Chicago in November 1981. "We didn't know whether or not to call it a museum in the beginning—because that sounded dusty and dead," Philbin continued. "It's actually a lively and dynamic place with a lot going on all the time." For the initial exhibit, entitled "Against the Wall: Three Centuries of Posters on War and Peace," the museum volunteers worked with collectors around the country to obtain the items which were displayed. The chronological exhibit opened with a poster rallying popular sentiment for the French Revolution and ended with a modern notice urging public support to declare Martin Luther King's birthday a national holiday. The *New York Times* delivered an important review of the exhibit, reporting that it drew more than 3,000 visitors in its first two months. The museum staff reprised the early success by arranging an encore display of antiwar cartoons and caricatures.

Perhaps the Peace Museum's most poignant exhibit was erected in August 1982, thirty-seven years after atomic bomb explosions destroyed the Japanese cities of Hiroshima and Nagasaki. Many of those who survived the initial blasts would perish from the radiation sickness which appeared soon after. The Nuclear Age had arrived with a deadly announcement, and for years the military and scientific significance of the events overshadowed the human agony. These moments were collected into a series of Japanese paintings and drawings after Iwakichi Kobayashi, a seventy-seven-year-old survivor of the Hiroshima blast, drew the first picture in May 1974. Japanese television displayed Kobayashi's work, then urged others to share their own memories in sketches or paint. Within three months nearly a thousand pieces had been received.

Declared a national treasure to remind future generations about the holocaust, the display of art had never traveled outside Japan's borders. In 1982 Mark Rogovin negotiated to have the exhibit, entitled "The Unforgettable Fire," brought to America for the first time. "Mark went over there and worked with the director of the Hiroshima Peace Memorial to actually collect sixty or so drawings and bring them back here for the exhibit," Philbin remembered. "[The Japanese] do feel that they are missionaries — that they are the only people in the world that really know what nuclear warfare means." The Peace Museum staff was gratified when a thousand patrons turned out for the exhibit's opening night, and large crowds viewed the grim artwork throughout its stay in Chicago. Rogovin told the Associated Press: "These drawings speak louder than lectures. They're more personal, they're more intimate. It's not a Picasso, it's not a Goya. But it's a fellow human being who wants to make a warning to you not to let this happen again." Before returning the treasures to Japan, Rogovin obtained permission to photocopy them for a permanent museum exhibit. An actual roof tile from a Hiroshima building, still slightly radioactive, is also part of the display.

In 1981, the idea for a future exhibit spotlighting the peace efforts of musicians was conceived. Usually an unpopular subject for any songwriter to tackle, the expression of antiwar sentiment often puts a musician's career on the line. The "Give Peace a Chance" display (named after John Lennon's 1969 song) would laud these heroes of our culture and, it was hoped, stimulate further interest in their message. The project took shape rapidly after Yoko Ono became involved, as Philbin remembered: "In 1982 we wrote a letter to Yoko and asked her if she'd be willing to lend us certain items for an exhibit which would focus on her work and John Lennon's work for peace through music. We got a call from her office not three days later saying yes, and that it was a wonderful idea and the whole notion of a Peace Museum was fantastic. We set up a time to meet and things just snow-balled. Needless to say, [Yoko's involvement] made it a lot easier to start knocking on doors."

Ono, who eventually became a major financial contributor to the museum, provided many pieces of memorabilia for the exhibit, including the actual Gibson guitar her husband had used to record "Give Peace a Chance," and various gold record sales awards for the couple's most moving peace anthems. She also supplied the exhibit with Peace Acorns, some of which the Lennons had sent in 1969 to various heads of state around the world with a request to plant them for peace. *Grapefruit Box,* a conceptual art piece by the couple from 1971, was lent as well. The museum staff added to Ono's contributions official F.B.I. memos and photocopies of documents concerning Lennon's lengthy immigration battle, various promotional posters, and a pair of political cartoons by Doug Marlette of the *Charlotte Observer.* Jann Wenner of *Rolling Stone* lent the museum staff Lennon's original March 1970 letter informing the magazine about the Toronto Peace Festival. Wenner also provided another Lennon letter which thanked *Rolling Stone* and its readers for helping him win his fight to remain in America.

The Lennon memorabilia was only one portion of the entire exhibit, which took a year and a half to assemble. Documents and objects illustrating efforts made on behalf of peace by Harry Chapin, Bob Dylan, Woody Guthrie and son Arlo Guthrie, George Harrison, Tom Lehrer, Bob Marley, Country Joe McDonald, Holly Near, Laura Nyro, Phil Ochs, Odetta, Tom Paxton, Peter, Paul and Mary, Paul Robeson, Pete Seeger, Stevie Wonder, and U2 completed "Give Peace a Chance." Early manuscripts and posters were displayed to establish a historical base, with a Woodstock Festival placard and documents from Graham Nash's involvement with Peace Sunday in 1982 representing modern efforts.

On September 11, 1983 the Peace Museum unveiled "Give Peace a Chance," with the recent arrival of U2's giant stage backdrop picturing the *War* album cover and the original handwritten manuscript for "New Year's Day." Over 200 volunteers helped build the display, which became the organization's most successful exhibit to date with over 30,000 people eventually attending. Peace Museum officials produced an accompanying 122-page paperback guide featuring reprints and photos of objects in the exhibit, articles about John Lennon, an essay from Yoko, and a bibliography/discography of songs concerning peace. Terri Hemmert, hired from her job as morning disc jockey at WXRT to be the museum's music consultant, wrote an extensive essay about the embrace of the antiwar theme by current musicians. Stevie Wonder had more than a few words to say about the need for a national holiday on Martin Luther King, Jr.'s birthday, and Pete Seeger wrote an exclusive article describing the sentiment of his song "Waist Deep in the Big Muddy." Contributions from other musicians and writers filled out an impressive history of the modern peace movement.

Before "Give Peace a Chance" closed at the end of January 1984, the Peace Museum opened another display devoted to Martin Luther King, Jr., and the civil rights movement of the sixties. Philbin recalled: "When we started talking about doing a show on King, I naively said that there had to be a hundred exhibits around the country on the man [since] he is a major figure in history. But, there wasn't. [There were] only a couple of exhibits [sponsored] through the King Center in Atlanta." Enlisting the talents of Barbara Armentrout, a member of the Women's International League for Peace and Freedom, and Northwestern University professor Sterling Stuckey as co-curators, the Peace Museum began assembling its own display. For three months the workers obtained documents and objects for the feature while extensively researching King's life. Included in the eventual "Dr. Martin Luther King — Peacemaker" exhibit was a recording of his famous "I Have a Dream" speech, original rallying posters for meetings and protests, and photographs of the leader and civil rights events. The winners of a Chicago poster competition, for which schoolchildren expressed their feelings about King, were displayed along with original works from British artist Paul Peter Piech, who had been inspired by King's speeches.

The museum has presented many other displays in its decade of existence, including an expose on the massive 1985 peace effort known as "The Ribbon." A fabric panel knitted into patterns relaying a message of peace, the idea began with a Denver grandmother. While sewing together the first ribbon, she envisioned it as a symbol of peace which could surround an image of war. She imagined that if enough people created panels, they could be placed end to end, encircling the Pentagon. The idea spread widely among peace activists and family members who had lost loved ones in war, until the dream was finally realized on the fortieth anniversary of the Hiroshima bombing. Interviewed for this book, Peter Ratajczak, executive director of the museum, related that "there were 28,000 panels and when they set them all together, it stretched eighteen miles! A lot of the Peace Museum people were there and we got to pick 500 of the original panels. It's a very popular idea, people are still making ribbon banners and there are even international exchanges of them."

The Peace Museum staff also created an exhibit highlighting the thirty articles of Amnesty International's "Universal Declaration of Human Rights." The document, drawn up as World War II closed, was signed by many nations to reaffirm the essential needs for freedom and human rights. The declaration stands as a cornerstone of the Amnesty International organization, which has worked for years to correct worldwide human rights injustices. The Peace Museum exhibit, mounted in 1989 during the forty-fifth anniversary of the document's signing, displayed the works of individual artists who each interpreted one article of the declaration through drawings, paintings, or sculpture. A claymation video presentation created by Amnesty International to highlight the points of the document was shown constantly in the gallery, becoming a big hit with schoolchildren who toured the exhibit.

The Peace Museum staff has exposed a great number of patrons to its "permanent" displays in the Chicago location, but a far larger audience has been touched by the museum's many traveling exhibits. Ratajczak has coordinated this "Outreach Program," which provides portable representations of the museum's past displays. In 1989, fifteen exhibits crisscrossed the country, hitting fifty cities with an attendance of over a quarter-million visitors. The displays ranged from two different sized versions of "The Ribbon," "The Unforgettable Fire," "Dr. Martin Luther King — Peacemaker," the largest exhibit, "Give Peace a Chance," and the small anti-war poster sets. Each show can be requested by any organization for a specific rental, after which Ratajczak arranges a suitable schedule for the exhibit to visit. Often, though, he has had to put those interested on a long waiting list — the King display was recently booked solid through two years into the future. But advance planning can eliminate scheduling problems, as evidenced by Arizona State University's acquisition of the King exhibit to coincide with the celebration of his January 1992 birthday. With Arizona one of the few states failing to recognize King's birthday as a state holiday, the display's presence at that particular time was a poignant statement. Funds to build the traveling exhibits have not come easily, but reasonable rental charges have offset some of the costs of maintaining them. At the beginning of 1992, rental of "The Unforgettable Fire" was $500 plus shipping charges, and the King display could be leased for $800, for example. Because of the constant backlog of the museum's more popular traveling exhibits, there are plans to duplicate and expand the most requested items. (If interested in renting one of these mobile displays, contact Peter Ratajczak at (312) 541–1474.)

The Peace Museum staff produced twenty exhibits since 1981, including an expanded and updated 1991 presentation of "Give Peace a Chance." Admission fees at the Chicago location combined with traveling exhibit rental fees provide thirty percent of the institution's revenue; the other seventy percent comes from individual donations and larger grants from patrons like Yoko Ono and her Spirit Foundation. Although the Peace Museum receives some funds from the State of Illinois and the City of Chicago, it is not subsidized in any way by the federal government. Tax-deductible memberships beginning at twenty-five dollars are offered, granting a year-long admission to the gallery space and subscription to the museum newsletter, which publishes exhibition schedules, notices of special events, and invitations to openings. There are special discounts available for students and senior citizens.

Fund raising has never been the number one priority on the museum staff's list, the members being preoccupied with their artistic presentations, but recent hard times have forced the institution to spend most of its time focusing on financial concerns. Although Yoko Ono and her son Sean were the guests of honor at a highly successful fund-raising dinner commemorating the institution's fifth anniversary in 1986, five years later the date was, by contrast, a bittersweet affair. Museum officials had decided that rising costs and falling revenue would force them to close the gallery by the middle of July 1991. With monthly bills for operating the space at $25,000 against an income of only about $15,000, the museum's financial woes were obvious. Although between 10,000 and 20,000 patrons visited the gallery per year, ten times that number viewed the traveling exhibits — so closing the gallery would conserve funds for the more important mission of maintaining the portable displays. An announcement detailing the closing was followed a few days later by an urgent appeal for donations. Miraculously, the overwhelming response from its membership, combined with successful negotiations with the landlord, allowed the Museum gallery to remain open through mid-October. The staff was able to mount an updated "Give Peace a Chance" exhibit plus a celebrity auction while still sending its traveling displays across the country.

After October, the Peace Museum closed its gallery space at 430 West Erie, happily reopening a couple of months later in the Chicago Cultural Center with a mounting of the "Ribbon" exhibit. In its new arrangement, the museum must share available floor space with other organizations, but that cost-cutting alternative was far better than permanently eliminating a home gallery. Exhibits will have to be struck frequently to make way for other cultural groups' displays, but Peace Museum members can still keep abreast of the schedule through the newsletter. The new arrangement represents a fresh lease on life and a far better financial situation for the Peace Museum, whose staff will maintain their permanent office at the location.

Furthering the Peace Museum's ideals through individual lifestyle and action is perhaps the best way to complement its hard-working staff. The effort can be as simple as voting against a candidate who supports building more nuclear weapons or participating in organizations dedicated to furthering the goal of peace. One such group, formed by a Wisconsin woman in 1988, has worked directly with the museum to help alleviate the burden of basic chores necessary to run the institution. S. Kathleen Maki got the idea for her volunteer group, Another Day, after seeing U2 perform in Chicago and then visiting the museum in 1987. Maki sent out postcards to local U2 fan newsletters and was gratified to see sixteen respondents turn out at an initial meeting. Since then, monthly attendance has varied, but four years later remains strong with almost two dozen volunteers. The group has conducted the Peace Museum's worldwide membership mailings, helped set up exhibits, cleaned and painted the gallery, and aided in a wide variety of essential tasks. Marianne Philbin commented to me that: "The Another Day people are a perfect example of those who are inspired by U2 and the museum. They do so much work here, I don't know what we'd do without them." Maki, who makes a 130-mile drive into Chicago for every meeting of her group, has proved that the Peace Museum's desire to educate and affect people through the arts can achieve dramatic results.

This novel concept — an institution promoting peace in the midst of thousands of war monuments and battlegrounds — has struggled, thrived, and struggled again during its decade-long history. Philbin has stepped down as director and now manages a foundation that provides grant money to non-profit organizations engaged in social services and the arts. She admitted, however, that the Peace Museum "is a place she'd never leave," and she remains highly active as a board member. Co-founder Mark Rogovin retired in May 1986, but also remains an active board member and volunteer. Peter Ratajczak runs much of the museum's day-to-day business and manages the traveling exhibits. Terri Hemmert is a stalwart at WXRT–FM and remains active in local public affairs work, including benefit appearances and concerts. The actions of these dedicated few, plus the scores of other workers and volunteers who make each exhibit possible, have made the museum an honorable institution worthy of a determined look. Who knows, while you're strolling through the gallery in Chicago or viewing one of the museum's traveling displays, perhaps a little of that peace might rub off on you.

The Peace Museum is located at the Chicago Cultural Center, 78 East Washington Street, Fourth Floor, Chicago, Illinois 60602. Telephone: (312) 541-1474.

APPENDIX 2

AMNESTY INTERNATIONAL

Amnesty International, a worldwide movement of human rights activists independent of political or governmental affiliation, has been in existence for thirty-one years. Conceptually based on the Universal Declaration of Human Rights, an agreement signed by the world's governments in 1948, Amnesty International boasts a current membership of more than 1.1 million members in 150 countries and territories around the globe.

The movement began in 1961 when a British lawyer, Peter Beneson, published an article appealing to his countrymen to help focus attention on people he called "The Forgotten Prisoners." Within a month, enough offers flooded in to make the idea of forming an organization a reality. After only a few months, the movement would spread into continental Europe. Amnesty International's mission now, as it was then, is to seek the release of prisoners of conscience — people who have been jailed for their beliefs, ethnic status, or religion who did not advocate violence. Amnesty International also works to expedite fair trials for the accused and rejects torture or inhumane treatment before either trial or sentencing. The organization is also firmly opposed to use of the death penalty.

Amnesty International obtains its knowledge about foreign prisoners from many sources, including analysis of regular news broadcasts or examination of information carefully smuggled from political hot-spots. Representatives are sent whenever possible to interview local officials and even the prisoners themselves about their conditions and treatment. If permitted, these Amnesty International teams remain on location to monitor the actual trials, encouraging fairness throughout. The organization draws attention to the individual cases of thousands of prisoners by writing letters and sending telegrams to the heads of state or government agents responsible for handling them. In some cases, only a relatively small effort is required before justice is served, but on many occasions Amnesty calls upon its large membership to begin a worldwide letter-writing campaign designed to inundate the responsible parties with attention. The resulting flood of mail announces to the perpetrators that their actions are not going unnoticed by the world community.

Entirely funded by subscriptions from members and donations from organizations and individuals, Amnesty International has always looked to the artistic community as a sympathetic source of funds. In 1979, "The Secret Policeman's Ball," a benefit comedy show presented over four nights at Her Majesty's Theatre in London and featuring Monty Python, was filmed and presented on English television. The musical portion of the show included acoustic performances by Pete Townshend, Tom Robinson, and John Williams. The high-profile Amnesty International benefit also produced two record albums, whose profits were donated to the organization. Bono first heard about Amnesty when he saw "The Secret Policeman's Ball" on television — unaware at the time that in just a few short years he'd be fronting a rock and roll band that would make a huge difference in Amnesty International's fiscal affairs.

In 1986 Amnesty International asked U2 if it would consider taking part in some sort of twenty-fifth birthday tribute to the organization. The idea of a film or a benefit concert was discussed, but the band's enthusiasm escalated to create the highly successful Conspiracy of Hope tour. Sting, Peter Gabriel, Lou Reed, and the many other artists who participated made this tour an event that not only netted Amnesty International millions of dollars, but added thousands of eager new members to its letter-writing army.

In 1988, Amnesty sponsored its "Human Rights Now!" campaign, based on the fortieth anniversary of the Universal Declaration of Human Rights. An appeal by the organization, signed by more than three million men and women from 130 countries, was handed over to the United Nations in an effort to remind the member governments that it was their responsibility to uphold these rights for their citizens. At this time, another collection of internationally known musicians undertook a massive benefit tour. Bruce Springsteen, Tracy Chapman, Sting, Peter Gabriel, and Youssou N'Dour performed for more than a million people on their global swing.

With the dismantling of the Berlin Wall and the Soviet Union, it's easy to assume that the world has made significant steps toward ensuring human rights for all. However, the sad truth is that the 1990s have proved no different than years past; only the locations of the injustices have changed: rampant atrocities in Beijing, Iraq's genocidal war on its Kurdish population, and Yugoslavia's bloody civil war. Even in America, with its relatively good domestic human rights record, the death penalty still exists. Amnesty International is needed now more than ever.

U2 and its official fan magazine *Propaganda* have never stopped supporting Amnesty International (though the band's efforts may not have been as public after the 1986 Conspiracy of Hope tour). In each issue of *Propaganda*, a number of political prisoners are specifically examined. Their stories, the steps leading to their imprisonment, and the reasons why they should be freed or given a fair trial are explained. The magazine then urges its readership to contribute to a letter-writing campaign, suggesting what sort of letter to prepare and where to send it.

Achtung Baby mentioned the names of two prisoners of conscience on its sleeve and also urged fans to join Amnesty International. For information about how to join the organization or donate to its cause, write to either of the following sections of Amnesty International:

(U.S.A.) U.S.A. Section
322 Eighth Avenue
New York, NY 10001
U.S.A.

(U.K.) British Section
99–119 Rosebery Avenue
London EC1R 4RE
U.K.

AMERICAN DISCOGRAPHY AND VIDEOGRAPHY

Commercially released albums and mini-LP's*

Boy (January 1981)
I Will Follow / Twilight / An Cat Dubh / Into the Heart / Out of Control / Stories For Boys / The Ocean / A Day Without Me / Another Time Another Place / Electric Co. / Shadows and Tall Trees

October (October 1981)
Gloria / I Fall Down / I Threw a Brick Through a Window / Rejoice / Fire / Tomorrow / October / With a Shout / Stranger in a Strange Land / Scarlet / Is That All?

War (March 1983)
Sunday Bloody Sunday / Seconds / New Year's Day / Like a Song / Drowning Man / The Refugee / Two Hearts Beat As One / Red Light / Surrender / "40"

*Under a Blood Red Sky** (November 1983)
Gloria / 11 O'Clock Tick Tock / I Will Follow / Party Girl / Sunday Bloody Sunday / The Electric Co. / New Year's Day / "40"

The Unforgettable Fire (October 1984)
A Sort of Homecoming / Pride (In the Name of Love) / Wire / The Unforgettable Fire / Promenade / 4th of July / Bad / Indian Summer Sky / Elvis Presley and America / MLK

*Wide Awake in America** (May 1985)
Bad / A Sort of Homecoming / Three Sunrises / Love Comes Tumbling

The Joshua Tree (March 1987)
Where the Streets Have No Name / I Still Haven't Found What I'm Looking For / With or Without You / Bullet the Blue Sky / Running to Stand Still /

Red Hill Mining Town / In God's Country / Trip Through Your Wires / One Tree Hill / Exit / Mothers of the Disappeared

Rattle and Hum (October 1988)
Helter Skelter / Van Dieman's Land / Desire / Hawkmoon 269 / All Along the Watchtower / I Still Haven't Found What I'm Looking For / Freedom for My People / Silver and Gold / Pride (In the Name of Love) / Angel of Harlem / Love Rescue Me / When Love Comes to Town / Heartland / God Part II / The Star Spangled Banner / Bullet the Blue Sky / All I Want Is You

Achtung Baby (November 1991)
Zoo Station / Even Better Than the Real Thing / One / Until the End of the World / Who's Gonna Ride Your Wild Horses / So Cruel / The Fly / Mysterious Ways / Tryin' to Throw Your Arms Around the World / Ultraviolet (Light My Way) / Acrobat / Love Is Blindness

Commercially released singles

"I Will Follow" / "Out of Control" (Live Paradise Theater, Boston, March 6, 1981) (April 1981)

"New Year's Day" / "Treasure" (February 1983)

"Two Hearts Beat As One" / "Endless Deep" (June 1983)

"Two Hearts Beat As One" / "Two Hearts Beat As One" (Edit) / "Two Hearts Beat As One" (Extended Remix) 12″ single

"I Will Follow" (Live from *Under a Blood Red Sky*) / "Two Hearts Beat As One" (Edited Remix) (January 1984) Promos feature "I Will Follow" with no applause on the B-side

"Pride" / "Boomerang II" (October 1984)

"New Year's Day" / "Two Hearts Beat As One" (1985) "Revival of the Fittest" Island re-release.

"Sunday Bloody Sunday" / "Gloria" (1985) "Revival of the Fittest" Island re-release.

"Pride" / "I Will Follow" (from *Under a Blood Red Sky* 1985) "Revival of the Fittest" Island re-release.

"With or Without You" / "Luminous Times (Hold on to Love" / "Walk to the Water" (March 1987)

"I Still Haven't Found What I'm Looking For" / "Spanish Eyes" / "Deep in the Heart" (May 1987)

"Where the Streets Have No Name" / "Silver and Gold" / "Sweetest Thing" 12″ version adds "Race Against Time" (August 1987)

"In God's Country" / "Bullet the Blue Sky" / "Running to Stand Still" (November 1987)

"Desire" / "Hallelujah Here She Comes" 12″ version adds "Desire (Hollywood Remix)" (September 1988)

"Angel of Harlem" / "A Room at the Heartbreak Hotel" 12″ and CD versions add "Love Rescue Me" (Live at Smile Jamaica Concert 10 / 88) (December 1988)

"When Love Comes to Town" / "Dancing Barefoot" 12″ and CD versions add "When Love Comes to Town (Live From the Kingdom Mix)" and "God Part II" (March 1989)

"All I Want Is You" / "Unchained Melody" 12″ and CD versions add "Everlasting Love" (June 1989)

"The Fly" / "The Fly (The Lounge Fly Mix)" / "Alex Descends into Hell for a Bottle of Milk Korova" (October 1991)

"Mysterious Ways" / "Mysterious Ways (Solar Plexus Extended Club Mix)" / "Mysterious Ways (Apollo 440 Magic Hour Remix)" / "Mysterious Ways (Tabla Motown Remix)" / "Mysterious Ways (Solar Plexus Club Mix)" (November 1991)

"One" / "Lady with the Spinning Head" / "Satellite of Love" / "Night and Day (Steel String Remix)" (March 1992)

Compilations, Soundtracks, and Solo sidesteps

They Call It an Accident (Soundtrack album) U2 lends the recording of "October" as well as permitting a second version with additional keyboards by Wally Badarou. (1982)

The Last American Virgin (Soundtrack album) U2 lends the previously recorded "I Will Follow." (1982)

Snake Charmer (Jah Wobble with guests Holger Czukay and Edge) Edge performs on three of five tracks. (1983)

"Band Aid" (7″ and 12″ charity single plus video conceived by Bob Geldof and Midge Ure to benefit Ethiopia) Bono and Adam participate. (1984)

Macalla (Album from Irish band Clannad) Bono lends vocals to "In a Lifetime." (1985)

Sun City (Little Steven's Artists United Against Apartheid project: album, singles, and video) Bono writes and records "Silver and Gold." (1985)

Live for Ireland (Compilation from the Self-Aid Concert in Dublin on May 17, 1986) U2 performs "Maggie's Farm." (1987)

Robbie Robertson (First solo album from the former guitarist and songwriter of the

Band) U2 backs Robertson on two songs, "Sweet Fire of Love" and "Testimony." (1987)

The Courier (Soundtrack album) U2 lends its previously recorded "Walk to the Water." (1988)

Captive (Soundtrack album) Edge writes and performs the entire album with Michael Brook and Sinead O'Connor. (1987 U.S. release)

A Very Special Christmas (Holiday songs collected by producer Jimmy Iovine) U2 performs "Christmas (Baby Please Come Home)." (1987)

A Vision Shared (Smithsonian Institute Benefit album of Woody Guthrie and Leadbelly songs) U2 performs "Jesus Christ." (1988)

Red, Hot + Blue (AIDS Research Benefit album of Cole Porter tunes) U2 performs "Night and Day." (October 1990)

Until the End of the World (Soundtrack album) U2 performs the title track, also using it for *Achtung Baby*. (1990)

Videos and Movies

"I Will Follow" Live onstage in America (May 1981)

"Gloria" Dublin barge. Directed by Meiert Avis (October 1981)

"A Celebration" Kilmainham Jail, Dublin. Directed by Meiert Avis (April 1982)

"New Year's Day" Swedish mountainside. Directed by Meiert Avis (December 1982)

"Two Hearts Beat as One" Montmartre, Paris. Directed by Meiert Avis (March 1983)

Under a Blood Red Sky Red Rocks Amphitheater, Denver, Colorado. Directed by Gavin Taylor. Television special and commercially released videocassette (June 1983)

"Sunday Bloody Sunday" Red Rocks. Directed by Gavin Taylor (June 1983)

"Pride" (#1) St. Francis Xavier Hall, Dublin. Directed by Donald Cammell. Popular MTV Version. (August 1984)

"Pride" (#2) Slane Castle, north of Dublin. Directed by Barry Devlin. Filmed as part of "The Making of The Unforgettable Fire" TV special. (May–July 1984)

"Pride" (#3) London. Directed by Anton Corbijn. Seldom seen. (August 1984)

"A Sort of Homecoming" Paris, Brussels, Rotterdam, London, Glasgow. Directed by Barry Devlin (October / November 1984)

"Bad" (live) Paris, Brussels, Rotterdam, London, Glasgow. Directed by Barry Devlin (October / November 1984)

"The Unforgettable Fire" Sweden and miscellaneous locations. Directed by Meiert Avis. (January 1985)

The Unforgettable Fire Collection Various locations and directors. Commercially released videocassette compiling "Pride" (#1), "A Sort of Homecoming," "Bad" (live), and "The Unforgettable Fire." (Released 1985)

"With or Without You" Dublin. Directed by Meiert Avis / Matt Mahurin. (February 1987)

"Red Hill Mining Town" London. Directed by Neil Jordan. (February 1987)

"I Still Haven't Found What I'm Looking For" Las Vegas. Directed by Barry Devlin. (April 1987)

"Where the Streets Have No Name" Los Angeles. Directed by Meiert Avis. (April 1987)

"Jesus Christ" from *A Vision Shared* commercially released videocassette. Directed by Jim Brown. (1988)

"Desire" Los Angeles. Directed by Richard Lowenstein. (September 1988)

Rattle and Hum Various locations. Directed by Phil Joanou. Commercially released movie and videocassette. (1987–88)

"Angel of Harlem" New York. Directed by Richard Lowenstein. (November 1988)

"When Love Comes to Town" Various locations. Directed by Phil Joanou. (March 1989)

"All I Want Is You" Rome. Directed by Meiert Avis. (April 1989)

"Night and Day" (AIDS Research Benefit) Berlin. Directed by Wim Wenders. (November 1990)

"The Fly" Dublin and London. Directed by Ritchie Smith and Jon Klein. (September 1991)

"Mysterious Ways" Morocco. Directed by Stephane Sednaoui. (November 1991)

"One" (March 1992)

AN AMERICAN U2 FANZINE LIST

The following is a list of domestic U2 fan magazines whose existence has been confirmed as of April 1, 1992.

A.D.A.M.
c/o Jones/Kellie
7426 West Boulevard #3
Boardman, OH 44512

Another Day (The Peace Museum)
S. Kathleen Maki: Organizer
P.O. Box 92444
Milwaukee, WI 53202

Feedback/U.S.A.
P.O. Box 1586
Warren, OH 44482–1586
Attn: Lori Caldwell

Indian Summer Sky
P.O. Box 58263
Philadelphia, PA 19102–8263
Attn: Tochen

Out (Formerly *Out of Control*)
Maureen Wrinn
13 Sewall Street #5
Marblehead, MA 01945

Propaganda (Official U2 World Service Magazine)
P.O. Box 350
Nanuet, NY 10954
Martin Wroe: Editor

Red, Hot, U2
c/o Kim Sutton
46 Mozart Avenue
Scarborough, ONT M1K 2V9
Canada

Sing a New Song
c/o Ellen Fauver
8795 Orange Street
Alta Loma, CA 91704
– and –
Lori Hill
506 East Cherry
Enid, OK 73701

Sing No More
c/o Mary Kadar
P.O. Box 536
Franklin, MA 02038

The Street Melody
Rt. 7, Box 514R
281 S. Atlanta Drive
Tuscon, AZ 85747

String of Pearls (formerly *Into the Heart*)
P.O. Box 29303
Chicago, IL 60629–9998
Attn: Lisa Petraitis

Touch
c/o Patricia Culliton
5520 North Octavia
Chicago, IL 60656

U2 and Then Some
Amy Johnson
14154 Hubbell
Livonia, MI 48154

U2/U.S.A.
c/o Lisa Abere
Box 1293
Canal Street Station
New York, NY 10013

Wire
6562 Route 31
Cicero, NY 13039

SOURCES

"U2 Can Make It in the Rock Business," Paul Morley. *New Musical Express*, March 22, 1980.

"It's Not What U2 . . . (It's the Way U2 It!)," Steve Taylor. *The Face*, August 1980.

"Hot Shots: U2 at the Moonlight — London," Daniela Soave. *Record Mirror*, July 7, 1980.

"Getting into U2," Paulo Hewitt. *Melody Maker*, September 13, 1980.

"U2 Take Us over the Top," Lynden Barber. *Melody Maker*, October 4, 1980.

"Stories for Boys," Dave McCullough. *Sounds*, November 1, 1980.

"U2 Will Follow," Tristram Lozaw. *Boston Rock* (#10), January 1981.

"*Boy*" (album review). *Variety*, February 18, 1981

"U-2: Here Comes the Next Big Thing," James Henke. *Rolling Stone*, February 19, 1981.

"*Boy* (album review), John Fisher. *Bucks County Courier Times*, February 22, 1981.

"U-2," Harry Sumrall. *Washington Post*, March 4, 1981.

"U2 Shows It's Ready to Take Off," John Fisher. *Bucks County Courier Times*, March 5, 1981.

"U2 Soars in Albany Debut," Carlo Wolff. *Schenectady Gazette*, March 7, 1981.

"Rock: Irish U2, a Young Quartet, Plays the Ritz," Stephen Holden. *New York Times*, March 9, 1981.

"You, too, May Help U2 Take Off Here," Ken Tucker. *Los Angeles Examiner*, March 17, 1981.

"British Keep Coming, U2 Irish Group in Lead," Robert Hilburn. *Los Angeles Times*, March 17, 1981.

"Timothy Leary's Dead — The Psychedelic Revival," Mark Moses. *Boston Phoenix*, March 17, 1981.

"Boy" (album review). *People Magazine*, April 6, 1981.

"Boy" (album review), Debra Rae Cohen. *Rolling Stone*, April 16, 1981.

"U-2, You Two," Tristram Lozaw. *Boston Rock* (#14), April 1981.

"Boy" (album review), Jim Green. *Trouser Press*, May 1981.

"Boy/October" (album review), Ira A. Robbins, ed. *The Trouser Press Guide to New Wave Records*, Collier Books, Macmillan Publishing Company, 1991.

"Museum in Chicago Focuses on Peace," Nathaniel Sheppard Jr. *New York Times*, August 8, 1982.

"U-2 — Pluck of the Irish," Jim Green. *Trouser Press*, March 1982.

"At Peace Museum, Art Speaks Louder than Grim Lectures," Sharon Cohen. *San Francisco Sunday Examiner and Chronicle*, January 16, 1983.

"U2 — War & Peace," Adrian Thrills. *New Musical Express*, February 1983.

"U2 Run Aground on Rock" (album review), Gavin Martin. *New Musical Express*, February 1983.

"U2 Delivers Music with a Message," Steve Morse. *Boston Globe*, May 5, 1983.

Give Peace a Chance (the official Peace Museum catalogue), Marianne Philbin, ed. Chicago Review Press, 1983.

"U2: Love, Devotion, & Surrender," Tristram Lozaw. *Boston Rock* (#39), May 1983.

"U2: A Way of Life," Scott Isler. *Trouser Press*, June 1983.

"Echo & the Bunnymen — *Porcupine*/U2 — *War*" (combined album review), Ira Robbins. *Trouser Press*, June 1983.

"Blessed Are the Peacemakers," James Henke. *Rolling Stone*, June 9, 1983.

"King the Peacemaker Honored in Exhibit," Ruth Mugalian. *Chicago Herald*, January 22, 1984

"Steve Lillywhite," Adam Sweeting. *Melody Maker*, February 25, 1984.

"U2 Tones Down Its Guitar Attack on New Lp" (album review), Kurt Loder. *Rolling Stone*, October 11, 1984.

"U2, The Pride of Lions," Tony Fletcher. *Jamming*, October 1984.

"U2, The Pride of Lions, Part 2," Tony Fletcher. *Jamming*, November 1984.

"Is Paris Burning?" Adam Sweeting. *Melody Maker*, November 10, 1984.

"Letting It Go" (album review), Anthony DeCurtis. *Record*, November 1984.

"U2: *The Unforgettable Fire*" (album review), Wayne King. *Hi Fidelity*, December 1984.

"Pluck of the Irish," Phillip Bashe. *International Musician and Recording World*, December 1984.

"The Edge on U2," Tristram Lozaw. *U.S. Rock* (#58), January 1985.

"Soul Revelation and the Baptism of Fire," Bill Flanagan. *Musician*, January 1985.

"Keeping the Faith," Christopher Connelly. *Rolling Stone*, March 14, 1985.

"U2: We Don't Need a Hit Single," Moira McCormick. *Billboard*, April 13, 1985.

"U2: Keeping the Rock Faith with Unforgettable Fire," Pam Lambert. *Wall Street Journal*, April 2, 1985.

"U2 Put Peace Exhibition on the Road," Bairbre Power. *Dublin Evening Herald*, June 15, 1985.

"The Edge of U2," Tom Nolan and Jas Obrecht. *Guitar Player*, June 1985.

"*Wide Awake in America*" (album review), James Henke. *Rolling Stone*, July 18, 1985.

"Edge Cuts," William Leith. *New Musical Express*, October 4, 1986.

"On the Edge," Bill Graham. *Hot Press*, October 9, 1986.

"Silver & Gold." *Propaganda* (#16), Martin Wroe, ed. 1986.

"Cactus World Views," Adrian Thrills. *New Musical Express*, March 14, 1987.

"Out of Little Acorns" (album review), John McCready. *New Musical Express*, March 14, 1987.

"U2: The World About Us," Bill Graham and Naill Stokes. *Hot Press*, March 26, 1987.

"U2's *The Joshua Tree*: A Spiritual Progress Report," Steve Morse. *Boston Globe*, March 8, 1987.

"U2 Gears Up to Conquer the World," David Zimmerman. *USA Today*, March 13, 1987.

"U2 Flying High," Andrew Means. *Arizona Republic*, April 3, 1987.

"Irish Rockers Donate to Recall of Mecham." *Arizona Republic*, April 4, 1987.

"U2 Shows Grace Under Pressure at Tour Opener," Robert Hilburn. *Los Angeles Times*, April 4, 1987.

"A Subdued U2 Rebounds for the 80's," Chris Willman. *Los Angeles Times*, April 15, 1987.

"U2's Sports Arena Concert Is Both Spirited and Spiritual," Todd Everett. *Los Angeles Herald*, April 20, 1987.

"An Irish Pied Piper of Rock," Cathleen McGuigan with Frank Gibney. *Newsweek*, April 20, 1987.

"Truths and Consequences," Anthony DeCurtis. *Rolling Stone*, May 7, 1987.

"U2, Angels Over America," Simon Garfield. *Time Out*, May 20-27, 1987.

"U2, Back in the U.S.A.," Liam Mackey. *Hot Press*, June 4, 1987.

"U2: Deus Ex Machina (The Band Who Grew to Earth)," John Waters. *In Dublin*, June 25, 1987.

"U2's Uneasy at the Top," Michael Fitsouza. *Boston Herald*, September 17, 1987. (Reprints quotes from Dublin's *Sunday Tribune*.)

"U2 Comes Through," Steve Morse. *Boston Globe*, September 18, 1987.

"Bono— U2's Passionate Voice," David Breskin. *Rolling Stone*, October 8, 1987.

"U2 on Location," Steve Pond. *Rolling Stone*, February 11, 1988.

"U2's *Joshua Tree* Has the Edge," Edna Gundersen. *USA Today*, March 3, 1988.

"1987 Music Awards/The Edge: The *Rolling Stone* Interview," James Henke. *Rolling Stone*, March 10, 1988.

"U2's *Rattle and Hum* is Hard-edged and Forceful," Jim Sullivan. *Boston Globe*, October 9, 1988.

"When Self-Importance Interferes with the Music," Jon Pareles. *New York Times*, October 16, 1988.

"Ho-hum, U2's Dive Bomb," Owen Gleiberman. *Boston Phoenix*, November 4, 1988.

"*Rattle and Hum*" (album review), David Hiltbrand. *People*, November 11, 1988.

"U2's American Curtain Call" (album review), Anthony DeCurtis. *Rolling Stone*, November 17, 1988.

"U2: Band of Gold," David Rensin. *Premier*, November 1988.

"U2 Explores America," Jay Cocks. *Time*, November 21, 1988.

"Hating U2," Ted Mico. *Spin*, January 1989.

"Bono Less Than Boffo at Box Office," Jeffrey Ressner. *Rolling Stone*, January 12, 1989.

"U2 *Rattle and Hum*" (video review), Mike Clark. *USA Today*, February 24, 1989.

"Now What?" Steve Pond. *Rolling Stone*, March 9, 1989.

"Bono Bites Back," Adam Block. *Mother Jones*, May 1989.

"Giving Peace a Chance at Villager's Peace Museum," Bill Thompson. *Forest Park Review*, June 14, 1989.

"All Things to All Men," John McKenna. *In Dublin*, December 21, 1989.

"Love Comes to Town!" Dave Fanning. *RTE Guide*, December 29, 1989.

Propaganda (#12), Martin Wroe, ed. 1990.

Propaganda (#14), Martin Wroe, ed. 1991.

"New U2 Album on Black Market." *The Irish Voice*, May 25, 1991.

"Bringing Up Baby," Brian Eno. *Rolling Stone*, November 28, 1991.

Propaganda (#15), Martin Wroe, ed. Winter 1991/92.

"*Achtung Baby*" (album review), David Hiltbrand. *People*, December 16, 1991.

"U2's *Achtung Baby*: Bring the Noise" (album review), Elysa Gardner. *Rolling Stone*, January 9, 1992.

"Phones Rattle and Hum in U2 Ticket Rush," Steve Morse. *Boston Globe*, February 24, 1992.

"The View from the Edge," Bill Flanagan. *Musician*, March 1992.

"U2 Makes Up for Lost Time," Julie Romandetta. *Boston Herald*, March 2, 1992.

"U2 Restyled, with Props and a Nod to the Fringes," Jon Pareles. *New York Times*, March 11, 1992.

"U Too May C U2." *People*, March 23, 1992.

About the Author

Carter Alan is the award-winning music director for WBCN–FM, Boston, one of the country's most influential album rock radio stations. He has broadcasted from major music events including the Live Aid concert, two Amnesty International tours, and Roger Waters' Berlin Wall concert. He is also a regular contributor to *Musician* magazine, *CD Review,* and the *Boston Globe*.